Diversity Leadership

Management Series

Diversity Leadership

Janice L. Dreachslin
With contributions by Portia L. Hunt

Health Administration Press
Chicago, IL 1996

Racial and ethnic terms herein appear as they are used (e.g., capitalized or lower-case, Hispanic versus Latino, etc.) in the style used by the source cited. References to the U.S. Census are for 1990 census figures.

Library of Congress Cataloging-in-Publication Data

Dreachslin, Janice L.
   Diversity leadership / Janice L. Dreachslin ; with contributions by Portia L. Hunt.
      p.   cm. — (Management series)
   Includes bibliographical references and index.
   ISBN 1-56793-046-8 (hard : alk. paper)
   1. Health facilities—United States—Personnel management.
2. Diversity in the workplace—United States.   I. Hunt, Portia L.
II. Title.   III. Series: Management series (Chicago, Ill.)
RA971.35.D74   1996
362.1'068'3—dc20   96-16820
                                                                CIP

The paper used in this publication meets the minimum requirements of American National Standard for Information Sciences—Permanence of Paper for Printed Library Materials, ANSI Z39.48-1984. ∞ ™

Health Administration Press
A division of the Foundation of the
   American College of Healthcare Executives
One North Franklin Street
Chicago, IL 60606
312/424-2800

For my father

Contents

Part I   Discovery

Part II   Assessment

Part III   Exploration

Part IV Transformation

Part V Revitalization

Foreword

Leaders' ability to get employees and middle managers from different cultural backgrounds to work together effectively may be the crucial ingredient in organizational success in the future.

Russell C. Coile, Jr.
Futurist

S C H O L A R, investigator, and writer, Janice Dreachslin, Ph.D. has put into one clear focus two of the essential trends in health care: leadership and diversity in the organization. In *Diversity Leadership,* Dr. Dreachslin has captured the essence and importance of the subject through her appreciation of the interaction and connections between a strong, diversified workforce and a high-performing organization. Her book poses a challenge for health care leaders: to build a stronger organization through diversity. She has given readers a map of the road and challenges them to travel it.

As the text thoughtfully points out, America's health care labor force is turning ever more culturally diverse. This is a change that will rock some institutions to their foundations. Part I of *Diversity Leadership* provides the platform for the text's theme: that change in the labor force signals a "diversity imperative." The U.S. Department of Labor's demand projections for health care jobs in the year 2000 show the need to understand—and work with—diversity. Calculated with 1988 as the base year, we can expect a 70 percent increased demand for medical assistants, a 63 percent increased demand for home health aides, and a 60 percent increased demand for medical records technicians—and the list goes on. Employers in this new health care world will have to struggle with two issues: first, the shortage of trained workers and, second, a multicultural labor supply. Many in this new diverse workforce will be women; many will be members of ethnic minority groups.

Managing the diverse workforce may be challenge enough; but add to this the economic pressures being placed on the health care industry as it copes with the present and looks to the next century, and you get a sense of the magnitude of the task. How, for instance, will managers integrate and utilize a heterogeneous employee force at higher levels in their organization? As the author points out, organizations willing to encourage diversity will reap numerous benefits, ranging from improved customer relations to reduction in employee turnover rates. Those organizations unwilling to commit to workforce diversity will find tougher going in the long run. Why? It's simple. Higher-skilled individuals will make their usual well-reasoned choices, and they will naturally gravitate to those organizations that "walk the talk"—in other words, organizations that *demonstrate* an appreciation of diversity and a willingness to encourage it.

Managing diversity is a lot easier to talk about and write about than to put into operation. There's a reason for that: humans are bound by their own prejudices and stereotypes. Managers, like most people, struggle with their own "isms," whether racism, sexism, elitism, or any other ism. Quite properly anticipating this, Dr. Dreachslin explores this range of actions and reactions in a chapter she titles "Backlash."

No one has found a perfect way to run an organization, and there is no one special work culture that will guarantee organizational success. Because health care is a people-intensive industry, leadership, employees, and the organization's corporate culture are more closely linked than in many other industries. Patterns of feelings, behaviors, and thoughts contribute to the culture. It is the leader's task to reinforce the positive in these patterns. In Part 2, *Assessment,* the author addresses the need for a "cultural audit" and explains its relationship to leadership diversity. The cultural audit is the key tool required to ease the transformation to successful diversity in the organization. Such an audit will assist leaders to (1) understand the current culture better and (2) adapt the culture with an eye to improving organizational performance.

If an organization wants its corporate culture to embrace diversity, then it's the leader's job to *say* it, *act* it, and *reward* it. Successful, high-performing organizations show a strong and consistent corporate culture. The opposite is also true: weak corporate cultures are more commonly associated with average- or poor-performing organizations. Here is some advice to managers and leaders. Winning organizations tend to do a better job as "culture builders" by:

- Taking "the long view"—the leadership must keep the end in mind.
- Understanding which decisions are strategic and which are tactical—the leadership must prioritize its decision making.
- Effectively cooperating and communicating internally among all levels—the leadership must take responsibility for communications.
- Understanding that "big doesn't beat small; rather, fast beats slow"—the leadership must make faster, more flexible, more innovative decisions.
- Building personal accountability into the very structure of the culture/organization—the leadership must set and maintain well-defined goals and performance standards.
- Taking responsibility for setting the tone—the leadership should encourage positive story telling, while building organizational heros and heroines.

The spirit of change in this text has powerful appeal. As individuals, each of us can resist or encourage change; it is our choice. Liberally quoting Damon Runyon, "The race is not always to the swiftest, nor the battle to the strongest, but that's the way to bet." If it comes to a battle between change and no change— bet on change. Granted, change can be painful, especially when it involves human emotions and attitudes. And that will happen when an organization seriously embraces diversity.

The author offers some specific prescriptions in Part 4: *Transformation,* for managers and leaders committed to fostering diversity and developing pluralistic teams. "Team development" strikes me as a particularly essential task for the new-breed champion of diversity. Exactly what are we referring to when we recall the common phrase, "the health care *team*"? In some organizations, "health care team" too often means the act of one leader "which begets multiple followership." Effective work teams aren't born nor are they engineered: they must be crafted, and that's the leader's job.

Building teams in health care offers a special challenge, that of positioning the physician into the effective team. In most professional settings, physicians are used to being the captain of the ship, but today's organizational leader knows the seas are changing. Therefore, the physicians' authority role has to be carefully considered when crafting effective teams.

Diversity management is not a fad and it will not evaporate. It's an ongoing performance issue. America's winning health care organizations will master the challenge of cultural diversity. The only issues for them are how, when, where, and how effectively. The answers will depend on leadership and its commitment. In a time when health care itself has long been perceived as a right, it is strange, indeed, to maintain a corporate culture that excludes non-mainstream groups and individuals. Society will receive an extra bonus when the organization diversifies. Those newly included will be disproportionately non-white and women. This commitment, when made to happen, will strike a powerful blow to society's cycle of denial and poverty. Hallelujah!

I. Donald Snook, Jr.
President,
The Presbyterian Foundation
for Philadelphia

Preface

T HIS BOOK presents a framework for diversity leadership —that is, the process of finding common ground and shared purpose in today's increasingly multicultural health care organizations. Diversity leadership may, at first blush, strike the reader as incongruous because diversity by definition implies difference, divergence, and presumptively, lack of commonality while leadership literally means the process of showing the way. How can any leader "show the way" given the lack of uniformity implicit in diversity?

But diversity leadership is not an oxymoron. It is, rather, the exciting and essential process of showing management, staff, clinicians, patients, and other organizational stakeholders the way to discover the common ground and shared purpose that always exists in human communities, even in the context of diversity.

This book presents a five-part framework for the process of diversity leadership: **discovery**, **assessment**, **exploration**, **transformation**, and **revitalization**. The 12 chapters guide the reader through the steps that together define the process of effective diversity leadership.

The intended audience for this book is, not surprisingly, diverse. Health care executives and managers can use the book as a guide and as a comprehensive foundation for action at both the personal and organizational levels. The book is intended as a reference for teams and individuals engaged in or embarking on the process of diversity leadership. Case examples of diversity leadership in action are interspersed liberally throughout the book. These examples are intended to illustrate how the book's framework for diversity leadership is put into practice.

Consultants and trainers who serve health care provider organizations are a second target audience. Health care provider organizations are, simultaneously, businesses and social service agencies. The question as to whether health care in America is a social good or a commodity—a right or a privilege—has not been answered definitively. Because of their unique position in our society and the special nature of the "product" of medical care, health care organizations and their constituencies can relate only in part to books and diversity training programs developed with other industries in mind. This book connects the theory of diversity leadership directly to its practice in health care provider organizations.

Students and faculty in both graduate and undergraduate health services management programs constitute a third target audience. The book is appropriate as a textbook for specialized courses in diversity leadership or as a useful reference book for more general courses in human resource management, organization behavior, strategy and change, and training design and development. Although case examples in the book are generally drawn from health care provider organizations, the framework for diversity leadership presented in the book is applicable in other industries as well. Consequently, anyone interested in diversity leadership could benefit from reading the book.

The case examples that are woven throughout the book are, of necessity, brief and intended to illustrate specific points. We have much to learn from the experiences of health care organizations and managers who are engaged in the process of diversity leadership. A book that focuses exclusively on extended case studies of organizational practice in diversity leadership would be a worthwhile future endeavor.

Research studies that quantify the effects of diversity leadership on organizational performance are long overdue as well. The review of the literature conducted for this book uncovered few such studies in the management and health care administration literature. Such studies are another important future priority.

Our hope is that this book will serve as a valuable guide to all who embark on the journey of diversity leadership. Each diversity leader traverses his or her own unique path through discovery, assessment, exploration, transformation, and revitalization. We wish you success in your personal journey.

Acknowledgments

I OWE A DEBT of gratitude to many friends, family members, and colleagues who made publication of this book possible. Elaine Smith's expertise in the health care field and her personal commitment to diversity leadership were invaluable to me. She provided moral support, served as a sounding board for ideas, and shared her experiences with diversity, enriching both the process and the outcome of this book. I am also deeply indebted to my contributing author, Portia L. Hunt, whose insight, expertise, and moral character are an inspiration in my life. The dedication of my graduate research assistant, Teresa M. Jackson, whose efforts went far beyond reasonable expectations, is especially appreciated. A special thanks is due to all of the health care professionals and organizations that shared their experiences, providing case illustrations of the process of diversity leadership.

I am grateful as well to my friend and colleague Ed. Kobrinski, who identified both the issue and the author. Without his commitment and initiative, this book would not have been published. Suggestions made by two anonymous external reviewers also enrich this manuscript. A special thanks is also due to the staff of Health Administration Press whose skill and performance moved the book efficiently and effectively through the development and production process.

Finally, I wish to thank my colleagues, students, and friends at the Great Valley Graduate Center and in the Department of Health Policy and Administration, the College of Health and Human Development, and the Smeal College of Business Administration of the Pennsylvania State University. Their concern and support for me and for this book will always be treasured.

Discovery

R alph Bryant, CEO of Urban Medical Center, has a reputation for managing by the numbers. Senior executives
at the center know that without hard data, they won't get an
audience with Bryant, much less a decision.

The vice president of human resources has just left Bryant's
office. She made a very convincing presentation that astounded
him. The numbers were indisputable: the center's labor pool
demographics are shifting and its ability to provide appropriate
services to a changing patient mix is increasingly compromised.

Bryant enjoys a well-deserved national reputation as a
trend-setter. Case-mix management techniques were firmly in
place at Urban Medical Center before Medicare's prospective
payment system was instituted in 1983. Bryant had insisted
that patients' financial and medical records be merged long
before the first preferred provider contract was written in the
city. Urban Medical Center was one of the first to consolidate,
building an integrated hospital/physician network with former
competitors. But this was different. Bryant, for the first time,
felt decidedly unprepared.

Bryant shook his head and muttered to himself, "I've got
some work to do on this one. Diversity . . . I've heard the buzz
word, but I guess I just discounted it as repackaged liberalism.
It's clearly much more than that. It's a business imperative
and I'd better attend to it."

CHAPTER 1

The Diversity Imperative

DIVERSITY, AS the hypothetical CEO Ralph Bryant learned, is much more than repackaged liberalism. America is becoming increasingly diverse, and not only along traditional dimensions of diversity like race and ethnicity. Generation, sexual orientation, socioeconomic status, physical ability, marital status, work style, parental status, education, and other dimensions are receiving increasing attention from health care executives who wish to improve their organization's competitive position and better serve their community.

America's increasingly diverse patient/customer base and workforce are no longer as uniformly content with assimilation or homogenization. The melting pot metaphor has been replaced with that of a salad bowl or a vegetable stew. Patients increasingly demand that health care organizations value and consider their differences in the marketing and provision of services, the delivery of care, and the design of health care facilities themselves. Employees are looking for reciprocity. Statements like, "I'll adapt to the organization, if the organization will also adapt to me," increasingly reflect the perspective of America's changing workforce.

Trends such as these require reflection as well as action. This and subsequent chapters provide a framework for aspiring diversity leaders: executives, managers, and staff who want to lead—not be led by—change. The diversity leader's journey begins with **discovery**. Exploring the diversity imperative, engaging in self-discovery, and developing a framework for understanding differences are the first steps in a process of exploration, personal growth, and organizational change. To explore the diversity imperative requires first a discussion of changing demographics.

POPULATION TRENDS
IN RACE/ETHNICITY

Race and **ethnicity** remain key dimensions of diversity. Analysis of data from a variety of sources confirms that the general population is changing even faster than the workforce and that workforce 2000 (as described in the landmark *Workforce 2000* report of 1987) has already arrived. Consider these statistics, gleaned from a review of U.S. Census data: in 1990, almost one in every four Americans was Asian, black or Hispanic. The comparable figure for 1970 was 12.5 percent, slightly more than one in ten. Analysts for the Urban Institute (Edmonston and Passel 1994) project that, soon after the turn of the century one in three Americans will be Asian, black, or Hispanic. Late in the twenty-first century, whites are projected to be one among many minorities in the United States—a plurality, not a majority.

Asian Americans

America's Asian population is the fastest growing, experiencing a rate of increase in excess of 100 percent between 1980 and 1990, according to U.S. Census statistics. Asian Americans currently constitute about 4 percent of the population, but the Asian Pacific American Public Policy Institute of Los Angeles (Ong 1994) projects that by 2030, Asian Americans will constitute 8 percent of the population.

This fast-growing segment of the population is itself a microcosm of diversity. The facts are at odds with the commonly held stereotype of Asian Americans as the "model minority" that is uniformly successful. A report prepared by the Asian American Public Policy Institute of Los Angeles (Ong 1994) presents statistics that are relevant to the diversity leader. For instance, the proportion of Asian American households with income over $75,000 per year is about the same as the proportion of Asian American households with income less than $10,000. The percentage of Asian Americans with household incomes below the poverty line varies from 46 percent of those whose families immigrated from Laos or Cambodia to 7 percent of those who report Japan or the Philippines as their family's country of origin (Ong 1994). In comparison, 29 percent of African Americans, 25 percent of Hispanics, and 9 percent of whites live below the poverty line.

Businesses and health care organizations are increasingly engaged in ethnic marketing. McCarroll (1993) reports that nearly half of the Fortune 1000 companies are engaged in ethnic marketing. Examples of such initiatives in the health care industry will be discussed in detail in subsequent chapters. But, aspiring diversity leaders who try to target the "Asian market" may be surprised to find that there is no such thing.

Novak (1992) describes the discoveries made by Metropolitan Life when, beginning in 1985, the insurance company began to develop Asian American niche markets. One costly faux pas consisted of printing a picture of people dressed in Korean clothing in advertising material directed at a Chinese American audience. James H. Major, Jr., agency vice president of Metropolitan Life, recommends that the best approach to understanding the needs of a niche market is by "actually going into the area" (Novak 1992, 20).

Hispanics

Hispanics are the second-fastest growing racial or ethnic group in America. From 1980 to 1990, the Hispanic population's growth rate was 53 percent, fueled, in part, by immigration. The 1990 U.S. Census reports that 9 percent of the population is Hispanic. By 2050, Hispanics are projected to surpass African Americans and become the United States' largest minority, constituting 22 percent of the population.

Hispanics are both racially and culturally diverse. As defined by the U.S. Bureau of the Census, Hispanic origin refers to Spanish-speaking people from Central or South America, Spain, the Caribbean, or elsewhere. Mexican Americans are the single largest Hispanic group in the United States—six of every ten Hispanics are Mexican American. As with other racial and ethnic groups, these statistics vary by region. Puerto Ricans are, by far, the largest Hispanic group in the Northeast, for instance.

Wallace and Lew-Ting (1993) report that the proportion of Latinos (Hispanics) older than 65 will increase fivefold by 2030. For most major diseases, with the exception of diabetes, the researchers report that Latinos' morbidity rates are lower than those of non-Latino whites. The exception, however, is disability, with both Puerto Rican and Mexican elderly reporting more days of restricted activity than other Latino groups, non-Latino whites, or African Americans.

Data like these, explain the researchers (Wallace and Lew-Ting 1993, 343), are relevant to the design and delivery of long-term care: "Older Latinos often hold expectations of assistance from their families, but those expectations do not mean that formal services would not improve the status of the elders and their care givers or that in-home health care would be refused if offered."

The astute diversity leader will investigate this growing market and develop strategies appropriate to the local service area.

Blacks

U.S. Census data show that the black population grew at a rate of 13 percent between 1980 and 1990, considerably behind the growth rate of Asian Americans and Hispanics, but faster than the 6 percent growth rate of the white population. Americans who are black are ethnically diverse and include African Americans, West Indians, Haitians, and Jamaicans, among others. The vast majority of blacks are African Americans whose ancestors were involuntary immigrants, brought to this country as slaves.

The stereotype of blacks as impoverished residents of the inner city is challenged by the growing presence of the black middle class. Although 29 percent of black households have incomes below the poverty line, 3 percent have household incomes in excess of $75,000 (Ong 1994). Over one of every ten black households has annual income in excess of $50,000.

Twenty-four percent of blacks are uninsured, as compared to 33 percent of Latinos and 13 percent of whites (Wallace and Lew-Ting 1993; Friedman 1991). Insurance status, combined with a legacy of distrust for the health care industry, presents challenges to the diversity leader. Given the same presenting condition, African Americans have historically received less intensive care (Yergan et al. 1987).

There is increasing pressure for the health care industry to collect data on patient race and ethnicity so that differences in treatment paths and clinical outcomes can be studied. Data on patient race and ethnicity are the subject of a lawsuit, *Madison-Hughes v. Shalala* filed by a consortium of civil rights and health groups that includes the American Public Health Association (APHA). The plaintiffs contend that the U.S. Department of Health and Human Services' (DHHS) failure to require health care providers to collect and report race and ethnicity data is in violation of the Civil Rights Act of 1964. In the absence of such data, documentation of health care providers' compliance with antidiscrimination regulations is not possible. The plaintiffs explain that, "doctors, hospitals, and nursing homes receive hundreds of billions of dollars in federal subsidies each year, yet do not collect or report any information regarding the race/ethnicity of the patients they serve" (APHA 1994).

Race and ethnicity are particularly sensitive dimensions of diversity. As Polednak (1989, 7) explains, a biological justification for dividing people into three major racial groups is questionable, but "the concept of biological race has some value despite its limitations and should be maintained as long as it is useful."

The U.S. Census categories of race and ethnicity are more appropriately considered social or cultural identity groups rather than biologically based groupings. Despite the tenuous nature of racial groupings themselves, there are striking differences in health indicators between racial and ethnic groups, some of which remain even when socioeconomic status is held constant. After controlling for education level, for instance, the rate of hypertension among blacks was still twice that of similarly situated whites (Polednak 1989).

Whites

Whites, the slowest growing racial group in America, represent a declining proportion of the population. Statistics from the Immigration and Naturalization Service show a declining proportion of immigrants from Europe: in 1992, only 15 percent of immigration was from European countries, as compared with 70 percent in 1940. Declining immigration from predominantly white European countries, combined with a relatively low birth rate among whites, help explain the current trend.

White Americans represent a broad array of ethnic groups. Of the top ten countries of ethnic origin tabulated from the 1990 U.S. Census, seven are predominantly white European countries. White Americans have had a profound influence on the shaping of American culture. As the anthropologist Edward T. Hall (Hall and Hall 1990, 140) explains, "While the United States has absorbed millions of people from countries around the globe, the core culture of the United States has its roots in northern European or Anglo-Saxon culture."

But, the face of America is changing. America, as *Time* magazine (McManus 1993) reports, is becoming the world's first multicultural society (see Table 1.1). Health care organizations will have to adapt to this increasing racial and ethnic diversity.

THE HEALTH CARE INDUSTRY'S WORKFORCE

Health Care Administrators

Women comprise approximately 80 percent of the workforce in the health care industry, but top management positions continue to be the purview of white men (Friedman 1991). Approximately

Table 1.1
The World's
First Multicultural
Society: Percent of
the Population

Race	1990 (actual)	2050 (projected)
Non-Hispanic White	75	57
Black	12	12
Latino/a	9	20
Asian	3	11

Note: In accordance with census categories, persons of Hispanic origin may be of any race. Figures are rounded to the nearest whole percentage point and may not total to 100 percent due to rounding as well as the "other" category in the U.S. Census.
Source: Edmonston, B., and J. S. Passel. 1994. "The Future Immigrant Population of the United States." In Immigration and Ethnicity: The integration of America's Newest Arrivals, edited by B. Edmonston and J. S. Passel, 317–353. Washington, DC: The Urban Institute Press.

four of every 100 hospital CEOs are women, when members of religious orders are excluded from the analysis. Friedman (1992) cites American College of Healthcare Executives (ACHE) data from 1990 to demonstrate that less than one of every 100 top administrative positions is filled by minorities.

The Association of University Programs in Health Administration (AUPHA) reports that approximately nine in ten health administration students and faculty members are white (Sabatino 1993). White women, however, are an increasing proportion of health care administration students, representing over half of master's program graduates since the mid-1980s.

Constituting only 12 percent of ACHE membership in 1983, women represented almost one-third of ACHE membership by 1994. A membership survey conducted by ACHE and the University of Iowa's Graduate Programs in Hospital and Health Administration (1991) concluded that women health care administrators earn less and are less likely to move up the career ladder.

To address this underrepresentation of minorities in the field of health care administration the Atlanta-based Institute for Diversity in Health Management was formed in 1994. The Institute is a joint project of ACHE, the National Association of Health Services Executives (NAHSE), and the American Hospital Association (AHA) (Blankenau 1994). A study (ACHE and NAHSE 1993) by ACHE and NAHSE found that black health care administrators earned less and were less likely to hold executive-level positions than their white counterparts. The study will be updated in 1997 to see if any change has occurred. As of 1995, only 6.5 percent of ACHE members were African American, Asian American, or Latino. The relative percentage of women and minority group members declines as members move up ACHE's membership ladder from associate to diplomate to fellow.

Clinicians

Areas of clinical practice continue to be segregated by gender, race, and ethnicity. According to 1993 data from the U.S. Bureau of Labor Statistics, nearly 95 percent of practicing nurses are women, while 78 percent of practicing physicians are men. The data also reveal that more than nine of every ten speech/language pathologists are women; fewer than four of every 100 physicians and about eight of every 100 registered nurses are black; and less than 5 percent of practicing physicians, about 3 percent of registered nurses, and slightly more than 1 percent of speech therapists are of Hispanic origin.

The U.S. Bureau of Labor Statistics does not tabulate employment statistics by profession for Asian Americans, but 1990 census data concluded that approximately 11 percent of physicians and over 4 percent of registered nurses are Asian. Two of every ten licensed physicians are foreign-born and foreign-educated (Wagner 1991). Asian American physicians and nurses tend to be concentrated in public hospitals: a study of public hospitals in four metropolitan areas (Ong 1994) revealed that almost one in four physicians and nurses was of Asian ethnicity.

Women are graduating from medical school in increasing numbers. Currently one of every three medical school graduates is a woman. If this trend continues, by 2050, the majority of physicians will be women (Friedman 1991).

In terms of the allied health professions, 16 different associations were contacted in a recent study, and only three were found to routinely collect data on members' race and ethnicity (Walker and Brand 1993). Due to sample size, the U.S. Bureau of Labor Statistics' periodic estimates of the racial and ethnic distribution of workers in the health and other professions cannot provide accurate estimates of Asian workers by profession. The lack of statistical data makes global estimates difficult.

The American Occupational Therapy Association (AOTA), one of the three professional organizations that does collect data on members' race and ethnicity, reports a 7.7 percent minority representation among registered occupational therapists (OTRs) and approximately 9 percent among certified occupational therapy assistants (COTAs) (Walker and Brand 1993).

The second of the three professional associations that collect data on members' race and ethnicity is the American Physical Therapy Association (APTA). The APTA reports that minority group members comprise slightly over 6 percent of its 1990 active membership. Slightly more than one of every 100 APTA members is African American, approximately three of every 100 is Asian American, and about one of every 200 is Native American. Latino representation in APTA is only slightly higher than that of African Americans (Walker and Brand 1993).

The Association of American Medical Colleges (AAMC) has developed a methodology to evaluate the extent to which practicing physicians appropriately represent the racial and ethnic diversity of the labor pool (Petersdorf et al. 1990). Variations of this methodology could be used by professional associations or health care organizations that wish to quantify the appropriateness of representation in their membership or in the workforce. The methodology could be extended to other dimensions of diversity, such as gender or age, as well.

The AAMC calculates each racial and ethnic group's **representation factor** which is calculated by dividing the percentage of U.S. medical school graduates from that racial or ethnic group in a given year by the percentage of that racial or ethnic group in the 20- to 29-year-old age group. A representation factor of 1.0 indicates parity, while a representation factor of less than 1.0 indicates underrepresentation of the racial or ethnic group among medical school graduates.

Representation factors calculated by the AAMC for 1989 were as follows (Petersdorf et al. 1990): African Americans, .39; Mexican Americans, .25; mainland Puerto Ricans, .61; and Indian Americans and Alaska natives, .54. As was the case for white Americans, none of the Asian American groups for which the ratios were calculated was found to be underrepresented—that is, all had a representation factor equal to or greater than one.

Even given the paucity of available data, the statistics paint a clear picture: labor force trends predicted in the ground-breaking Hudson Institute Report (Packer and Johnston 1987) and confirmed through more recent analysis (Beilinson 1990; Thornburg 1991; Towers Perrin and the Hudson Institute 1990) will present a compelling challenge to the health care industry. Diversification at all levels of the health care workforce is truly an imperative for today's health care organizations.

THE HUDSON INSTITUTE REPORT

Publication of the Hudson Institute's landmark, *Workforce 2000: Work and Workers for the 21st Century* (Johnston and Packer 1987) fueled a growing interest in and attention to America's changing demographics among major employers such as health care providers. The report, which focuses on gender, race, ethnicity, and age, identified five current demographic trends that are changing the face of America's labor pool:

1. the slowest growth in the population and workforce since the 1930s;
2. the rising average age of the workforce;
3. the increase in women entering the workforce;
4. the increase in the proportion of new entrants into the labor force who are minority group members; and
5. the increase in the proportion of new entrants into the labor force who are immigrants.

Further, the Hudson Institute report highlighted a growing "skills gap" between America's workforce and the needs of employers: at the same time that movement to a technologically complex, service-based economy is accelerating, the representation of appropriately skilled workers in the labor pool is declining.

According to the report, African Americans and Hispanics, while comprising a growing percentage of a shrinking labor pool, are the least prepared in terms of education and skills to join "workforce 2000." When the skills workers bring to the workplace are compared with the expected skill requirements of new jobs, women, African Americans, and Hispanics all have lower implied shares of new jobs than their expected share of labor force growth (Johnston and Packer 1987).

In light of changing demographics, the shrinking labor pool, and anticipation of heightened competition for qualified workers, health care executives must address this skills gap. Because the health care industry has a relatively high proportion of female and racial and ethnic minority workers, the industry is well positioned to take action. This chapter concludes with a description of an initiative designed to do just that. The Presbyterian Medical Center of Philadelphia is addressing the skills gap through a work study program that targets the working poor of the Hospital's West Philadelphia community.

Consider statistics like the following through the lens of Johnston and Packer's (1987) forecasts:

- The U.S. Bureau of Labor Statistics using 1994 data, has estimated that two of every ten people employed in the health care industry are service workers. Food service workers and supervisors, housekeepers and custodians, nurses aides, orderlies, and transporters are key among these lower-paid, entry-level service workers.

- Health care workers are already a diverse group, with the proportion of ethnic minorities increasing with each rung down the career ladder. For example, approximately 16 percent of hospital employees are black and tend to be concentrated in lower-paying and less-skilled job categories. According to 1993 data from the U.S. Bureau of Labor Statistics, nearly one of every three nursing aides, orderlies, and attendants is black, and an additional 8 percent are Hispanic. As the Hudson Institute report (Johnston and Packer 1987) found, the salaries of workers in industries like health care reflect a greater earnings gap between the highest and lowest paid workers when compared with manufacturing.

- The National Center for Health Statistics projects a growing demand for allied health professionals in fields already experiencing shortages of personnel. Physical therapists, medical record technicians, occupational therapists, speech therapists and audiologists, and laboratory technologists are among the professions cited.

- The U.S. Bureau of Labor Statistics, through studying the 1992 workforce, estimates that one of every three new jobs will be in health, business, and social services; with health services itself having a projected job growth rate of 89 percent. Five of the ten fastest-growing occupations are in the health care industry.

Health care leaders that value diversity must discover and implement strategies to develop tomorrow's workforce today. Today's service workers can be partners in, as well as beneficiaries of, such efforts.

INITIAL ACTION STEPS FOR HEALTH CARE EXECUTIVES

Such dramatic shifts in the nation's demographics are a call for action and leadership. Some suggested first steps, culled from the experience of practicing executives, follow:

- Gather data that will enable you to predict trends in your available labor pool. National trends alone are not sufficient to inform executive decision making with respect to workforce composition, supply, and demand.

- Design and implement professional development initiatives to prepare yourself, your management team, and your employees to perform successfully in the context of a diverse workforce. Executive management must model the institution's desired approach to diversity leadership if efforts are to succeed.

- Make diversity management an integral part of your facility's strategic planning process. Human capital, particularly in a service-intensive industry like health care, is integral to achieving strategic goals. Demographic trends such as those previously presented in this chapter drive the need for an increased focus on the role of human resources in the health care provider facility's viability and success.

- Address the skills gap through supporting educational initiatives that will ensure availability of the skill mix your institution will need to realize its mission and goals. By facilitating access to education and advancement, health care institutions can "grow their own" clinical and management team members, concentrating on those categories of personnel where supply is not anticipated to meet demand.

- Profile your institution's successes and target its weaknesses in managing diversity. Like patient-centered care, effective diversity leadership demands cultural change and ongoing initiatives toward continuous improvement.

This and subsequent chapters present a five-step model for successful diversity leadership: discovery, assessment, exploration, transformation, and revitalization. The model envisions diversity leadership as an integral part of the health care organization's management style and quality initiatives.

DIMENSIONS OF DIVERSITY

What is **diversity**? Should diversity be viewed solely in terms of race, ethnicity, and gender? Are there other dimensions of diversity that are key to effective diversity leadership?

Consider these two scenarios.

P. S. is a successful member of your senior management team. She is well-liked and spearheaded development and implementation of your hospital's profitable cardiology program. You've noticed that she seldom talks about her personal life and always attends social functions alone. You've often wondered why, but have attributed it to her workaholic style.

L. T. is the youngest member of your management team. You're pleased with his performance but notice that he frequently requests leave time for family responsibilities. You'd like to promote him but wonder how others would relate to his work style. The other men on your team come to work early and stay late. They never request time off when their children are sick. You wonder about his loyalty and question whether he'll fit in.

A diverse workforce requires leaders to test their assumptions.

Gays and lesbians, dual-career couples, baby boomers, baby busters, older adults, disabled individuals, and veterans all contribute to the fabric of America's diverse workforce. Religious preference, social class, and learning style are additional dimensions of diversity. The richness of human experience and individual uniqueness allow diversity to be manifested in many ways.

Diversity leadership guides the health care organization in channeling workforce diversity toward achievement of corporate goals and fulfillment of the institutional mission of community service. The process of diversity leadership, which often begins with attention only to race, ethnicity, and gender, tends to uncover additional dimensions of diversity. Learning to value diversity, not judge it, and to direct its power can result not only in heightened worker satisfaction but, particularly in a service organization like health care, can enhance the quality and appropriateness of customer service.

SOME BENEFITS OF DIVERSITY LEADERSHIP

Health care institutions that have undertaken diversity initiatives report a range of benefits including an improved customer base, improved quality of care, increased labor pool, labor cost savings, reduction in turnover, and more effective teams.

Improved Customer Base

The U.S. minority marketplace exceeds the gross national product of Canada. McCarroll (1993) reports projections indicating that, by the turn of the century, Asian, African, and Hispanic Americans will account for as much as 30 percent of America's economy. Perhaps more than any other industry, health care's customers reflect increased diversity, since demographic changes are even more pronounced in the general population than in the workforce.

Particularly as market or regulatory reforms begin to address the inequities in third party payment that plague the current reimbursement system, those health care providers that value diversity will experience greater success in an increasingly competitive marketplace. A study by Covenant Investment Management (Carfang 1993) attests to the financial benefits of diversity leadership in investor-owned corporations: companies with strong track records in diversity leadership outperformed the Standard and Poor's 500 stock market average return on shareholder's investment by 2.4 percent while those with poor diversity performance underperformed the average return by 8 percent.

Improved Quality of Care

Culturally appropriate care improves customer satisfaction and quality. When clinicians have an enhanced understanding of patients' diverse cultural backgrounds and beliefs, they can better serve patients, and compliance with prescribed treatment can be improved. The experience of Children's Health Care–St. Paul, discussed in Part 2 and Part 4, is a case in point.

Altering standard services to better meet the needs of the community results in customer loyalty and an improved bottom line. For example, in some minority communities, patients may routinely use emergency services for nonemergency medical care. One Philadelphia area hospital developed a fast-track service program so that routine care could be efficiently delivered in the ER without jeopardizing quality of care for true life-and-death emergencies. An approach that targets a community's specific needs can be cost effective and positively boost community relations.

Other health care providers have redesigned services to enhance appeal to the local market. For example, low-fat cooking classes that take into account food choices of African American or Hispanic patients are essential to successful programming in many urban hospitals. Hypertension clinics in predominantly black areas and emphysema clinics in coal mining regions are further examples of programming that, when designed with respect for cultural differences, can improve community health status and produce financial returns for the health care provider as well.

Increased Labor Pool in a Scarce Labor Market

When minority staff perceive the workplace as fair, firm, and supportive, they believe they can succeed and move up in the organization. As a result, they take a personal interest in recruiting other minorities and are open to mentoring new recruits and to being mentored by other employees with more experience. Environments that are fair and supportive empower all employees. In many cases, minority employees become more willing to establish trust across racial lines. The benefits to the organization are enormous because the work climate facilitates risk taking, open communication, and creativity.

Labor Cost Savings

Some of the costs that directly affect the health care organization's bottom line but are often not discussed are those associated with sporadic performance, high rates of absenteeism, and property theft. There are basically two types of employee theft—time and property. According to a report by Rusting (1987, 6), "Theft by employees . . . is not just an unpleasant fact that can be ignored. It is probably the major single source of dollar loss to your facility. Conversely, reducing such theft is the greatest opportunity that exists today to make many of these dollars available to you once more." The study of employee theft in hospitals and nursing homes also (Rusting 1987) revealed that 33 percent of survey respondents admitted to stealing property, and 69 percent to stealing time—for example, arriving late and leaving early or calling in sick when they were actually well.

In addition, a significant correlation was found (Rusting 1987) between job dissatisfaction and the likelihood of theft: employees looking for a job change within the year were twice as likely to steal, and employees who felt that management treated employees unfairly or felt a lack of concern on the part of management for employee safety and well-being were also more likely to steal. Poor work habits and property theft were also highly correlated.

In research conducted on theft among nurses, it was found that nurses with poor honesty attitudes and a high degree of job burnout were three times as likely to steal as nurses with equally poor honesty attitudes, but a low degree of job burnout (Rusting 1987). When staff morale is low due to job-related stress and poor communication, employees may react indirectly by coming to work late, being absent, stealing property, or simply not performing. Behaviors like these cost health care providers millions of dollars each year. Two-thirds of those who admit to above average time and property theft make above-average wages (Rusting 1987).

What does your health care organization lose as a result of employee theft each year? A high-end estimate of property theft is 20 percent of supplies purchased, and a low-end estimate is $3,000 per bed (Rusting 1987). Health care provider facilities that value diversity know the importance of creating an inclusive climate. When employees feel included, they participate and more consistently perform their jobs. Employees who feel a sense of affiliation or membership in the organization will be less likely to undermine the system. When employees feel underappreciated and alienated from an organization, they are more likely to permit indiscretions to happen.

Reduction in Turnover

As with other employers, health care providers find recruiting, orienting, and training new employees to be costly. Costs mount quickly especially with high turnover rates. Kazemak and Shomaker (1990) estimate that nearly 60 percent of a hospital's costs are labor related. The costs of turnover are discussed in greater detail in Chapter 10.

Patient care may suffer when there is a lack of stability in the clinical and support services team due to high turnover. Problems between professional and support staff are exacerbated by the poor communication, inadequate skills, and faulty performance that can result when turnover is high. If the turnover is a result of employees' lack of respect for their co-workers who are different, the administration must take steps to address diversity or costs due to staff turnover will increase.

More Effective Teams

Diversity initiatives encourage respect for differences. Astute executives may have observed that minority employees are silent in staff meetings when white employees are in the majority. If differences are valued, minority employee involvement levels should increase, setting the climate for enhanced creativity and participation in problem-solving. Studies of team performance support the contention that diverse teams produce more creative solutions, especially those that have learned to respect the differences among team members.

Subsequent chapters will discuss the benefits of diversity leadership in greater detail. Case examples will chronicle the experience of health care organizations that are already benefiting from diversity leadership. Presbyterian Medical Center's experience is described below.

PRESBYTERIAN MEDICAL CENTER'S LADDER OF OPPORTUNITY

Like many other hospital-based nursing schools, the Presbyterian Medical Center of Philadelphia closed its school doors in 1988 after a century of service. As CEO I. Donald Snook considered the paradox of Presbyterian's continuing nursing shortage in light of its now defunct nursing school, he looked out his office window and saw the flurry of activity and movement typical of the hospital's West Philadelphia neighborhood. CEO Snook had gazed at the same street countless times during his seven-year tenure as CEO, but had never seen what he saw that day: the nurses of the future are the working poor of Philadelphia.

Snook's vision led to a strategic decision and, ultimately, resulted in Presbyterian's well-publicized Ladder of Opportunity. The *New York Times*, the *Philadelphia Inquirer*, "ABC World News Tonight," and the "CBS News Sunday Morning" have all featured this innovative program that addresses two challenging demographic trends: the "skills gap" and the increasing number of minority women in the labor pool.

Although not designed to be a minority recruitment or retention program, the Ladder of Opportunity has filled that role because of Presbyterian's service area and labor pool demographics. Almost 70 percent of the residents in the hospital's service area are African American; approximately 27 percent are white, and the remaining 3 percent are Latino/a or Asian. Nearly one of every three nurses aides, orderlies, and attendants at Presbyterian is African American.

The first rung of Presbyterian's Ladder of Opportunity is the School of Practical Nursing. When Presbyterian's School of Nursing closed, Snook knew that change in the facility's training program for licensed practical nurses (LPNs) was also imminent. For it to remain cost effective, it would have to expand or close also. However, unlike the program for registered nurses (RNs), Presbyterian had no problem filling enrollment quotas in the LPN training program. As a result, Presbyterian decided to expand the LPN training program into a full-fledged School of Practical Nursing. This decision was also driven in part by Presbyterian's long-term business strategy of servicing the community's growing elderly population through expanding long-term care services, and was consistent with the CEO's vision and the community's needs and human resources.

Through a cooperative agreement with the Community College of Philadelphia, the LPN training program currently provides 1,500 hours of state-required hospital training with 20 college credits. Students who complete the LPN program are only 30 credits, or one year, from being eligibile to sit for the RN licensing examination, which provides a nationally recognized credential and the potential to earn an annual salary in excess of $36,000.

Presbyterian invested approximately one million dollars to expand its existing training program for LPNs into today's School of Practical Nursing. Since its 1990 initiative to recruit students from within the hospital and its service area, there are now ten applicants for each available training slot with 100 students admitted each year—60 in the full-time program and 40 in the part-time program. Most live in West Philadelphia or other low-income areas in the city. Since close to one-third of the program's graduates were previously receiving welfare payments, the $25,000 starting salary of an LPN represents a significant boost in family income, which in turn provides a boost to the community.

Because Presbyterian realized that many students required remedial education to strengthen their basic skills, it provides tutoring and financial assistance as well as flexible work schedules to facilitate students' success. In addition, social workers assist students with personal or family problems that might interfere with their studies.

In 1994, the school's curriculum was changed to incorporate a certified nursing assistant program. Students who complete this program can work for one of Presbyterian's nursing homes, earning a starting salary of approximately $15,000 per year, while completing requirements for the LPN. Presbyterian made this adjustment in response to the shift in available positions from hospital-based tertiary care to long-term care.

As of 1994, eight of every ten graduates of the School of Practical Nursing have been hired by Presbyterian Medical Center or its affiliate nursing homes. Graduates who remain Presbyterian employees are eligible to take additional steps on the Ladder of Opportunity. Tuition reimbursement and other types of support assist students up the ladder's rungs to RN, BSN, MSN, and Ph.D. degrees through cooperative arrangements with the nearby University of Pennsylvania and Philadelphia Community College.

Because the Ladder of Opportunity is a relatively new program, data on its long-term impact are limited. Now in its fourth year, the LPN program has graduated 217 students, almost half of whom are African American. All of the graduates have passed the state boards. Approximately one in every three graduates pursues an associate degree and licensure as a registered nurse. To date, one graduate has gone on for a BSN. A recently established alumni office will allow Presbyterian to better track the program's longer-term achievements.

In the meantime, Presbyterian's commitment and the contagious enthusiasm of Snook, the program's faculty and students, and the media provide ample support for this innovative response to the changing demographics of America's workforce. The nationally syndicated columnist Claude Lewis (1993) wrote, "Presbyterian's nursing program is proving that sometimes all that is needed to change lives is new opportunities along with imaginative, creative and innovative recruiting efforts among America's disenfranchised."

"In the final analysis," says Snook, "you serve the community or you're not around."

REFERENCES

American College of Healthcare Executives, and National Association of Health Services Executives. 1993. *A Racial Comparison of Career Attainment in Healthcare Management: Findings of a National Survey of Black and White Healthcare Executives.* Chicago: ACHE.

American College of Healthcare Executives, and University of Iowa Graduate Programs in Hospital and Health Administration. 1991. *Gender and Careers in Healthcare Management: Findings of a National Survey of Healthcare Executives.* Chicago: ACHE.

American Public Health Association. 1994. "APHA Calls on HHS to Collect Minority Health Data on Forms." *The Nation's Health* 24, no. 5 (May–June): 1, 12.

Beilinson, J. 1990. "Workforce 2000: Already Here?" *Personnel Journal* 67 (10): 3–4.

Blankenau, R. 1994. "Project Aims to Prepare Minorities for Health Care Leadership Roles." *Hospitals and Health Networks* 68 (22): 74.

Carfang, A. J. 1993. "Equal Opportunity, Stock Performance Linked." Press release. Chicago: Covenant Investment Management.

Edmonston, B., and J. S. Passel. 1994. "The Future Immigrant Population of the United States." In *Immigration and Ethnicity: The Integration of America's Newest Arrivals,* edited by B. Edmonston and J. S. Passel, 317–53. Washington, DC: The Urban Institute Press.

Friedman, E. 1991. "Health Care's Changing Face: The Demographics of the 21st Century." *Hospitals* 65 (7): 36–40.

———. 1992. "America's Growing Diversity: Melting Pot or Rainbow?" *Healthcare Forum Journal* 35 (1): 10–14.

Hall, E. T., and M. R. Hall. 1990. *Understanding Cultural Differences.* Yarmouth, ME: Intercultural Press.

Johnston, W. R., and A. H. Packer. 1987. *Workforce 2000: Work and Workers for the 21st Century.* Indianapolis: Hudson Institute.

Kazemak, E. A., and B. Shomaker. 1990. "Reducing Turnover Can Bring Bottom Line Results." *Healthcare Financial Management* 44 (8): 80.

Lewis, C. 1993. "Solution to the Nurse Shortage: Train Them in the Neighborhood." *Philadelphia Inquirer* (13 January).

McCarroll, T. A. 1993. "It's a Mass Market No More." *Time* 142 (21): 80–81.

McManus, J., (ed). 1993. "The New Face of America" Special Issue. *Time* 142 (21).

Novak, C. A. 1992. "Profiting from Diversity." *Best's Review* 92 (11): 18–22, 99–100.

Ong, P. (ed.). 1994. *State of Asian Pacific America.* Los Angeles: Leadership Education for Asian Pacifics.

Pallarito, K. 1994. "Top Priorities." *Modern Healthcare* 24 (16): 31–38.

Petersdorf, R. G., K. Turner, H. W. Nickens, and T. Ready. 1990. "Minorities in Medicine: Past, Present, and Future." *Academic Medicine* 65 (11): 663–70.

Polednak, A. P. 1989. *Racial and Ethnic Differences in Disease.* New York: Oxford University Press.

Rusting, R. R. 1987. *Theft in Hospitals and Nursing Homes.* Port Washington, NY: Rusting Publications.

Sabatino, F. 1993. "Culture Shock: Are U.S. Hospitals Ready?" *Hospitals* 67 (10): 23–28.

Thornburg, L. 1991. "What's Wrong with Workforce 2000?" *HRMagazine* 36 (8): 38–42.

Towers Perrin and the Hudson Institute. 1990. *Workforce 2000: Competing in a Seller's Market: Is Corporate America Prepared?* New York: Towers Perrin.

Wagner, M. 1991. "Managing Diversity." *Modern Healthcare* 21 (39): 24–29.

Walker, P. W., and M. K. Brand. 1993. "The Status of Data on Minority Practitioners in Selected Allied Health Professions." *Journal of Allied Health* 22 (1): 1–7.

Wallace, S. P., and C. Lew-Ting. 1993. "Getting by at Home: Community-Based Long-Term Care of Latino Elders." *Western Journal of Medicine* 157 (3): 337–44.

Yergan J., A. B. Flood, J. P. LoGerfo, and P. Diehr. 1987. "Relationship Between Patient Race and the Intensity of Hospital Services." *Medical Care* 25 (7): 592–603.

CHAPTER 2

A Journey of Self-Discovery

AS CHAPTER 1 revealed, demographic changes have transformed diversity leadership from repackaged liberalism to
business imperative. But, unlike more typical business imperatives
such as responding to Medicare's prospective payment system or
addressing the trends toward health care networks and managed
care, successful diversity leadership requires executives to engage in
an unprecedented level of self-exploration. The concept of human
diversity, after all, is a very personal one.

Individual identity makes each person simultaneously unique
and similar. Composed of both individual characteristics and
traits that are the consequence of each person's group affiliations,
individual identity plays a key role in diversity leadership. Deeply
rooted, closely held values and beliefs guide behavior and help
determine our personal and organizational style. As Cox (1993,
43) explains, "Various group identities play a part in how we
define ourselves as well as how others view us."

The personal journey outlined in this chapter guides health
care executives as they begin to explore the effect that group
identity has on their own and other's values, beliefs, and behaviors.
Insights gained through the personal journey provide a strong
foundation for the process of diversity leadership.

THE ORGANIZATIONAL CLIMATE

Exercise 1: The Power of Observation

- **Observe management and staff.** Begin the journey
  by taking a walk around the health care facility. Pay
  close attention to the racial, gender, and other visible

group identities of employees *at varying levels* and *in different roles* in the organization. Who occupies the management, professional staff, skilled, and semiskilled positions? Note your reactions to what you see. How do you explain the gender and racial/ethnic distribution in the organizational hierarchy? Do you find yourself justifying why certain racial and gender groups tend to occupy certain roles? What *assumptions* do you make about identity groups that are clustered in particular positions?

- **Observe patient behavior.** Next, walk around the facility with your focus on patients this time. What are the characteristics of patients by gender, race, age, or other visible group identities? Is there similarity between the overall mix of employees and the mix of patients being served? When patients enter a health care organization do you think it is important for them to see service providers who are members of their identity groups? Is staff composition at certain levels in any way related to patient cooperation, patient disclosure of information, or the amount of information physicians and other clinicians give to patients about their condition? Have you any evidence relating older patients' feeling valued and respected to the ages of the staff who provide care to them? Do you observe physically challenged patients being treated with dignity and respect? Do you think the quality of patient care would be different if care providers were more diverse?

- **Observe patient and staff interactions.** What are the skills staff need to be effective in serving the patient base? How do staff attitudes and behavior affect patient cooperation? Do clinicians need to know about patients' belief systems to influence their cooperation in taking medication, recognizing and reporting physical problems and symptoms, and seeking information about their condition? Do you think the quality of patient care would improve if physicians and other clinicians knew more about patients' identity groups?

- **Observe staff interactions and teamwork.** How well do staff from different racial or other identity groups work together? Do identity groups cluster in the cafeteria or in the hallways of your health care organization? What successes and failures have you observed among staff in communication, decision making, cooperation, and joint planning? How do nurses and service workers such as nurses aides or patient transporters communicate? How do administrators relate to support staff? How would you describe the quality and effectiveness of communication between doctors and nurses, between administrators and staff, between service workers and supervisors? Do you observe any patterns in communication styles and group identities?

• **Observe the environment.** Does the physical plant reflect the life experiences of patients and staff? Do artwork, magazines, and the style of interpersonal etiquette and greetings communicate acceptance and understanding of patients' varying identity groups? Are the magazines in the hospital waiting rooms reflective of the many cultures of patients? If there is a large Latino or Asian patient base, does the hospital purchase magazines and newspapers in Spanish and different Asian languages? Does artwork reflect the images of all of the identity groups served by the health care organization?

THE RACIAL AND ETHNIC LIFELINE

Cultural programming, though very subtle, is extremely powerful in shaping how we view ourselves, members of our own identity groups, and members of other identity groups. We learn about our own and other identity groups in a variety of ways. Our earliest attitudes usually come from impressions of family members, school relationships, peer group influence, and media exposure.

The lifeline activity will begin to uncover the milestone events that helped to mold your current attitudes, beliefs, and behaviors about one key aspect of identity: race/ethnicity. This activity can be modified to uncover other milestone events that help explain how you view other group identities such as gender, age, religion, sexual orientation, or social class.

Exercise 2: Racial and Ethnic Lifeline

• On the Lifeline Graph, Figure 2.1, plot the earliest memory you have of a racial or ethnic event that affected you on a personal level. The event can be an experience

Figure 2.1   Lifeline Graph

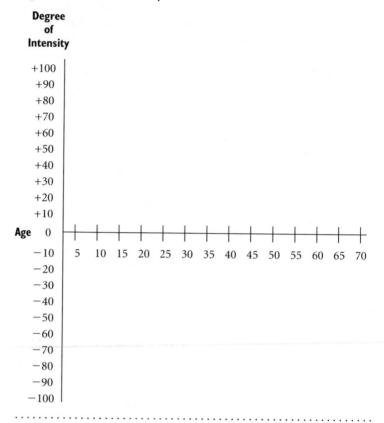

Instructions:
1. Recall the event and the age it occurred.
2. Determine whether the event was positive or negative.
3. Place a dot on the graph at the age and intensity level.
4. Connect each of the positive and negative events with a line, so that you can see the pattern over time.

Source: ©*Eclipse Consultant Group, Inc. Reprinted by permission.*

in which you participated or an event in the larger society that you became aware of through the media. Events in which you personally participated can be either intra- or intergroup—that is, either with others from your own racial or ethnic identity group or with people from another racial or ethnic identity group. On the horizontal axis, locate your age at the time that the event occurred. On the vertical axis locate the degree of emotional intensity, either positive or negative, that you felt when the event occurred. Plot the event at the intersection on the Lifeline Graph. Recall what you learned about yourself and others involved in the event. Jot down the key emotions you felt and the attitudes and beliefs that the incident reinforced for you.

- Move to a later age and event and repeat the process described above. Continue the lifeline activity until you reach your current age. Reflect on how the events you plotted on the Lifeline Graph influence your attitudes, beliefs, and behaviors about race or ethnicity today. Did the emotional intensity of events increase or decrease as you grew older? What pattern of emotionally positive or emotionally negative events do you see on your Lifeline Graph? If the event involved racial or ethnic discrimination, were you a perpetrator, victim, or bystander? Which events would you feel most comfortable sharing with others? Why?

- Share the exercise with someone you trust from a racial or ethnic identity group that is different from your own. Ask him or her to also complete the Lifeline Graph. Afterward, discuss both of your Lifeline graphs as well as the conclusions you each drew from the events plotted on your graphs. Discuss what you learned and how you felt while undertaking the lifeline activity. Were your experiences and reactions similar or different? Do the Lifeline graphs of individuals who are members of racial or ethnic identity groups that have been the target of discrimination or negative stereotyping differ from the Lifeline graphs of individuals who identify with a group that has not been targeted? How might different life lines affect inter- and intragroup relationships in health care organizations?

GROUP IDENTITIES ············

Exercise 3: Group Identity and Personal Experience

Exploring how people experience their group affiliations can provide the health care executive with more insight into the roles that racial, ethnic, gender, and other group identities play in human interactions within health care organizations. This section leads the reader through a series of interviews designed to increase awareness of the power and impact of group identities on our individual experiences and responses.

- Interview three individuals: a person of color, a woman, and a differently abled person. Ask each one the following question: What does it mean to be (blank)? Fill in the blank with only one characteristic, that is, race, gender or physical ability. Jot down their responses.

- Interview three other individuals: a white person of either gender, a male of any race, and an able-bodied person of any race or gender. Ask each one the same question: What does it mean to be (blank)? Keep the question focused only on the specific group identity characteristic under discussion. If the interviewee starts talking about another group identity characteristic—for example, if the individual addressing the question, What does it mean to be white? or begins to discuss what it means to be a woman or to be Jewish—take steps to bring the discussion back to being white. Jot down the responses of each interviewee.

- Ask a colleague or friend to interview you. Be aware of your responses and your feelings during the interview process.

- Compare the interviews. Was it easier for minority group members to talk about the meaning of their race or gender than it was for majority group members? Did majority group members seem to be aware of any privileges and entitlements they may have experienced as a consequence of their group identity? Did minority group members discuss discrimination, prejudice, or stereotypes they may have experienced as a result of their group identity? Does group identity carry the same meaning with the same intensity of feeling for majority and minority group members?

THE ROLE OF THE MEDIA

Cultural programming is pervasive and occurs within every segment of our society. One way to illustrate this is by studying how groups are portrayed in the mass media. Your task in this exercise is to study general messages that the media deliver about particular identity groups. In thinking about the media, consider newspapers and other print media, radio call-in shows and other programs, movies, and all television programs, among others.

Exercise 4: Images in the Media

- Select two American racial or ethnic groups that are commonly portrayed in the media. Include a white ethnic group and a group whose skin color is not white or whose speech is noticeably different from standard English. Observe how these groups are portrayed in the media. What images of the groups you've selected are reinforced through the portrayals you've observed in the media? Would you label the images you see as positive or negative?

- Think of and list, side by side, the stereotypes you have heard about each of the groups whose media portrayals you have observed. Which group has the most positive stereotypes and which has the most negative? Ask yourself why.

- Discuss your observations with a white colleague and an ethnic or racial minority colleague to ascertain if your conclusions about how minority racial and ethnic identity groups are handled by the media are the same or different. Do your white and racial or ethnic minority colleagues share the same point of view?

ADDITIONAL DIMENSIONS OF DIVERSITY · · · · · · · · · · · ·

The following exercises explore three additional dimensions of diversity. These exercises require the reader to imagine a scenario in which a key aspect of their own identity might be perceived by others as a professional liability.

Exercise 5: Thinking about Other Dimensions of Diversity

- **What if you worked in another country?** Suppose you are employed in another country where language, religion, and sex role relationships between men and women are strictly regulated. The customs are very different from your own, and the people in the host company view your country as inferior to theirs. What would you have to do to stay connected to the organization in which you work?

- **What if your age was thought to be a liability?** Imagine that your seniority as a manager is not viewed as an asset by executive leadership and that your supervisor is younger than your youngest child. You've proposed workable solutions that would correct several major problems that are adversely affecting the bottom line, but your input is routinely dismissed by your younger supervisor. What barriers would you have to overcome to be recognized as a valuable employee? Reverse this situation. What would you have to do to have your skills and talents noticed, if your supervisor was considerably older than you and, in your estimation, lacked the technical skills to advance the department and remain current in the job?

- **What if your sexual orientation could cost you a promotion?** Imagine you are a manager who is gay. Suppose also that one of the ways middle managers tend to succeed in your organization is by frequently attending social functions to raise money and develop corporate donors. You have been in a stable relationship for ten years, yet at many of the social functions you find your colleagues introducing you as an eligible bachelor. Suppose your boss is homophobic and doesn't acknowledge it. What do you do to advance your career and maintain your sense of self?

CONCLUSIONS

Personal journeys like the one outlined in this chapter can often lead to insights such as the following:

- Behavior is more easily changed than are attitudes and beliefs about group identity.
- Clinical and administrative staff, as well as patients, bring preconceived attitudes and beliefs about their own and other identity groups into the daily interactions in the health care organization.
- Managers' cultural styles result, in part, from their group identities and influence the ways in which they recognize and reward employees.
- Cultural styles are deeply embedded in social behavior and influence the ways in which health care is delivered and received.

The personal journey exercises undertaken in this chapter are first steps on the road to discovering that managing people and delivering care in a multicultural context pose new challenges for the health care industry. The next chapter, "Group Identity: A Framework for Understanding," continues the discovery process.

REFERENCE

Cox, T. 1993. *Cultural Diversity in Organizations: Theory, Research, and Practice.* San Francisco: Berrett-Koehler.

CHAPTER 3

Group Identity:
A Framework for Understanding

GROUP IDENTITY, explains Cox (1993, 43), "is a personal affiliation with other people with whom one shares certain things in common. Such identities are central to how cultural diversity impacts behavior in organizations." There are two types of identity groups that, in part, define individual identity or self-concept—phenotype identity groups and culture identity groups (Cox 1993). Members of **phenotype groups** share a distinguishing and visible physical characteristic in common such as skin color or gender. According to Cox (1993, 45), phenotype identity groups are important because "we use visible signals as a basis for categorizing people as men, women, Blacks, Asians, Caucasians, physically disabled, and so on. Once that visual identification has been made, our minds automatically call forth any stored data about other members of that group. A set of expectations or assumptions is therefore often attached to these phenotype identifications and may predispose us to interact with a person in a particular way."

Members of **culture identity groups**, on the other hand, share a distinctive subjective culture or world view. Gays and lesbians, Episcopalians, or Americans may be physically indistinguishable from heterosexuals, Baptists, or Canadians but, nevertheless, share an important group identity with its own values, beliefs, and behaviors. The number of culture identity groups with which an individual identifies and the strength or relative importance of that identification, Cox (1993) explains, will vary. Based on considerable research, Cox (1993, 50) concludes that, "most individuals have relatively high awareness of the identity that most distinguishes them from the majority group in a particular setting and considerably less awareness of other identities." When the phenotype and culture identities of an individual are inconsistent, explains Cox (1993), others who interact with the individual will experience some psychological discomfort.

Individuals' phenotype and culture group identities and their feelings about their own as well as others' group identities affect interactions in health care organizations. Cross (1971), Atkinson, Morton, and Sue (1979) and Helms (1984, 1990) have all advanced models of racial identity development that can help to illustrate how an individual's stage of racial identity will influence work relationships and health care encounters. Although these models were originally advanced to explain the stages of black and white racial identity development, they provide a conceptual framework that can be extended to other minority-majority identity groups, such as homosexuals and heterosexuals, the physically challenged and the able-bodied, and women and men. Valuing diversity involves understanding how race, gender, and other key aspects of identity influence the ways in which people interpret, choose, explain, and justify their own behaviors and the behaviors of others in the workplace.

The examples used below to illustrate the models are hypothetical or composite examples drawn from experience. Individuals cannot be categorized into a stage of the models based solely on a few observed behaviors. The process of racial identity development is complex. The models are an attempt to explain the relationship between an individual's stage of racial identity development and how that individual interacts with others. The models should not be used to label or stereotype others.

MINORITY RACIAL IDENTITY DEVELOPMENT

Table 3.1 is the Model of Racial/Cultural Identity Development of the Eclipse Consultant Group. The theory of minority identity development that supports Table 3.1 was initially developed by Cross (1971) and subsequently extended by Atkinson, Morton, and Sue (1979). The model has since been extensively studied, refined, and validated (Helms 1990). Each stage in the model is discussed in detail, and implications for intra- and intergroup relationships in health care organizations are illustrated through hypothetical or composite examples drawn from experience. The examples were developed to show behavior in a health care setting that reflects the theoretical stage of identity development under discussion.

Because the Cross (1971) model was originally developed to explain black identity development and in order to more clearly convey the model's implications for health care organizations, all illustrations of the model are of interactions between black and white staff or patients. However, Table 3.1 can be used to describe the identity development of other minority groups as well.

Adaptation

The first stage, **Adaptation** occurs when the minority group member attempts to conform and accommodate to the majority culture, rejecting one's own. For an individual at this stage of identity development, assimilation is the name of the game.

According to the model, black persons at this stage of identity development will reinforce negative racial stereotypes against their own group if the majority group promotes it. For example, if the majority thinks that blacks are shiftless, lazy, and dangerous, the adapter will believe the same. A black recreational therapist in the adaptation stage might nod and express agreement when her white colleagues say, "Most blacks are so angry and difficult to get along with. We're glad you're not like them."

An individual in the adaptation stage wears a mask to survive in the majority culture. The adapter's goal is to tell the majority group members whatever they want to hear. If the individual adapter's language and skin color are indistinguishable from majority group members, the individual may try to pass himself or herself as a majority group member (Taylor-Haizlip 1994).

How might adaptation behavior manifest in a black patient? A black patient in the adaptation stage can be seemingly compliant. Black patients in this stage may follow white physicians' orders while in their presence but when left alone, will fail to carry out the orders. For example, a physician tells the patient to take medicine in four-hour intervals; the patient smiles and nods to convey agreement but fails to take the medicine at the prescribed intervals. Or, an older black patient in the adaptation stage may not reveal to the white doctor that he or she is still having pain two weeks following an operation. To do so would show disrespect for the doctor. Soon individuals in the adaptation stage may discover that there is a price to pay for reverence given to what is perceived to be white authority. They may withhold information about their condition and not convey their anger toward professional staff. In order not to appear ungrateful, they may attempt to be conciliatory in front of the doctor or nurse.

The adapter's sense of self is framed within the context of racial superiority and inferiority. Deference to authority is, in

Table 3.1 Eclipse's Model of Racial/Cultural Identity Development

Stage	Racial Self-Identity	Attitudes and Behaviors			
		Blacks as a Group	Blacks to Whites	Blacks to Other Minorities	White Reactions to Blacks
1. Adaptation	To pass or not pass Accepts bias	Suppressed anger Passivity	Superficial politeness Compliance	Indifference Acceptance of white bias	Comfort Superiority Patronizing
2. Confusion	Conflict between passive and anger Search for identity	Challenges bias vs. acceptance Self-hatred expressed	Compliance and challenge	Search for similarities Testing minority superiority Loyalty to ethnic group identity	Confusion Discomfort
3. Crystallization	"I am black" Strong race pride Arrogance Compassion	Pushes blacks to be black Judges other blacks	Rejects white superiority Challenges and blames Us against them	Superiority Challenges others to resist whites	Fear Rage Anger
4. Reevaluation	Self-assurance Stop polarized thinking	Stops judging blacks Integrates identity	Questions white rage Trust of individual whites	Equal dialogue Compassion Confronts conformity	Search for genuine dialogue Discusses hard racial issues
5. Transcultural	Struggle with internalized "isms" Race/ethnic identity valued	Able to discuss race Confronts internal "isms" Supports group	Genuine dialogue Individual relationships Sees others' "isms"	Genuine dialogue Compassion Open talk about ethnic/race relations	Respect Openness Selected fear

Source: Model adapted by Eclipse Consultant Group, Inc. from William Cross' (1971) "Theory of Nigrescence" and the Minority Identity Development Model by Atkinson, Morton, and Sue (1979). ©Eclipse Consultant Group, Inc. Reprinted by permission.

part, influenced by sociohistorical experience with white people. Patients may believe that the white doctor knows best and will not question the physician's evaluation. Internally, however, they may be feeling annoyed and afraid to speak up.

Confusion

The second stage, **Confusion** is characterized by ambivalence and conflict. Black persons in confusion vacillate between rejecting their group and almost simultaneously embracing it. They will make both positive and negative comments about their own racial identity group. They may begin to silently challenge the accepted racial stereotypes, while simultaneously reinforcing them.

Confusion is filled with ambivalence as it relates to self-evaluation. Racial identity is in a state of flux. Thinking may follow along these lines: "White people believe that all black people are lazy. I'm not lazy and I'm black." As a result, the individual starts to recognize that negative stereotypes have limited their racial identity group's employment opportunities, educational experiences, and access to health care. New feelings are in conflict with old beliefs. "Blacks deserve to be treated like this," is contrasted with "No, we don't; white people are only doing this because they're prejudiced." Black persons in the confusion stage start to confront negative messages they've internalized from the majority culture, while experiencing emerging feelings of self-acceptance.

Individuals in the confusion stage also begin to question beliefs about white superiority. Contradictions are seen in how whites treat each other, other minority groups, and blacks. This questioning of white superiority is accompanied by an exploration of the negative stereotypes about blacks. Covert suspicion of whites surfaces in the context of continuing discomfort with their own emerging racial identity. Initially, the distrust against whites is not expressed openly, especially in the presence of whites, but it will be discussed among blacks in closed settings.

In the health care setting, a black service worker in this stage may appear to cooperate with white supervisors on the surface but may undercut their authority in front of patients. For example, if a white supervisor criticizes the work, in front of a black patient, of a black service worker who happens to be in the confusion stage, the worker may be silent and appear compliant in front of the supervisor. However, once the supervisor leaves, the service worker may make racially loaded comments about the supervisor to the black patient.

Negative feelings about blacks may be discussed in the presence of blacks or whites, but not at the same time nor in the same setting. The black person is still in conflict about positive acceptance of the racial group as an important point of reference. One's feelings in this stage are ambivalent—a mixture of pride, joy, wonderment, anger, and shame. The individual recognizes that the racial group is both like and unlike the stereotypes; some stereotypes fit and some do not.

Blacks in the confusion stage become increasingly aware that individual differences within their race are very broad— some individuals accept and some reject their phenotype and its associated culture identity. The view of whites as a referent group also changes: in adaptation, whites are seen as superior to blacks. They are the standard of comparison. In confusion, the white standard is questioned and challenged.

A black patient in the confusion stage might say to another black patient, "I wouldn't go to a black doctor if you paid me. You know they don't know what they're doing." Moments later the same patient may say to some other patient, "Did you see how that nurse treated Dr. Johnson (a black doctor)? She didn't treat Dr. Jones (a white doctor) that way. White people sure are prejudiced." On one hand, black professionals are denigrated, and on the other, they are most ardently defended.

What often propels black people to resolve their confusion in stage two is another black person who intensifies the conflict by pressuring them to get off the fence and commit to a black identity. The confusion stage comes to an end when people in this stage reveal their ambivalence about being black to other blacks who are in a more advanced stage of racial identity development.

Crystallization

When the confusion dissipates, stage two is complete. What follows next is the somewhat turbulent period of stage three, **Crystallization**. Blacks in this stage embrace their racial identity and reject the majority culture. White interactions with blacks are interpreted in an historical/political context where whites are viewed as the oppressor and are unilaterally distrusted. On the other hand, blacks are elevated to superior status.

Black individuals in crystallization revel in ethnic pride and begin an intense study of black culture prior to, during, and after slavery. They start to express their ethnic identity in dress, language, and in some cases through religious affiliation with, for example, the Black Muslims, Black Jews, Black Christians, or Black Catholics. People in crystallization may assume ethnic names and disassociate with "slave names." It's a time of deep appreciation for afrocentricity in their behavior, spiritual practices, politics, and professional affiliations.

Recall that black patients in adaptation may not cooperate with minority caregivers, even dismissing them as not having authority. In the crystallization stage black patients may demand to see a caregiver from the same racial group and, likewise, refuse to cooperate with white caregivers. Such behavior may be confusing to majority or minority staff who lack understanding of the role that identity development plays in cross-racial interactions.

One key change that characterizes stage three is the black person's blatant rejection of whites as a reference group for self-identification. The confusion and conflict in stage two dissipates in stage three, and the individual emerges to fully embrace the racial group. The person also rejects, unilaterally, any comments from whites about that group or its members. An example is of a black billing clerk in the crystallization stage who had a reputation for viewing every disagreement with his white colleagues as racially motivated and didn't hesitate to express the disgust, anger, and rage his perception generated within him.

Unlike their response to blacks in the adaptation and confusion stages, whites are more likely to openly express fear toward blacks who are in stage three. The person in crystallization is immersed in racial acceptance and justifies most in-group behavior. It's possible that white subordinates of black supervisors who are in the crystallization stage may perceive the supervisor as always siding with black colleagues when conflicts arise. There may be a total rejection of whites and white culture, and this rejection may be angrily expressed. Without exception, whites are the enemy. One black laboratory technician reflected stage three when she made the following comment during a diversity training session: "There's no way I'd trust any white person in this hospital to cut on my body. Have you seen how we look when they finish hacking on us? The only doctor who could cut on me is a black doctor. I would rather die before I'd let a white doctor touch me."

Some blacks remain in crystallization for long periods of time, while others move through the stage rather quickly. Several interpersonal factors may influence individuals to move forward, such as

- relationship pressure from a close friend who has moved through stage three;
- pressure from a white person who has sustained contact with the black person through this turbulent stage;

- ongoing work relationships where the black person has to rely on or assist a white person through crisis; or
- a peak experience of a profound nature that upsets the stage three person's world view, such as having one's life saved by someone who is white.

Reevaluation

Once blacks begin to actively question whether unilateral acceptance of blacks and rejection of whites reflects their interpersonal experience with both groups, they enter stage four, **Reevaluation**. In this stage, they fully accept their ethnic group as the point of reference for their identity, while concurrently questioning the need for racial polarization. They begin to realize that racial groups are neither all good nor all bad.

Questions such as the following are reviewed and are beginning to be resolved in stage four: Is it possible to accept my racial group and still relate to some members of the dominant culture? Can I trust any white people? Are blacks right all of the time? Are some blacks destructive to other blacks? Is it possible to be strongly identified with my racial group and reject some of the members of my own race?

Blacks in this stage will begin to trust white people who are able to listen to their complaints about racism. Once they discover that some white people can be trusted, the belief that all white people are racist is shattered. Resolution of this stage generally means the black persons can discriminate between whites who can be trusted from those who cannot. In addition, they can articulate the effects of institutional racism on blacks. For example, a black vice president illustrated the reevaluation stage when she shared the following perception with a white male counterpart with whom she is developing a close working relationship: "I think our hospital has a poor track record for hiring community people who are black and Latino. The problem seems systemic. We need to confront our employment practices and look at both recruitment and retention. I'm not ready to discuss this issue with the rest of the leadership team, but I would like to know what you think." She now trusts her white counterpart enough to raise a racially sensitive issue.

Transcultural

Stage five, **Transcultural**, is characterized by self-acceptance, appreciation of other minority groups, and open communication with whites. Stage five individuals see value in other identity groups, but their own personal racial identity is clearly established and cherished. Those in the transcultural stage speak freely about race as advocates who are not defensive but who understand black issues in a sociopolitical context.

Imagine this scenario: A white x-ray technician says to his black female supervisor, "Only blacks and women get promoted to supervisory positions in this place. I don't have a chance even though I'm qualified." The black supervisor responds in a nondefensive tone by asking, "How many minorities or women do you know in supervisory positions? I am only aware of three out of the 45 on the nonnursing staff. I can see you really think you are at a disadvantage as a white man. Help me to understand your point of view."

Transcultural blacks can serve as leaders and as role models in health care organizations that are engaged in diversity leadership. Consider the following examples of the kinds of contributions that transcultural blacks can make in the workplace.

- A black president in the transcultural stage successfully mentors emerging leaders of all races. She has recruited many talented young managers to the health care network. They, in turn, have made impressive contributions to diversity leadership and to the overall success of the organization.

- A black director of community relations has developed a strategy that dramatically increases black participation in the hospital's patient education series. The series previously drew interest only from white residents of the racially mixed service area. The director has helped both white and black health educators to develop cross-cultural communication strategies that meet the needs of the increasingly diverse and multicultural audience. The hospital's market penetration has increased significantly.

- A black patient transporter in the transcultural stage is a popular peer trainer in the health care organization's cultural diversity initiative. He received an organizationwide award for his role in promoting interracial understanding and improved employee morale.

Acceptance of one's racial identity has a profound impact on interpersonal relationships in health care organizations. Understanding the minority racial identity development process can provide insight into the challenges of intra- and interracial communication in health care settings.

WHITE RACIAL IDENTITY DEVELOPMENT

Whites also engage in a developmental process that, if continued, can result in a positive white group identity (Helms 1990). This developmental process occurs because whites, like minorities, encounter and are shaped by individual, institutional, and cultural racism (Helms 1990). These three manifestations of racism can be described as:

- **Individual racism** consists of attitudes, beliefs, and behaviors that reinforce the presumed superiority of whites and inferiority of nonwhites.
- **Institutional racism** refers to policies, laws, and regulations that systematically give the advantage to whites and the disadvantage to nonwhites.
- **Cultural racism** refers to societal beliefs and customs that reinforce the assumption that white culture—for example, dialect, traditions, and appearance—is superior and nonwhite culture is inferior (Helms 1990).

According to Helms:

Because each of these three types of racism is so much a part of the cultural milieu, each can become a part of the White person's racial identity or consciousness ipso facto. In order to develop a healthy White identity, defined in part as a nonracist identity, virtually every White person in the United States must overcome one or more of these aspects of racism. Additionally, he or she must accept his or her own Whiteness, the cultural implications of being White, and define a view of Self as a racial being that does not depend on the perceived superiority of one racial group over another (p. 50).

Helms (1984; 1990) formulated a model to describe the process of white racial identity development. Unlike the bigotry explanation of white racial identity, which divides whites into two categories, overtly racist or not overtly racist, the Helms (1984; 1990) model explains the richness and complexity of white racial identity development and describes the process whereby whites can come to terms with their whiteness as individual members of a racial group.

Helms' pioneering work can assist health care executives in understanding the interpersonal dynamics of whites and other majority group members in organizations. Helms (1984; 1990) believes that whites must move through two phases of racial consciousness in order to develop a positive white nonracist identity. The first phase is called "the abandonment of racism" and the second, "establishing a positive white identity" (Helms 1984; 1990). Each phase is characterized by three stages. The Model of White Racial Consciousness shown in Table 3.2 builds on Helms' earlier work. Each stage in the Eclipse Consultant Group's model is discussed in detail below and implications for intra and intergroup relationships in health care organizations are illustrated. As with the minority racial identity development model discussed above, the white racial consciousness model is illustrated below with hypothetical or composite examples drawn from experience. The examples are intended to reflect the theoretical stage of identity development under discussion.

The Abandonment of Racism

The first phase of white racial consciousness, **Abandonment of Racism**, is characterized by three stages: contact (naivete), disintegration (dissonance), and reintegration (defensive). This phase is the process of moving from not being conscious of race as a white person to the conscious acknowledgment of white racial identity. The stage descriptions in parentheses were developed by Eclipse Consultant Group as an alternative to Helms' (1984; 1990) original names of the stages, and are the ones that will be used in this discussion.

Naivete

In stage 1, **Naivete**, white persons are unaware of the implications of minority racial identity. And, more importantly, they do not perceive their own group as having a racial identity. White persons in the naivete stage may minimize racial identity and, instead, focus on national identity—that is, on being an American. White people in the naivete stage of white racial identity development may make statements like the following: "Why can't we all just be Americans? I don't understand why these minority groups are making a fuss about racial pride."

White people in this stage believe that they are color blind, yet at the same time insist that minority groups should assimilate into "American" culture. Their motto is, "When in Rome, do as the Romans do." One white nurse reflected the naivete stage when she was overheard expressing the opinion that black patients had far too many visitors at once, crowding whites out of the visiting area. She asked her colleagues, "Why can't they follow the rules and have just one or two visitors like the rest of us?"

Table 3.2 White Racial Consciousness

| | | First Phase: Abandonment of Racism | | | |
| | | Attitudes and Behaviors | | | |
Stage	Self-Identity	Whites as a Group	Black Individuals	Blacks as a Group	Racism
1. Contact (Naivete)	"White is not a color!"	Does not consider whites a group	Avoids contact except with blacks who "seem" white	"People are people; I don't see color."	No awareness, benefits from privileges
2. Disintegration (Dissonance)	"Maybe being white *does* matter."	Ambivalence	Approaches and avoids contact	Ambivalence, stereotypic perceptions	Beginning awareness, causes conflict
3. Reintegration (Defensive)	"*So what* if I'm white?"	"We have more because we *deserve* more!"	Avoidance and/or hostility	"Those people . . ."	Denial or justification of inequities

Second Phase: Establishing a Positive White Identity

Stage	Self-Identity	Attitudes and Behaviors			
		Whites as a Group	Black Individuals	Blacks as a Group	Racism
4. Pseudo-Independence (Liberal)	"I'm white, but I'm not like *those* whites."	"Those people . . ."	Initiates contact, seeks answers from, may patronize	Idealizes as victims who need help to succeed in white culture	Understands intellectually, seeks simplistic solutions
5. Immersion/Emersion (Self-exploration)	"How can I redefine myself as a white person?"	Explores positive and negative aspects of white culture	Initiates contact on an individual basis	Increases appreciation of culture and history	Explores complexity; Challenges self and others to be non-racist
6. Autonomy (Transcultural)	"Being white is a positive part of my identity."	Values positive aspects of white culture	Forms intimate friendships, builds alliances	Continually expands knowledge and understanding	Actively explores and combats racism at all levels

Source. Adapted from Helms, J. Black and White Racial Identity: Theory, Research and Practice, Greenwood Press, 1990. ©Eclipse Consultant Group, Inc. Reprinted by permission.

White people in the naivete stage express individual racism, but in an unsophisticated fashion. They are unaware that comments they make can be perceived as racist. For example, a white diabetic patient characterized the naivete stage when he expressed surprise and wonderment that the nutritionist who came into his room to deliver predischarge education on diet was black. The white patient said innocently, "Wow, you're black! I can't wait to tell my wife that I saw a black nutritionist!"

If white persons in this stage of racial development engage in sustained contact with one or more people of color, they are likely to be made aware of racial entitlement. This awareness will confront the naivete of a white person who professes to be colorblind. A black colleague of a white manager who is in the naivete stage may express anger or hostility at the type of comments she might hear, such as, "I don't see color" or "We treat all people alike regardless of their race."

Suppose a black employee group in your organization requested that artwork depicting blacks and other racial and ethnic minority groups, as well as whites, be placed on display. Now suppose that a white manager in the naivete stage is unable to understand why this is important, and says, "People are people." If a black colleague confronts the naivete by asking, "How would you feel if we had only pictures of blacks in our building?" And if confronted often enough, the white person in the naivete stage will begin to experience discomfort.

Institutional entitlements that seem to be race-related become more apparent to the white person. For example, a white social worker emerging from the naivete stage may be appalled to learn that his white patients had been given extensive information on what to expect after a heart bypass, while Latino and African American patients were rarely given any information on what to expect after surgery. He may have been shocked when he questioned the nurses and physicians about the difference in protocol and was told that "they [the nonwhites] rarely follow instructions anyway."

Once the white person in the naivete stage begins to acknowledge that whites receive different treatment than other racial groups, they start to notice how deeply negative beliefs from the past shape present race relations. A white accounts payable clerk illustrated emergence from the naivete stage while part of a small group of male employees who were laughing at a racial joke. The clerk became aware that a black employee had overheard and was offended. The white clerk felt ashamed. Racial jokes and other behavior that he once had perceived as funny now came under scrutiny.

Feelings of discomfort, anxiety, and shame toward one's own racial group's behavior are awakened in white people who are emerging from the naivete stage. When discussing racial issues with whites or minority group individuals, they are caught in a dilemma: "If my racial group is responsible for these problems, what can I as an individual do to correct them? And on the other hand, what responsibility does the minority group have for creating and maintaining its own problems?" Sustained contact between whites and blacks leads to further exploration of race relations in an increasingly complex context.

Dissonance

Anxiety and discomfort mark the beginning of stage two, **Dissonance**. White persons realize, perhaps for the first time, that they do see color, and that other whites see it too. White people in dissonance begin to suspect that there might be an element of truth in their black friends' and colleagues' perceptions of bias and unequal opportunity. If, through personal choice or through circumstance, they maintain contact with black people, and if that contact is consistent at work or in social situations, then they start to notice that others, both whites and minorities, are reacting to their cross-racial relationships.

A white nurse manager once reported that her neighbors scurried over to ask if she was planning to sell her house to a black colleague who had just departed with her husband and children after an enjoyable afternoon visit. She was shocked by her neighbors' questions. When she invited white colleagues and their families to her home, the neighbors had never inquired about plans to sell her house.

Once white persons become aware that other whites are assigning meaning to their cross-racial relationships, they must make a choice between continuing the cross-racial relationship and facing rejection by some whites or succumbing to pressure and limiting the relationship. If the former is chosen, they can continue to struggle with what it means to be white in a mixed racial context. If the latter cause of action is chosen, they may attempt to retreat into a "whites-only" world. However, retreating to a whites-only world has become an increasingly difficult option for whites in the dissonance stage to exercise due to the changing demographics previously discussed.

Sustained contact with blacks will cause white persons in dissonance to experience more anxiety, especially as they continue to learn about the racial experiences of their black friends and colleagues. On the surface, white people in dissonance want to identify with their black associates and be accepted as individuals who are not thought to be biased. Under the surface, they gradually become aware that some minority people have strong negative feelings toward whites.

Acceptance by some minorities and rejection by others, in addition to the white person's growing self-awareness as a racial being, can cause feelings to intensify: "Did I make the right choice to continue my close association with this person of color? Should I admit I made a mistake and drop the association?"

White persons in stage two experience **cognitive dissonance** (Festinger 1957) wherein their treasured belief that "all people are created equal" conflicts with the growing awareness that black people are not regarded as equals in our society, so either they are inferior or the way they have been treated is wrong.

One way for those in conflict to reduce dissonance is to limit contact with blacks to the greatest extent possible. Dissonance may lead a white service worker who used to take coffee breaks with her black coworkers to begin to cluster only with white coworkers. Dissonance may explain why a white speech pathologist who carpooled to an inservice training with her black colleague then avoided sitting with her at the training where all other participants were white.

Another way to reduce cognitive dissonance is by attempting to identify with blacks through imitation or taking up the cause of social justice as a way to show acceptance of blacks. Around other whites, the individual experiencing dissonance may espouse liberal views and acknowledge past racial inequities.

Another action of white persons in the dissonance stage can be engaging in patronizing discussions with blacks and whites in an attempt to demonstrate how much they understand racial tensions. These discussions are often accompanied by their offering unsolicited advice on how blacks can improve some aspect of their personal style in order to be accepted by whites. A white social worker in dissonance, for instance, may suggest that her black colleague replace her afrocentric appearance with a more conservative look in order to improve acceptance by white patients. Then during a department meeting, she may express the opinion that more services and more sensitive care are offered to white patients than to black patients. A result of this type of episode could be the dismissal of her views as ridiculous by her white colleagues, their accusing her of blaming them for social problems, and their refusal to continue the discussion.

Attempts to "help the underdog" are often really strategies designed to reduce the anxiety that the white persons in dissonance feel about white entitlement. These strategies eventually result in the white person's being rejected by both racial groups: blacks may accuse them of being paternalistic and phony, and whites may accuse them of overidentification with black causes. Rejection by both blacks and whites usually results in a strong defensive response by the white person, which brings the dissonance stage to a close and initiates stage 3.

Defensive

A key characteristic of stage 3, **Defensiveness**, is that the white person's anger about being rejected by both groups is mixed with a growing awareness of his or her own personal racial identity. Anger may be openly expressed and targeted at blacks, or the individual in the defensive stage may be angry and resentful but not openly expressive of feelings.

In the health care field, white patients in this defensive stage may refuse care from black nurses or question the credentials of black physicians or allied health professionals. In one health care organization, managers were encouraged to hire or promote more minorities into supervisory positions to achieve greater diversity in management ranks. Almost all of the current supervisors were white, while a majority of patients and support staff were ethnic minorities. Shortly after a strongly qualified black billing clerk won promotion to supervisor over a well-liked white colleague, an employee reflected the defensive stage by expressing the opinion that the black billing clerk was promoted based on race. Here the employee was assuming that race was not a factor in hiring white supervisors and that promoting a minority automatically meant that management was filling a quota. Often double standards for racial identity groups are not recognized by majority group members while in the defensive stage, and consequently, they tend to feel cheated.

Therefore, stage 3 is characterized by a return to racism. Charges of reverse discrimination will often be advanced as a rationale to maintain the status quo. For white persons in the defensive stage, different comes to be equated with deficient; and they may start to rationalize that minority employees lower standards and that majority privileges exist because white people work harder and are smarter.

If the dissonance experienced previously was resolved by retreating back into an all-white context, the individual is likely to develop overtly racist attitudes and behaviors. However, progression to a more advanced stage is possible if the white persons in the defensive stage maintain contact with other whites who are at more advanced stages of white racial identity development, or if they maintain contact with black people who have worked through their own racial identity. In one health care training session, a white male nurse reported a decrease in the number of racially loaded comments made by other nurses once he revealed that his fiancée was black. Prior to that, staff regularly talked about blacks and other racial or ethnic minorities in a derogatory way.

Establishment of a Positive White Identity

The second phase of white racial consciousness (see Table 3.2) is also composed of three stages: pseudo-independence (liberal), immersion/emersion (self-exploration), and autonomy (transcultural). Helms (1990) describes this phase as the process of establishing a positive white identity that is nonracist. The stage descriptions in parentheses were developed by Eclipse Consultant Group as an alternative to Helms' (1984; 1990) original names of the stages and are the ones to be used in the discussion that follows.

Liberal

The first stage in this process is characterized as the **liberal** stage. There are two distinct areas in which fundamental change occurs in the liberal stage. The first is the relationship the white person has to other whites, and the second is the white person's relationship with blacks.

White persons in the liberal stage recognize institutional racism and other forms of exclusion that are ingrained in the organization's system. For instance, a white supervisor in the liberal stage in an accounting department may notice that the music piped into the department by the health care organization appears to be enjoyed by most of the white staff, but many of the black staff bring their own radios with earphones.

A white person in the liberal stage is able to see how double standards operate at the institutional level. For example, a white nurse in the liberal stage may conclude that the hospital's visitation policy disadvantages black patients who, she has observed, tend to have closer relationships with their extended family than white patients generally do. Initially, the white person in the liberal stage confronts other whites who deny the existence of institutional racism and it's common for the individual to actively work to bring about major shifts in the system to achieve balance. Here's an example: one health care organization that had only whites at the director level was attempting to hire another director quickly, before an anticipated hiring freeze went into effect. No blacks were included in the quickly assembled applicant pool. As a result, a white vice president in the liberal stage approached the executive council and pressured the group to extend the application deadline so that a more diverse pool of qualified applicants could be developed.

On a personal level with blacks, the white person in the liberal stage attempts to create an intellectual bond by acknowledging racism and white collusion in creating and sustaining racial problems. There is also a curiosity about the black experience. White people in the liberal stage try to deepen their knowledge about racism and their understanding of black culture by asking blacks to teach them about black cultural heritage. In addition, white people in the liberal stage may assume that every black person is an expert on white racism and African American culture. The white person may join political causes to end racism and may also glorify the black culture as a way of showing support.

Sustained contact and honest interactions with blacks are very important in this stage. The white person in the liberal stage has to confront the desire to "save the world" while simultaneously struggling with understanding white racial privilege at an institutional and personal level. A white lab technician in the liberal stage might therefore reveal to a black friend that he only goes to Latino or African American doctors, because whites usually avoid them and he wants to show others in his family how stupid they are for avoiding them. However, the individual in this stage may be surprised to learn that the black friend is not impressed, saying that white people need to stop working so hard trying to prove that black people are equal. The individual may be asked, "If you believe they are equal, then why do you have to keep proving it?"

If contact with black people is maintained, white people in the liberal stage may begin to notice that their black friends and colleagues become annoyed when asked to validate their need to help correct past racial injustices. Black friends or colleagues may tell the white people to talk to other white people if they want to know about racism, or to look inside themselves at their own unconscious attitudes toward blacks.

If the white person in the liberal stage does turn inward, awareness as a racial being can be awakened through self-reflection and through relationships with other whites who have struggled with internalized racism. It is at this point that the white person starts to explore white identity with other whites who are involved in a similar struggle.

Self-Exploration

The white person has now entered stage five, **Self-exploration**, and the internal struggle is formed by the question, What does it mean to be white and nonracist? The white person in the self-exploration stage may begin to seek out other whites who are trying to answer the same question. For example, a white physician in this stage, may regularly meet with other white physicians to discuss sources of racial bias in their approaches to medical care delivery.

The relationships that whites in the self-exploration stage develop with blacks also take on a different dimension. Instead of asking black people to describe their experiences with racism, white people in this stage start to disclose their own experiences within a racial context and acknowledge passive forms of internalized racism. For instance, a white building engineer in the self-exploration stage may reveal to a black coworker that he had stood by silently while white coworkers at a previous place of employment wrote racist graffiti on black building engineers' lockers. Or a white phlebotomist in the self-exploration stage of white racial identity development might reveal in a diversity training seminar that she has seen other white phlebotomists treat black patients roughly but white patients gently, acknowledging that she had never brought up her observations in meetings or mentioned them to any co-workers.

Transcultural

In stage 6, **transcultural**, the often intense self-exploration that occurs in the previous stage has subsided, and the individual has successfully developed a positive and nonracist white identity. The transcultural white person is able to recognize internalized forms of racism and discuss how they affect the individual, the organization, and American culture. Racial and cultural issues are now understood at a deep level; transcultural whites do not need to defend, glorify, or rescue themselves or other whites. Institutional exclusion of others is observed and challenged in constructive ways, and the integrity of others who are different is no longer denied or questioned.

White people who have arrived at the transcultural stage are now able to discuss racial privilege comfortably and to help develop a workplace that is flexible enough to include people with different life experiences and at different levels of racial identity development. Racial and cultural differences can be observed in others and valued as different, without being evaluated as inferior.

Like transcultural blacks, transcultural whites can serve as leaders and as role models in health care organizations that are engaged in diversity leadership. Consider the following examples of the kinds of contributions that transcultural whites can make in the workplace.

- A white physical therapist in the transcultural stage becomes equally comfortable delivering care to her homebound patients, black or white. She is aware of and successfully monitors her own racial stereotypes and assumptions and, consequently, treats each person as an individual, respecting the uniqueness of each. Her exemplary performance produces accolades for the home health care agency by the local minority media.

- A white director of nursing in the transcultural stage forms a close friendship and working relationship with the black director of patient services. The two colleagues freely discuss the similarities and differences between their racial identity groups. Their collaboration results in a nationally recognized model for culturally sensitive patient care.

- A white human resource director in the transcultural stage encourages a group of black nurses who want to form a support group to share their concerns as black professionals in a predominantly white institution. At their request, he carries their concerns to a higher level, resulting in fundamental changes in policy and improved morale.

- A white security officer in the transcultural stage successfully mediates a dispute between black and white officers. His efforts avert potentially costly, time-consuming, and publicly embarrassing litigation.

CONCLUSIONS

Racial identity development, whether for majority or minority group members, is a complex and very personal process. Health care executives who understand the process will be more astute observers of their own and others' interpersonal dynamics in today's increasingly multicultural health care organizations.

The theories and illustrations presented in this chapter have aimed to simplify the process of racial identity development. Every individual will not exhibit all of the characteristics of the stages presented here; neither does everyone begin at the first stage and progress through the last. In the real world, the same person may exhibit behaviors that reflect two or more stages of racial identity development. For example, a white person whose expressed beliefs, attitudes, and behaviors generally fit the description of the liberal phase may occasionally respond to a given situation with behaviors indicative of earlier or of later stages. People can regress to earlier stages as a result of life stresses or situational demands.

The racial identity development of biracial individuals does not occur in accordance with either the white or the black model (Poston 1990). Although the minority identity development model (Atkinson, Morten, and Sue 1979) expanded Cross' (1971) original framework to include other racial and ethnic minorities, research has not supported its application to all ethnic and racial minority groups (Morten and Atkinson 1983; Gibbs 1987).

Even greater challenges are presented by attempts to apply the models to other majority/minority identity groups, such as between men and women or between heterosexuals and homosexuals. Certain details of the identity development experience described by the models will not fit the reality of individuals from these groups. The process in general, however, does provide some valuable insights. The models are clearly most useful in explaining how members of a minority identity group that has been the target of prejudice, stereotypes, or discrimination and members of the corresponding majority group that was not similarly disadvantaged respond to their group identities.

Reality further complicates application of the model in the workplace because multiple and overlapping group and personal identities are operating at once in interpersonal interactions. For example, a black woman manager may have all of the following group identities: black, woman, professional, Catholic, and American. She will also have personal aspects of her identity that, like group identities, will affect her interpersonal relationships in the workplace. Group affiliation and identification is clearly an important aspect of each person's identity, and diversity leaders can clearly benefit from greater awareness of the process of minority and majority identity development.

In "Part 2: Assessment," the discovery process is built on and the framework of understanding from individuals and identity groups is extended to the health care organization itself.

REFERENCES

Atkinson, D. R., G. Morten, and D. W. Sue. 1979. *Counseling American Minorities: A Cross-Cultural Perspective.* Dubuque, IA: William C. Brown.

Cox, T. 1993. *Cultural Diversity in Organizations: Theory, Research, and Practice.* San Francisco: Berrett-Koehler.

Cross, W. E., Jr. 1971. "The Negro-to-Black Conversion Experience: Toward a Psychology of Black Liberation." *Black World* 20 (9): 13–27.

Festinger, L. 1957. *A Theory of Cognitive Dissonance.* Stanford, CA: Stanford University Press.

Gibbs, J. T. 1987. "Identity and Marginality: Issues in the Treatment of Biracial Adolescents." *American Journal of Orthopsychiatry* 57 (2): 265–78.

Helms, J. E. 1984. "Toward a Theoretical Explanation of the Effects of Race on Counseling: A Black and White Model." *The Counseling Psychologist* 12 (4): 153–65.

———. 1990. "Toward a Model of White Racial Identity Development." In *Black and White Racial Identity Theory, Research and Practice,* edited by J. E. Helms, 33–48. New York: Greenwood Press.

Morten G., and D. Atkinson. 1983. "Minority Identity Development and Preference for Counselor Race." *Journal of Negro Education* 52 (2): 156–61.

Poston, C. 1990. "The Biracial Identity Development Model: A Needed Addition." *Journal of Counseling and Development* 69 (2): 152–55.

Taylor-Haizlip, S. 1994. *The Sweeter the Juice.* New York: Simon & Schuster.

PART II

Assessment

CEO Ralph Bryant is perplexed. A recent meeting with his VP of Human Resources brought some disheartening news: Minority recruitment and retention efforts have been uniformly unsuccessful. Urban Medical Center's employee demographics don't match those of the service area, making the Center's workforce composition ratio look decidedly unfavorable. Turnover ratio analysis confirms that the minority applicants who are hired leave the Medical Center at a rate that far exceeds that of white male hires. Absentee rates for female and minority employees also exceed white male norms. Bryant is aware that the Center's workforce and customer demographics are changing. He knows the Center cannot rely on the shrinking pool of white male workers over the long run, but he can't seem to identify appropriate corrective action.

In addition, patients are complaining of a lack of sensitivity on the part of the staff. The growing population of Asian immigrants in the area is gravitating to a competing institution that offers admissions assistance in their native languages, accommodates different preferences in diet during inpatient stays, and provides special counseling in handling the maze of insurance forms and jargon that complicates patient encounters with health care provider institutions.

And Urban Medical Center's census is down. The Center seems to lack the know-how to repackage standard services to address the needs of specific ethnic groups.

Bryant wonders what's wrong. Why is Urban Medical Center losing ground to its competition? Why are the Center's key human resource performance ratios so uniformly poor for minority staff? The Center's staff, Bryant feels, are caring and competent. What could explain the widespread discontent and polarization of staff by race, gender, and professional status?

II

Assessment

CHAPTER 4

The Need for a Cultural Audit

THE HYPOTHETICAL Urban Medical Center is among a growing number of health care facilities that could benefit from a cultural audit or organizational climate assessment. Cultural audits can help health care executives uncover and understand the impact of key assumptions, beliefs, values, and behavioral norms on the health care organization's success in recruiting, retaining, and earning the loyalty of an increasingly diverse workforce and patient mix.

CULTURE AND DIVERSITY

Culture, defined by anthropologists as the "way of life of a people," is evidenced by shared behavioral norms, values, beliefs, and customary practices. **Cultural norms** constitute the usually unwritten rules and assumptions of the health care organization. Deal and Kennedy (1982) and others (Healy and Miller 1987) refer to culture as "the way we do things around here." Because the rules of the game are generally unwritten and unspoken, playing by the rules can prove challenging to an increasingly diverse workforce and patient mix.

The research of renowned anthropologist Edward T. Hall (Hall and Hall 1990; Kennedy and Everest 1991) provides insight into the reasons why women and racial and ethnic minorities can experience special difficulties in a traditional, hierarchical health care organization. Hall categorizes cultures on a continuum that ranges from high to low context where high- and low-context cultures differ in how they see the purpose of communication as well as in the rules and regulations that drive how they communicate (Hall and Hall 1990).

High- and low-context cultures operate from different sets of unwritten rules and assumptions. Think of the traditional, hierarchical U.S. health care organization as operating from low-context cultural norms. European American men's cultural norms tend to be lower context than those of European American women. Swiss, German, British, and other European American cultures tend to be lower context than Japanese, Chinese, Puerto Rican, or African American cultures.

Given that, imagine how differences in approach and meaning such as the following might affect communication in a health care setting between representatives of the dominant low-context culture and representatives of high-context cultures who account for growing proportions of new entrants to the health care workforce and the patient mix.

- Low-context people communicate to exchange information, while high-context people communicate to build a relationship.

- Low-context people compartmentalize, separating the personal from the professional, one relationship from another, and the current decision from previous ones. High-context people integrate, seeing the personal and the professional as a seamless whole, using one relationship or encounter to give meaning to the next, and treating decisions as links in a continuous chain.

- In low-context cultures, the words carry most of the meaning in interpersonal communication; in high-context cultures nonverbal factors such as setting, body language, social status, and tone of voice drive the meaning and define the communication intent, with words playing a secondary role.

As with any discussion of culture, it is important to remember that there is a wide range of individual variability within groups. Not every individual member of a low-context cultural group, for instance, will invariably reflect typical low-context behaviors, beliefs, or values. It is important *not to stereotype* based on group membership; certain European American women will operate from lower-context cultural norms more so than certain European American men, and African Americans will fall at different levels on the high- to low-context continuum. In a health care organization that values diversity, people are responded to as individuals, but general differences in cultural traditions are accepted, valued, and understood.

When differences in culturally based norms such as those listed above are not understood, discomfort and misunderstanding can result. High-context applicants, for example, can "fail" interviews if a low-context interviewer judges their responses in accordance with low-context cultural norms. In fact, one health care organization recently audited its approach to interviewing applicants in an attempt to ferret out hidden cultural biases they suspected might be hampering achievement of their corporate goal to hire for diversity. Insights gained through the audit included the following:

- Applicants from high-context cultures are less likely to be comfortable with the standard interview approach, in which the interviewer asks detailed questions of the applicant while giving little information in return, than are applicants from low-context cultures. Responses of applicants from high-context cultures are not as likely to be the responses expected or valued by the interviewers as are the responses of applicants from low-context cultures. Consequently, qualified but culturally different candidates might be screened out by not meeting expectations because they do not maintain eye contact, take the initiative to highlight their own accomplishments, and share information assertively and without prompting.

- Trust and rapport are often key issues with high-context applicants, such as Asian, Latino, or African Americans. These issues are often heightened when the high-context applicant is being interviewed by a low-context interviewer who is seen as a representative of the dominant culture and/or as a reminder of past violations of trust. Low-context cultures are more likely to see the interview as a means for information exchange, while high-context cultures are more likely to see the interview as an opportunity for interaction and relationship building. An interview approach in which the interviewer withholds information from the applicant while requiring the applicant to share detailed information can produce distrust and lack of cooperation on the part of the high-context applicant.

- A low-context interviewer may conclude that the high-context interviewee is lying or withholding information when, in fact, he or she is just responding from different cultural norms. Low-context interviewers who are unfamiliar with high-context cultural communication norms may misread the high-context applicant's communication intent and, consequently, screen out qualified but culturally different applicants. Fox example, an Asian American applicant may emphasize how well the group worked together to complete a project but be reluctant to highlight her individual contributions to the project's success. As a result, a low-context interviewer, unfamiliar with differences in cultural norms, may conclude that the applicant didn't play a significant role in the project and thus will not hire or promote her. Or, an African American applicant may be angered by a European American interviewer's questions that require repetition of the information contained in the resume. The African American may feel his integrity is being questioned and that the resume should speak for itself; the interviewer may feel the applicant is sour and uncommunicative. The interviewers' culturally based stereotypes and assumptions will influence their feelings, perceptions, and the conclusions they draw when making hiring decisions, which could have a negative effect on the recruitment of high-context employees.

As the applicant pool becomes more diverse, the need for cultural awareness and flexibility in both recruitment and retention strategies is heightened for today's institutions. An interview approach that seeks the fit between the corporate culture, which is considered a given, and the applicant, who may or may not fit, conflicts with the goal of recruiting a diverse workforce. Applicants whose communication style and personality traits fit the current cultural norms are screened in while others are screened out.

Organizations that are competitive in recruiting and retaining a diverse workforce exhibit cultural flexibility whereby shared core values can be communicated in diverse ways and differences in personality traits and communication styles are accepted, valued, and encouraged. *Both* the organization and the culturally different employee must change in response to one another's cultural style— corporate culture in the era of the diversity imperative can no longer be seen as an immovable, unchangeable standard to which the employee must conform and assimilate.

Employees from high-context cultures will experience discomfort with the health care organization's cultural norms if they conflict with their own and may be perceived by others as not contributing to the organization's success. A question commonly asked by high-context employees of health care organizations with low-context cultural norms is: How much of myself do I have to give up to work here?

Patients from high-context cultures are likely to experience the health care organization's culture as do high-context applicants and employees. Health care organizations must study their cultures to answer this key question: Do we only want people who 'act white' here?

STYLE AND PERFORMANCE, THE VISIBLE AND INVISIBLE

Increasingly, organizations must learn to distinguish between style differences that are irrelevant to performance and a candidate's qualifications for the job. Health care organizations are challenged by the need for a strong culture (Deal and Kennedy 1982; Shortell 1985) that "spells out how people are to behave most of the time" (Deal and Kennedy 1982, 15) and the need for cultural flexibility and respect for differences—the essential building blocks of successful diversity leadership. As the composition of the available workforce and the patients themselves change to include a growing proportion of people with high-context cultural norms, diversity leadership—and the concomitant need to question sacred cows and alter standard operating procedures and behavioral expectations—truly becomes an imperative.

Roosevelt Thomas (1991), author of the ground-breaking book on managing diversity, *Beyond Race and Gender,* conceptualizes organizations as trees, with the roots representing the key cultural assumptions. These "invisible roots," says Thomas, are the source of the parts of the tree that we can see. In organizations, the values, myths, rites, rituals, heroes or heroines, traditions, business strategy, policies, and customary practices constitute the visible manifestations of the invisible cultural assumptions or roots in Thomas' paradigm. The purpose of a cultural audit is to make the invisible visible; to uncover and understand the implications of hidden cultural assumptions in order to improve the process of diversity leadership.

CULTURE AND PATIENT SATISFACTION

Culture can affect patients' perception of the health care organization, with implications for the organization's competitiveness, patient satisfaction and loyalty, malpractice litigation, and, ultimately, the bottom line. Health care organizations that value diversity are changing "the way we do things around here" to accommodate the needs and preferences of their culturally diverse patient mix.

For example, Children's Health Care–St. Paul learned that the process of effective diversity leadership requires more than just good intentions. United Hospital, an adult acute care facility that occupies the same building as Children's–St. Paul, also participated in the cultural change process through The Birth Center, a shared service of the two hospitals. United and Children's process of self-examination and change resulted in a nationally recognized model for culturally sensitive health care delivery.

The Minneapolis–St. Paul area is home to the second largest population of Hmong in the United States. The Hmong immigrants, primarily from Laos, Cambodia, and Vietnam, arrived in the mid-1970s and 1980s. They brought with them another medical tradition, leading them to generally avoid encounters with Western medicine until all other alternatives had been exhausted and the patient was grievously ill.

After the deaths of two Hmong patients at Children's–St. Paul, rumors began circulating that the hospital was experimenting on and killing Hmong children. The hospital's response was to initiate community outreach activities and develop new models for patient care. Through the use of Hmong interpreters, multilingual signage, and multicultural images in marketing and community relations, Children's–St. Paul has transformed its image in the Hmong community. More information about United and Children's–St. Paul and the Hmong community is discussed in Chapter 9.

Even the most basic aspects of patient amenities reflect cultural assumptions. Yale–New Haven Hospital's cultural diversity program resulted in this apparently small but important insight, according to Edward Dowling, senior vice president of human resources: "We distributed one type of comb to patients upon admission. We needed to realize that people with different types of hair need different things." Much like hotels that changed from catering to business*men* to catering to business*people*, hospitals are using cultural audits and insights from diversity training to explore the hidden, culturally based assumptions that underlie their standard operating procedures.

Jewish patients at a major medical center in the Northeast expressed dissatisfaction with the performance of the predominantly Filipino nursing staff in the medical center's long-term care facility. The patients wanted the nurses to "look them in the eyes," but the nurses routinely averted their gaze, as is customary in the

Filipino culture as a sign of respect. It's quite common for a sign of indifference in one culture to be a sign of respect in another. This awareness is vital for today's managers. Management with sensitivity and awareness of culture-bound behaviors and norms will approach such conflicts more appropriately. Cultural audits and climate assessments can help executives to identify and correct problem areas.

Cultural conflicts between smaller, more emotionally restrained European American families and extended, more emotionally expressive families from high-context cultures are common occurrences in today's health care organizations. One way health care organizations are adapting is by changing visiting rules and, sometimes, the physical plant itself. For example, Paradise Valley Hospital's Art Program ensures that artwork displayed in waiting rooms, exam rooms, and corridors honors the cultural and ethnic backgrounds of the hospital's patients and staff. The artwork showcases diverse families, music, dance, and neighborhoods, and reflects the hospital's sensitivity to the community it serves.

Paradise Valley Hospital recently conducted a series of focus groups in which African American health care consumers mentioned the greater degree of empathy they expected to receive from an African American physician when a specific illness such as sickle cell anemia was being treated or diagnosed. Unfortunately, health care organizations experience difficulty in accommodating these preferences due to the marked differences in the gender and racial/ethnic composition of the health care workforce as compared with the patient mix. The facts are that 50 percent of practicing physicians are not women; 12 percent of speech pathologists are not African American. The consequences of not responding to patient preferences can include patients' lack of compliance with recommended treatment and their dissatisfaction, resulting in adverse outcomes and potential litigation. Culturally sensitive patient information and approaches to care can help to bridge the gap between patient preferences and the current demographics of America's caregivers.

BUILDING A CULTURE THAT FOSTERS DIVERSITY

Yale–New Haven Hospital

Yale–New Haven Hospital is exploring aspects of the work environment that might impede minority recruitment and retention. According to Senior Vice President Dowling, "We want to make our health care facility an attractive place for minorities. It's a process—sometimes a high-anxiety time. I have had my thinking stretched. Five years ago we were talking about affirmative action goals. We are far beyond thinking in terms of quotas now!"

Corporate cultures that fail to identify and address shared beliefs or unresolved fears that serve as impediments to the progress and performance of underrepresented groups produce an ineffective diversity climate. Yale–New Haven Hospital's Dowling has described how unresolved race and gender issues adversely affect the performance review process: "If I'm white and I'm doing the performance review of an African American, I might hesitate to be critical. Therefore, that employee doesn't get the feedback and the constructive mentoring needed to develop." Dowling credits the diversity focus of Yale–New Haven Hospital's evolving human resource strategy for the hospital's on-site day care center for employees: "We have women who have four years of nursing school completed and don't want to choose between a career and family. We really recognize that this is good business. We can't afford to lose their talent because they want to raise a family."

Community involvement, through its presence or absence, is another reflection of a health care institution's diversity climate. Yale–New Haven Hospital sponsors a local high school scholarship program. Recipients receive $1,500 annually, up to a total of $6,000, with no strings attached, to enter a nursing program. Such outreach efforts may take perseverance: as Dowlings says, "The first year we offered the scholarships, we couldn't get high school guidance counselors interested. We learned that we'd have to be in this for the long haul."

Organizational assessment is one of the four key areas for concerted action identified in Yale–New Haven Hospital's cultural diversity strategy. With the assistance of an external consultant, Yale–New Haven Hospital adapted a standardized employee survey that assessed employee perception of pay and benefits and included questions that targeted employee perceptions of the diversity climate at the facility. In addition, Dowling reported that a more in-depth cultural audit had been conducted, and another firm was used to lead community focus groups.

Linda Galindo, president of Innovations Consulting International, is a strong advocate of cultural audits at an early stage in the diversity leadership process. Galindo contends that quality, empowerment, and diversity are interrelated. Because quality teams are usually a vertical cut in the organization, health care organizations implementing total quality management (TQM) often find that diversity becomes an issue in team effectiveness and trust. "Health care organizations," explains Galindo, "become more colorful as you go down the ladder." The statistics presented in Chapter 1 confirm her perspective.

Kaiser Permanente

Alva Wheatley, vice president and manager, Cultural Diversity Project, Kaiser Permanente's central offices in Oakland, California, says, "Diversity is part of the fabric of Kaiser Permanente. Our organization development consultants have imbedded diversity in all of our programs." Wheatley contends that the commitment of CEO David Lawrence to both personal and organizational assessment and change is central to the success of Kaiser's diversity initiatives. Kaiser's commitment to a diversity climate that fosters high performance is reflected in Kaiser's 1993 video, "Diversity: The Competitive Advantage"; the images in marketing and recruitment brochures; and diversity climate assessments, such as the Kaiser Permanente Minority Recruitment and Promotion Task Force's interregional survey.

Many of Kaiser Permanente's nursing staff in the California region are foreign-born; some received their professional training in Mexico, the Philippines, the Middle East, and Asia. The foreign-born nurses' cultural norms, developed within high-context cultures, can lead to misunderstandings and difficulties with the performance norms in low-context U.S. health care organizations. Focus groups conducted with Kaiser's foreign-born nurses in southern California identified some of the challenges to successful adjustment that the nurses were experiencing and enabled Kaiser's management to offer support and understanding.

In a corporate culture that values diversity, it is as important to identify common ground as evidenced by shared values, beliefs, norms, and behaviors as it is to accept and value differences. Kaiser Permanente's strategic plan for diversity, Diversity and Excellence: Planning for the Year 2000, identifies the "overarching goal of giving quality medical care" as "one that can be agreed upon by all Kaiser Permanente staff, however diverse."

University of California at San Diego Medical Center

Many health care organizations begin their diversity leadership initiatives in response to a crisis. In November 1992, the University of California at San Diego Medical Center (UCSD) found itself needing to answer the criticisms of employees, primarily African American staff, who felt that the organization was not offering adequate promotional opportunities and was not attentive to minority representation, particularly among management and professional staff. UCSD's response resulted in fundamental changes in interview practices, such as using multilevel, multiracial panels to conduct interviews for upper-level positions. These changes resulted in an increase in minority representation among management and professional staff. In addition, a major emphasis on diversity as an organizational initiative, including focus groups to listen to employee concerns, helped ensure that employees would feel that the organization respected its diverse workforce.

Intermountain Health Care

Intermountain Health Care (IHC), widely recognized for its innovations in patient care information systems, finds that diversity leadership is a natural fit with IHC's forward-looking, strategic orientation. Hospitals, according to Mary Ann Holladay, IHC's assistant vice president of human resources, are traditionally very hierarchical and territorial, and departmentally organized. Diversity leadership can help dismantle barrier boundaries between disciplines that are often gender- and race-segregated and change the unwritten rules that make implementation of a patient-centered transdisciplinary team approach to patient care difficult.

Scott Parker, IHC's CEO, isn't just a passive observer of the diversity leadership process, but an active participant. Holladay says, "Executive leadership and involvement is critical. Unless we clearly understand that executive-level commitment is there, we shouldn't even pursue the issue. Any program is doomed without top management commitment." Executive involvement in the whole process of personal and organization assessment is essential to uncovering and addressing the unwritten rules that block the high performance of a diverse workforce.

Additional Illustrations

Executive-level response to African American, Hispanic, or gay and lesbian employees who violate unwritten rules that define family in accordance with European American heterosexual norms, for instance, has ramifications throughout the organization. The extended family often plays a more central role in Hispanic and African American cultures than in European American culture. Missing work to attend the funeral of a "distant" relative, when viewed through European American cultural norms, can be seen as taking advantage of the system. Gay or lesbian employees dealing with the loss or illness of their partner may feel uncomfortable asking for family illness or bereavement time to deal with what, for them, is a legitimate family concern, and they may feel that they cannot count on receiving empathy and understanding from co-workers or supervisors. The role of the CEO and management staff in modeling acceptance and understanding of such differences is key to the creation of a positive diversity climate.

Constance Row, president and CEO of the Upper Chesapeake Health System, sees her role in modeling diversity leadership as central to the system's success and as an essential factor in promoting a positive diversity climate. Row says, "Gathering statistics isn't enough. We need to deal with the prejudices we all grew up with. Those of us who grew up in white, geographically isolated suburbs have a lack of life experiences that are requisite to effective diversity leadership. The state of society is generally reflected in our hospitals. This issue is destined to fall into the trash basket if people see it as a program rather than a process of management."

CHALLENGES TO THE DIVERSITY LEADER

The futurist Joel Barker (1989) speaks of the challenges faced by "paradigm pioneers" who pursue new or untried ideas that question current understanding and tradition. The diversity leader must be prepared to face the difficulties experienced by all paradigm pioneers. The health care organization's workforce is unlikely to be uniformly supportive of and ready for the cultural change required to value diversity. This makes the task facing the committed diversity leader a formidable one.

Towers Perrin and the Hudson Institute (1990) conducted a survey of Workforce 2000 issues. Their sample included representation from the health care industry. Results are reported in the publication, *Workforce 2000 Competing in a Seller's Market: Is Corporate America Prepared?* Over half of all senior human resource executives responding to the survey expressed concern about supervisors' ability to motivate diverse groups of employees, while 41 percent were concerned about differences in values and cultural norms. However, Towers Perrin and the Hudson Institute (1990) have reported that "the level of concern about diversity . . . generally isn't matched by action in the form of developing specific human resource programs. The number of companies with programs aimed at addressing diversity issues is relatively small. . . . Employers' hesitancy to take action in this area may have a lot to do with the sensitivity of the issue and their perceptions of tensions in the existing employee climate." In fact, one of every four survey respondents reported that their corporate culture is not open to diversity (Towers Perrin and the Hudson Institute 1990).

The Families and Work Institute (1993) conducted telephone interviews with a nationally representative sample of wage and salaried workers and uncovered some information about attitudes, beliefs, and perceptions of importance to diversity leaders. Slightly more than half of the survey's respondents reported that they preferred working with people of the same race, gender, and educational level as themselves. When the responses of workers over and under 25 were compared, no significant differences were found.

Regardless of their own race, survey respondents agreed that European American workers had a better chance of advancement than workers of other racial or ethnic backgrounds: minority men and women as well as white women rated white men's chances of advancement higher than did white men themselves (Families and Work Institute 1993). More than one in five minority respondents reported that they had been victims of workplace discrimination by their current employer. These same workers were more likely to report burnout and a lesser interest in taking initiative on the job and were significantly more likely to report an intention to leave their job (Families and Work Institute 1993).

In addition, the study found that women managers were more than twice as likely as men to rate their opportunity to advance in their career as "poor" or "fair." Two of every three respondents with children reported that their job didn't afford them enough time with their children (Families and Work Institute 1993).

A strong positive correlation was found between employee loyalty and the availability of benefits such as flexible scheduling, permission to work at home, and the right to take time off to care for family members. Respondents consistently reported that improvement in the quality and supportiveness of their work environment would make them more loyal to their employer (Families and Work Institute 1993).

Over 80 percent of health care industry respondents in the Towers Perrin and Hudson Institute study (1990) reported some or great difficulty recruiting technical and professional staff (Families and Work Institute 1993).

The health care organization that builds a culture that values diversity will be in a much stronger position to build and maintain a stable, loyal workforce. The diversity leader who pioneers a new multicultural paradigm is central to the process of organizational and personal growth and development.

ADDITIONAL RESEARCH FINDINGS

Recent studies have confirmed the continuing existence of differences in career attainment that are linked to race and gender. Franklin D. Wilson (1992, 25) and his colleagues from the Center for Demography and Ecology of the University of Wisconsin–Madison reported in a 1992 working paper that "high relative unemployment is a pervasive aspect of the labor force experience of all blacks. . . . There remains a substantial labor market penalty for being black after . . . differences in demographic composition are taken into account. Even blacks of high educational levels have been unable to close the unemployment gap separating them from their white counterparts." Wilson (1992, 26) also reports that "the unemployment rate for blacks in most occupations is at least twice that of similarly situated whites." Health care organizations that undertake a cultural audit are likely to uncover explanations for the black-white unemployment gap identified by Wilson and his colleagues. The authors have interpreted their own findings in this way:

> A clear implication of our findings is that the widespread perception that [the] governmental intervention policies and programs designed to promote racial equity in employment have disadvantaged whites is incorrect. Indeed, current work suggests that organizational responses to anti-discrimination laws and affirmative action and compliance program mandates are structured in "ways which test, negotiate, and collectively institutionalize forms of compliance" that are more symbolic than substance in form. . . . In other words, legal ambiguity in equal employment opportunity laws and affirmative action and compliance programs allow organizations avenues of responses to legal mandates that are image driven, with only minimal impact on promotion and hiring decisions which still favor whites and males. (Wilson 1992, 28)

Undertaking a cultural audit can help health care organizations to distinguish between image-driven "window dressing" and true cultural change that fosters a positive diversity climate. "Knowing what we don't know" explains management consultant and theorist Stanley Davis (1982) is the first step to transformation and change.

Results of the Urban Institute's audit of employment discrimination in the Chicago and Washington, DC areas in 1990 (Turner, Fix, and Struyk 1991), reported in *Opportunities Denied, Opportunities Diminished*, confirm the continuing existence of racial bias in hiring. The study used a hiring audit process modeled on the audit methodology used extensively in housing discrimination studies. Ten matched pairs of black and white males, age 19–24 applied for 476 entry-level positions, randomly selected from the classified ads. The study found that blacks were three times more likely to be discriminated against as job applicants than were whites. How would the nation's health care organizations perform if such an audit were conducted of our hiring practices? How would yours?

Gender Differences in Career Attainment

The ACHE and the University of Iowa Graduate Programs in Hospital and Health Administration (1991) conducted a national study of men and women affiliates of ACHE in spring 1990 that produced some interesting insights into the very different experiences of men and women health care administrators. Such insights point to the need for cultural audits and climate assessments in health care organizations.

The researchers studied three cohorts who entered the field of health care administration in the following years—1971–1975, 1976–1980, and 1981–1985. Statistically significant differences were found in the proportion of men and women health care administrators who had achieved the level of CEO in all three cohorts, as shown in Table 4.1.

The study further reported an earnings gap between men and women health care administrators: based on self-reported 1989 salary data, women in cohorts 1 and 2 earned significantly less than the men in those cohorts. Although the results from cohort 3 were not statistically significant, 15 percent of the men, as compared with 9 percent of the women, earned more than $75,000 (ACHE and University of Iowa 1991).

Table 4.1

Percentage of Health Care Administrators by Gender Who Have Attained the Level of CEO

Cohort	Year Entered Health Administration	Men (percent)	Women (percent)
1	1971–75	37	17
2	1976–80	24	9
3	1981–85	17	7

Source: American College of Healthcare Executives and The University of Iowa Graduate Programs in Hospital and Health Administration 1991. Gender and Careers in Healthcare Management: Findings of a National Survey of Healthcare Executives. *Chicago: ACHE.*

The ACHE and University of Iowa (1991, 4) researchers highlighted their findings as follows: "In summary, females are less likely to have achieved CEO status, are less likely to have general management or financial management responsibilities, and in Cohorts 1 and 2 earn lower salaries than men. In addition, Cohort 1 females are significantly less satisfied with pay, their co-workers, and their chances for promotion than males who began their careers between 1971 and 1975. Finally, Cohort 3 women are significantly less likely than men to have taken positions in hospitals or hospital systems."

ACHE and University of Iowa researchers identified and investigated four explanations for the gender gap in health administration career attainment uncovered by their study:

1. The human capital explanation, which posits that differences in career attainment are due to one group's having less education, training, and/or experience than the other

2. Work style and work environment issues, which is the only one of the four explanations that can be uncovered and addressed through cultural audits and climate assessments

3. Work and family conflicts

4. Career aspirations.

With the exception of major field of study in health administration for the master's and post-master's residency for cohort 1 subjects only, no significant gender differences in the human capital variables investigated were found.

Investigation of the second explanation, workstyle and work environment issues, did uncover some interesting and statistically significant gender differences. Women were more likely than men to have had a woman predecessor or to have taken a newly created job. The researchers (ACHE and the University of Iowa 1991, 18) report that "it appears that the gender of the incumbent is related to the gender of the successor." Although the work environment factors studied by the researchers were not significantly different, significant gender differences in perception of the fairness of policies were: women considered affirmative action based on gender, sick childcare policies, salaries, and promotional opportunities to be less fair than did the male respondents. Nearly 34 percent of the women respondents as compared with 2 percent of men respondents agreed or strongly agreed that they "feel discriminated against in obtaining a better position due to gender" (ACHE and the University of Iowa 1991,

24). Workstyle variables for which significant gender differences were found included the following: women were more likely than men to prefer working with and for people of the opposite gender, and women were less likely than men to socialize with other executives after work.

Through undertaking a cultural audit, health care organizations can uncover work environment factors that might impede women's career achievement. Climate assessments can uncover gender differences in the perception of the fairness of organizational policies and procedures.

The third explanation, work/family conflicts, uncovered additional statistically significant gender differences, reported by the American College of Healthcare Executives and the University of Iowa (1991):

> In summary, fewer women than men are married or live in a marriage-like relationship. Fewer women than men have children, and for those that have children, fewer women have children living at home who are under age 16. In households with a sick child, more women executives need to take care of them by themselves or by alternating with their spouse. Male executives can more often rely on their spouses for the care of their sick children. Finally, more women than men sacrificed their own career progression for their spouse's careers and feel that home obligations fall disproportionately on them. That we saw no major shifts among the cohorts suggests that work/family conflicts may not only contribute to the lesser career achievement of women today but that this pattern may well persist in the future. (pp. 31–32)

The fourth explanation, differences in career aspirations, also uncovered some possible reasons for the career achievement gap by gender in health care administration. The American College of Healthcare Executives and the University of Iowa (1991, 36) report that "the most important finding is the consistent and significantly lower future position level aspired to by the females in the study. Moreover, the disparity widens with each younger cohort." Women were less likely to be willing to move to advance their careers than were the men respondents.

Study results (American College of Healthcare Executives and the University of Iowa 1991) also provide insight into the gender stereotypes held by health care administrators:

> In seven of eleven traits measured, the majority of men and women responded that the gender groups were equal.

However, when respondents did have an opinion about one gender being more adept or favored, it was the males who were singled out. Indeed, both men and women ascribe more positive features to men than to women including leadership qualities, financial skill, ability to take risks, opportunities for advancement, support from superiors, support from peers, support from subordinates and competitiveness. The only exception is nurturing skills at work. . . . Overall the stereotypical view of women as possessing fewer of the qualities considered essential for top executives is affirmed by not only men but also by a sizable proportion of women in this study. (p. 40)

As women comprise an increasing percentage of health care administrators and scarce technical and professional employees of health care organizations, the culture of health care organizations will have to change to accommodate their differing perceptions and lifestyles. Health care organizations that have undertaken a cultural audit will be better positioned to meet the challenges of the changing workforce and uncover hidden barriers to the full achievement of their women executives and employees.

Racial Disparities in Career Attainment

In 1993, the American College of Health Care Executives (ACHE) and the National Association of Health Services Executives (NAHSE) released results of their study of the career attainment of their black and white members, in which they drew this somber conclusion: "Career attainments of a group of individuals who are similarly trained with approximately the same number of years of experience should, in an unbiased society, show no differences between the races. However, the findings of this study refute this ideal." (iv)

Key findings from this report included the following:

- Significantly fewer blacks held CEO positions or positions reporting to the CEO.
- Fewer blacks were in general management; more were in specialized areas of management such as human resources or finance.
- Proportionately more blacks worked in alternative delivery systems and nonprovider settings such as consulting firms, educational institutions, and associations.
- Blacks earned a median income of $53,000 in 1990; whites earned $67,000.

As with the ACHE/University of Iowa gender study (1991), perceptions of equity are very different when black and white health care administrators are compared. Consider the percentages of black and white health care administrators who agree/disagree with the following statements:

- "Blacks usually have to be more qualified than others to get ahead in my organization." blacks, 69% agree; whites, 10% agree.

- "Race relations within my organization are good." blacks, 44% agree; whites, 79% agree.

- "The evaluation of both whites and blacks are equally thorough and careful." blacks, 66% disagree; whites 6% disagree.

- "White managers share vital growth and career-related information with black managers." blacks, 69% disagree; whites 8% disagree.

- "The quality of relationships between black and white managers could be improved." blacks, 92% agree; whites 43% agree.

- "White managers have greater opportunities to advance than blacks in health care." blacks, 96% agree; whites 43% agree.

- "There are limited opportunities for black managers to advance in their careers." blacks, 74% agree; whites, 19% agree.

Health care institutions are challenged to address issues of equity and perception such as those uncovered through these studies. The next chapter will present tools and techniques to assist in the organizational assessment process. Assessment, combined with benchmarking on key dimensions of diversity leadership, will help each health care organization to know where it stands relative to national norms and in comparison to high-performing health care organizations.

REFERENCES

American College of Healthcare Executives, and the University of Iowa Graduate Programs in Hospital and Health Administration. 1991. *Gender and Careers in Healthcare Management: Findings of a National Survey of Healthcare Executives.* Chicago: ACHE.

American College of Healthcare Executives and National Association of Health Services Executives. 1993. *A Racial*

Comparison of Career Attainment in Healthcare Management: Findings of a National Survey of Black and White Healthcare Executives. Chicago: ACHE.

Barker, J. 1989. *Discovering the Future: The Business of Paradigms*, 2d ed. videotape. Burnsville, MN: Charthouse Learning Corporation.

Davis, S. 1982. "Transforming Organizations: The Key to Strategy Is Context." *Organizational Dynamics* 10 (3): 64–80.

Deal, T. E., and A. A. Kennedy. 1982. *Corporate Cultures: The Rites and Rituals of Corporate Life*. New York: Addison-Wesley.

Families and Work Institute. 1993. *National Study of the Changing Workforce*. New York: Families and Work Institute.

Hall, E. T., and M. R. Hall. 1990. *Understanding Cultural Differences*. Yarmouth, ME: Intercultural Press.

Healy, S. A., and G. L. Miller. 1987. "Developing a Corporate Culture," In *Human Resource Management Handbook*, edited by E. M. Lewis and J. G. Spicer, 27–32. Rockville, MD: Aspen.

Kennedy, J., and A. Everest. 1991. "Put Diversity in Context." *Personnel Journal* 70 (9): 50–54.

Shortell, S. 1985. "High-Performing Health Care Organizations: Guidelines for the Pursuit of Excellence." *Hospital & Health Services Administration* 30 (4): 7–35.

Thomas, R. R. 1991. *Beyond Race and Gender*. New York: AMACOM.

Towers Perrin, and the Hudson Institute. 1990. *Workforce 2000: Competing in a Seller's Market: Is Corporate America Prepared?* New York: Towers Perrin.

Turner, M. A., M. Fix, and R. J. Struyk. 1991. *Opportunities Denied, Opportunities Diminished: Racial Discrimination in Hiring*. Washington, DC: Urban Institute.

Wilson, F. D. 1992. "Racial Equality in the Labor Market: Still an Elusive Goal?" Working paper. Madison: University of Wisconsin–Madison Center for Demography and Ecology.

CHAPTER 5

Cultural Audit Instruments and Strategies

THE DIVERSITY leader can choose from among a plethora of tools, techniques, strategies, and philosophies of organizational assessment. Regardless of the selected approach, the desired outcome is the same—to uncover and explore the health care organization's shared attitudes, beliefs, and behaviors, behaviors that enable the organization to capitalize on diversity or that prevent it from doing so.

CULTURAL AUDIT OR CLIMATE ASSESSMENT

Two commonly used terms in organizational assessment are **cultural audit** and **climate assessment**. The cultural audit is a multifaceted review of beliefs, values, attitudes, and practices—that is, the way of life in the health care organization. Climate assessment, generally accomplished through administration of a questionnaire or survey, is a review of the personality of the organization as perceived by different constituencies or interest groups. Defined in this way, climate assessment can be seen as providing useful information in the cultural audit process but not as constituting a substitute for it. Climate can be viewed as one manifestation of the organization's culture as perceived by its constituents—executives, managers, administrative staff, physicians, nurses, allied health personnel, patients, community, regulators, board members, and others.

Charlene Thomas (Thomas et. al. 1990) reminds us that employees whose beliefs and values are consistent with the organization's will assess the climate as positive, while employees whose beliefs and values are not consistent with the organization's will assess the climate as negative. The astute diversity leader will pay attention to differences in perceptions of the health care organization's climate that cluster by race, gender, age, or other dimensions of diversity.

Paradise Valley Hospital in National City, California, asked employees to report their level of agreement with statements like the following sample from its third annual Employee Opinion Survey, administered in September 1993: "I believe I will be given fair consideration for a promotion when an opening occurs for which I am qualified"; "I think the hospital overall extends a favorable image through positive interactions with patients, visitors, and other guests"; "I support the mission of this hospital"; "This hospital has an effective procedure for resolving employee problems and complaints"; and "I am paid fairly for the kind of work I do."

Survey respondents rated the statements on a five-point Likert-type scale. Areas rated included the following: administration, co-workers, communications, department director, employee benefits, guest relations, hospital reputation, hours of work, job satisfactions, job security, mission, opinion survey, pay, personnel policies, quality, status/recognition, and working conditions. By analyzing general satisfaction survey responses by race and gender and other dimensions of diversity, hospitals like Paradise Valley can uncover pockets of dissatisfaction and identify concerns that can be addressed before a crisis occurs.

THE PROCESS OF ORGANIZATIONAL DIAGNOSIS

Organizational diagnosis, according to Clayton Alderfer (1980), is a recursive process consisting of three phases—entry, data collection, and feedback. Issues that are unresolved or poorly handled in one phase will have a profound impact on subsequent phases and will, in part, determine how the assessment influences the organizational change process.

The diversity leader must answer two key questions related to entry and data collection before embarking on a cultural audit.

1. Should we contract for the services of an external consultant or use in-house expertise?
2. Should we use qualitative, quantitative, or a mixed model for data collection?

External vs. Internal Consultants

A consultant's role is to give professional, expert advise. While internal expertise in diversity leadership as it relates to the proper conduct of a cultural audit may exist, the internal consultant faces many challenges to credibility, primarily based on their perceived lack of objectivity. Based on his extensive experience as a management professor and consultant, Clayton Alderfer (1980) says:

> People cannot be consultants to systems in which they are full-fledged members. All individuals have vested interests in their own organizations. Even if individuals did not press their own interests, other members of the system would be unable to accept a consultant relationship from a peer, and the complete insider would be rendered ineffective as a result. Being at least partial outsiders, therefore, is part of the equipment of the organizational consultants. Without this role element, they cannot function effectively. Internal consultants, for example, can work in parts of a larger system where they have not been or currently are not members. (p. 461)

External consultants can create a climate of objectivity. On the other hand, external consultants who are unskilled at group dynamics and conflict resolution or who advocate a particular point of view rather than facilitate the health care organization's exploration of its own point of view and the consequent discovery of its strengths, drawbacks, and alternative perspectives, can appear to be as lacking in objectivity as Alderfer's (1980) hypothetical complete insider.

Grace Miller, manager of training and development at the University of California–San Diego Medical Center, describes an evolving process of selecting a diversity consultant that was the right "fit" with the organization's leadership. Different consultants, she explains, come with different biases, experiences, and techniques for involving leadership. "An organization needs to "shop" carefully for the individual or group that is going to be able to work effectively with its senior team," said Miller. "Our first consultant was incredibly skilled, with years of experience, but the executives didn't respond to this first attempt," added Miller.

The UCSD Medical Center began again with an internal diversity planning team that represented all levels and all cultural groups. This approach, combined with more careful attention to organizational assessment and the needs of executive leaders, improved the organization's readiness. The result was a contract with a second consulting firm that has produced very positive results. UCSD Medical Center's Grace Miller recommends that health care organizations start "small and subtle, rather than with a big bang" and consider utilizing an internal diversity planning team to set the stage.

Aspects of diversity such as race or gender can be especially volatile. Based solely on the consultant's own race or gender, his or her objectivity can be questioned by anxious, concerned constituents of the health care organization. For this reason, it is recommended that an external consultant team be used, whenever possible, for diversity assessment. The team should reflect the aspect of diversity that is viewed as most central to the health care organization's circumstance and should model effective cross-cultural communication. To hire a physician to address physician-nurse communication, for example, would not be as effective as hiring a nurse/physician team that models cross-disciplinary cooperation and mutual respect.

If your organization experienced a critical incident that led to the decision to assess climate, trust for internal human resource assessors may be low. At UCSD, hiring practices were perceived to be biased by the African American community. The perception of an internal human resource consultant's credibility would be likely to reflect that mistrust. If the health care facility conducting the cultural audit is a branch of a larger system, the overall trust level between branch personnel and internal human resource consultants from the corporate office will be reflected in the branch personnels' perceptions of the diversity climate assessor(s).

Whether an internal or an external consultant is chosen, the issues of objectivity and trust must be considered key to the selection process. Tied directly to trust is the issue of **confidentiality.** Your consultant should be able to describe how the anonymity of individuals who participated in the cultural audit will be ensured. Guarded, self-censored input from participants in the audit greatly reduces the utility and integrity of the audit's findings. On the other hand, once administered, assessment results must be publicly shared and acted on or the health care organization's credibility with respect to diversity leadership will suffer and it will be difficult to get open and honest input in the future. The effective diversity leader will share assessment results even if they are not uniformly positive.

For example, after its cultural audit, Paradise Valley Hospital noted in its March/April 1994 employee newsletter that "employees are right when they say that our hospital staff does not totally reflect the ethnicity of our community." The newsletter article included a table comparing the percentage of African Americans, Asians, Latinos, and Caucasians comprising their patient, service area, and hospital communities. The article further details Paradise Valley's ongoing cultural diversity initiatives.

Kaiser Permanente, known for its transformational approach to diversity leadership, also publicizes its challenges as well as its successes. In its April 1993 internal publication, *A Kaiser Permanente Imperative: Diversity and Excellence: Planning for the Year 2000*, Kaiser reported that "less than half of the minority managers (Asian, African American or Hispanic) were satisfied with the recognition or support they receive in their current jobs." This publication, which also includes tables that report the number and percentage of executives and managers as compared with total employees by race and ethnicity, offered the following self-analysis: "Looking at the tables together, it is clear that while three-fourths of the managers and executives are Caucasians, the remainder of the workforce is much more diverse."

Effective diversity leadership, as evidenced by Paradise Valley Hospital and Kaiser Permanente, clearly reflects a process of self-exploration and growth, as well as a commitment to the pursuit of excellence. "Progress, not perfection" is key to the successes of health care organizations that demonstrate effective diversity leadership.

When selecting an external consultant, it's important to find one who is willing to learn your organization, not just present a general or canned approach to assessment and analysis. Intermountain Health Care's (IHC) assistant vice president of human resources, Mary Ann Holladay, confirms the importance of a tailored approach to organizational assessment: "Just changing the name on the front of a workbook will not sell in IHC. The consultant must be willing to spend the time to understand us and our issues." Holladay further believes that experience, flexibility, availability, and accessibility are key to an effective consultant–health care organization relationship.

Miriam Lee, president of the Minneapolis-based Vaughn-Lee & Associates, a human resources consulting firm, also emphasizes the importance of choosing consultants who want to work with your organization: "Choose consultants who want to work with 'who you are and what you are about', not with 'who they are about'." She advocates face-to-face interviews with potential consultants and checking references. Organizational assessment is critical, states Lee. Health care organizations should not "jump into diversity training without it."

It's also important to choose a consultant who knows the health care industry. The differences between health care and other organizations are well documented in the literature (Shortell and Kaluzny 1987). Both Linda Galindo of Innovations International, Inc., and Miriam Lee emphasize the importance of selecting a consultant with health care industry experience, and Lee sees the health care organization–physician and the caregiver-patient relationships as two keys that illustrate how diversity consulting in health care contrasts with other organizations.

Whether an internal or external consultant is selected, the consultant must have access to and be able to effectively use a liaison system within the organization being audited. Clayton Alderfer (1980, 463) explains that while the liaison system may be an individual, a series of individuals, or a group, "to the degree that the liaison system is a microcosm of the system being studied, it will provide the consultant with samples of behavioral dynamics of the system. If the system or parts of the system resist the diagnostic process, the same process will be observable in the liaison system. Interventions with the liaison system to aid the diagnostic process will also have effects on the total system."

Qualitative, Quantitative, or Mixed Data Collection Models

Should the health care organization use qualitative, quantitative, or a mixed model that uses both quantitative and qualitative methods for data collection? The best answer to this question, in part, depends on your organization's culture. A health care organization with a strong bottom line orientation that manages by the numbers and values hard data will be more responsive to approaches to a cultural audit that quantify findings. Health care organizations that manage by intuition and insight may be more responsive to a qualitative approach.

However, most health care organizations will generally find the mixed model to be most appropriate. The diverse subcultures within health care organizations—finance, operations, nursing, medical staff, community relations—all have preferred "ways of knowing," of uncovering new insights, and discovering the truth. Therefore, a mixed model, with its reliance on both qualitative and quantitative analysis and its insistence on multiple measures, should provide information about the organization's culture that will be accepted and understood by many disparate groups.

Alderfer (1980) explains that "the more qualitative data are used, the more clients are encouraged to search for their own explanations, and the more quantitative data are used, the more the data themselves are likely to shape conclusions about the system." Both approaches can produce new insights and prompt dialogue about diversity. As psychology professor Stewart E. Cooper and Raymond M. O'Connor, Jr., (1993) explain:

> An emerging consensus seems to be developing that an either-or view of the quantitative-qualitative debate is less productive than a both-and approach. Specifically, many researchers believe that qualitative approaches have strength in answering discovery questions and in uncovering the meanings that individuals attach to their perceptions, whereas quantitative approaches are better for validation and theory testing. Moreover, the notion of a triangulation of psychometrically sound quantitative instruments, process oriented soft surveys, and qualitative methods is viewed as the best approach for uncovering the most complete knowledge of psychological phenomena, intervention processes, and their effects (p. 651).

Qualitative data are often most appropriate in the early stages of a cultural audit. On the other hand, quantitative methods, such as paper and pencil surveys that require the respondent to choose among predetermined responses, may be inappropriate in the initial stages of assessment, depending on the health care organization's circumstance. The consultant conducting the audit must gain insight into the issues, concerns, and style of your organization prior to developing a paper and pencil survey or recommending an "off the shelf" survey. Failure to do so may result in an audit that does not give your organization insight into key issues.

Many organizations begin their audit with focus groups, individual interviews with key personnel, and an expert qualitative review of company policies and procedures in order to evaluate the implications for diversity leadership. Miriam Lee, President of Vaughn-Lee & Associates, comments that paper and pencil surveys tend to provide a surface impression, while face-to-face interviews and focus groups will identify underlying and deeper issues.

External consultants with health care industry experience can use their knowledge and experience to qualitatively compare the health care organization's policies and procedures to best demonstrated practices and can identify aspects of the organization's culture that have adversely affected diversity leadership in other health care organizations.

Beware of consultants who want to limit the assessment process to a paper and pencil survey. Beginning with less structured and moving toward increasingly structured assessment approaches usually results in a richer information base and helps ensure that the consultant is committed to learning about your organization and tailoring the assessment to your needs.

Who Should Be Assessed?

Another key issue centers around determining who should take part in the assessment among the management, staff, physicians, patients, the community, the board. Including the customer in the diversity climate assessment process is essential and reflects patient- rather than provider-centered thinking. Only customers can shed light on aspects of the health care organization that are unknown to the organization's internal constituents.

Both Paradise Valley Hospital and Kaiser Permanente attest to the value of customer inclusion in the diversity assessment process. Paradise Valley Hospital's assessment philosophy has as its basis the belief that understanding the hospital starts with understanding the community. As health care organizations compete for business, effective diversity leadership, as reflected in customer loyalty, can provide a competitive edge.

Through targeted market research, Kaiser Permanente has uncovered valuable information about its increasingly diverse customer base, information that can be used to repackage services and improve market penetration. As the Kaiser publication *Diversity and Excellence: Planning for the Year 2000* states: "In the past it has sometimes been considered too difficult or too costly to include, for example, non-English–speaking member respondents in patient-focused research efforts. Additionally, we have often failed to be pro-active in determining whether or not there are ethnic/cultural differences in the way services are viewed or utilized among members. These groups are too great a proportion of our membership and potential membership to be ignored."

Kaiser's focus groups of Japanese American subscribers identified some culturally based perceptions that contributed to Japanese Americans being less likely to select Kaiser as their health care provider. Another Kaiser patient survey in southern California revealed that "the only patient characteristic that was significantly and negatively linked to overall evaluation of the quality of patient care was lack of ability to speak English." Insights such as these generate actionable items to investigate and change, improving service to the customer and the health care organization's bottom line.

Your consultant can help you to clarify the purpose of your cultural audit; understanding the purpose will then lead to determining who should take part in the assessment phase. A health care organization committed to diversity leadership will work toward the inclusion of all constituencies in the assessment and the whole diversity leadership process.

ALTERNATIVE TOOLS AND TECHNIQUES

Face-to-Face Interviews

Face-to-face interviews can minimize the problem of nonrespondents often encountered in paper and pencil surveys. Personal interaction is facilitated by this approach to data collection because it enables the interviewer to read nonverbal cues such as facial expression, body language, intonation, and inflection of the voice. This rich base of qualitative information can be used as an aid in interpreting the meaning of the respondent's answers and offers the opportunity to establish a bond of familiarity and trust between the interviewer and the respondent. This information can be particularly useful if the interviewer will be a trainer in the next phase of the diversity leadership process.

Nonverbal cues observed through face-to-face data collection can add richness to the interviewer's understanding, but they can also be misinterpreted. Many nonverbal signals are culturally based, making it possible for an unskilled interviewer to not pick up on them. In addition, an unskilled or poorly trained interviewer can "lead" the respondent by unknowingly giving verbal and nonverbal cues, thus biasing the results. When more than one interviewer is involved, all must be trained so that their approaches become standardized to increase the reliability or consistency of results.

Face-to-face interviews are generally guided by a script that introduces the purpose of the interview, discusses how confidentiality of responses will be addressed, and how and to whom survey results will be distributed. The introduction, in conjunction with the setting, the interviewer's dress and manner, and the questions themselves set the context for the interview. Questions that communicate a lack of understanding of the health care organization will adversely affect the credibility of the interviewer. Questions that are perceived to be leading, such as "Describe the last racist incident you observed at Hospital A," or "What should be done to improve cross-cultural relations in Health Care

Organization Z?" can bias responses due to the hidden assumptions implicit in the questions.

An effective interviewer will have obtained basic demographic information about each interviewee prior to the face-to-face meeting so as not to be perceived as wasting time. Interviewers generally use a list of questions that are open-ended, designed to elicit free responses. Questions that require a simple yes or no response are generally avoided, because answers to them can be obtained less expensively through paper and pencil surveys.

The health care organization's liaison with the consultant should ask to review the questions prior to the interview. In addition, the consultant should conduct a mock or practice interview with individuals similar to the actual interviewees to ensure that the questions are clear in meaning and that the interview process provides the breadth and depth of information desired. The questions themselves must be carefully worded to avoid biasing responses and carefully selected so that important areas of concern are not omitted and unimportant areas are not emphasized. The health care organization's liaison individual or team that works with the consultant play important roles in the process of developing the interview guide and designing the questions.

Occasionally interviews are audiotaped or videotaped, but concerns about confidentiality become heightened when they are. The benefits and drawbacks of such approaches must be thoroughly discussed, and interviews must never be taped without the prior knowledge and permission of the interviewee(s).

The health care organization is responsible for providing an appropriate, private setting for the interview. The degree to which the respondent is free to be frank, honest, and open with the interviewer will be affected by the setting for the interview itself. Interviewing the hospital's only Latina nurse in a glass cubicle on a patient floor in full view of the nursing station is not likely to produce valid results. While this may seem obvious, failure to consider the importance of setting to the validity of interview responses is a common error in cultural audits.

The disadvantages of face-to-face interviews include the relatively high cost and time commitment required. Interviews limit the number of respondents who can participate in the assessment.

Paper and Pencil Surveys

Paper and pencil surveys are frequently used in cultural audits or climate assessments, and their administration is less expensive than the cost of conducting face-to-face interviews, which allows for a greater number of respondents. Standardization is also easier since interviewers don't need to be trained and responses are generally easier to analyze, especially if a closed-response format is used. Paper and pencil surveys are especially amenable to a quantitative approach to data analysis, which can be a real advantage in communicating results to certain health care organization cultures and subcultures.

Disadvantages to this method include the fact that re- sponse rates are usually considerably lower than in face to face interviews—often fewer than 40 percent of survey recipients return their questionnaires. Also, the answers of respondents may not mirror the opinions of nonrespondents. It is important then for the consultant to compare known characteristics of respondents and nonrespondents in an attempt to identify any significant differences in demographic composition. If, for instance, a disproportionate number of white males are among the nonrespondents, resistance or backlash may be present that would not be identified solely through analyzing survey responses.

Survey questions can be open- or closed-response or a mixture of both. Questionnaires that are unstructured permit the respondent complete freedom in answering—thus the questions are open-response. A structured questionnaire, which requires the respondent to choose among a predetermined set of responses is considered closed response. Questionnaires can also consist of a mixture of open- and closed-response questions.

The Maryland Hospital Association's (1992) Minorities in the Workplace Task Force's survey published in *Work Force 2000: Valuing Cultural Diversity* is an example of a closed-response diversity survey developed specifically for the health care industry. Statements such as the following, to be rated by the respondent on a Likert-type scale, are included in the instrument entitled, "Assessing Your Organization's Diversity Quotient: A Self-Assessment Tool for Hospitals."

1. The hospital's mission statement includes a commitment to cultural diversity and equal opportunity.
2. Hospital policies and procedures acknowledge and reflect a positive approach to diversity.
3. Suppliers and contractors include a representative pro- portion of minority vendors.
4. The hospital provides educational programs about di- versity to all employees.
5. Managers' performance objectives and appraisals are related to effective management and development of a diverse work force.

6. Ethnic, racial, or sexist jokes are not told or tolerated.

7. The hospital sponsors events and outings that appeal to a variety of cultures and to men as well as women.

8. Accomplishments of all workers, including minorities, are highlighted through hospital newsletters and in appropriate print and electronic media.

9. The hospital routinely includes minority media in its recruitment advertising.

10. People openly celebrate different religious holidays.

The Maryland Hospital Association's closed-response survey requires respondents to select from four response categories: "yes," "no," "to some extent," and "not applicable."

United Hospital and Children's Health Care–St. Paul's employee diversity survey combined both closed- and open-response questions. Examples follow.

1. In my department, jokes and humor are used to: (circle those that apply)
   a. put people down
   b. lighten up stress
   c. show sarcasm
   d. show care and concern
   e. other _____

2. What is an "unspoken rule" about differences and diversity at your hospital?

3. If you are a manager/supervisor, what situations are most difficult for you in supervising employees who are different from you that you want training on?
   _____ a. conflict situations
   _____ b. performance evaluation
   _____ c. giving or receiving feedback
   _____ d. employee to employee communication
   _____ e. language barrier/difference
   _____ f. others? _____

4. Add any additional comments or opinions about Cultural Diversity you wish to express.

Both the open- and closed-response questions produced a rich database for diversity climate assessment and action. The survey, according to United Hospital Education Director Jeanne Bailey, was mailed to the homes of all employees at both United

Hospital and Children's–St. Paul. The results were publicized in the September/October 1993 issues of both employee newsletters.

Data from closed-response questions included these results: (1) One in five survey respondents said they had experienced discrimination in specific aspects of their employment; and (2) nearly one of every three Children's employees answering the survey said humor is used in their department to put people down or to show sarcasm.

Significant at both United and Children's–St. Paul was the high number of "unwritten or unspoken rules" in operation at the hospitals. Over 400 of these were listed by the employees who responded to the survey. These clustered into about a dozen groupings that included references to job class, shift-work challenges, and the prevalence of indirect communication.

Answers to open-response questions included the following perceptions of "unspoken rules" in the Hospitals' culture: "A member of an ethnic minority should be able to speak for that entire ethnic group. For instance: 'What do black people think about this?' 'Don't be different'; or 'Poor parents (or minority parents) are probably bad parents.'"

United Hospital and Children's—St. Paul, with the assistance of their external consultant from Minneapolis-based Vaughn-Lee & Associates, included survey questions specifically designed to assess employee opinion on the optimal diversity training design, the next step in United Hospital's and Children's–St. Paul's diversity leadership process. Survey results led the hospitals to adopt a peer trainer model, with employee volunteers working in staff/manager teams serving as trainers for their colleagues.

Checklists

Checklists are a special type of data collection instrument that diversity consultants may use in a cultural audit as an aid to consistency and completeness in observational analysis. The consultant may, for instance, develop a checklist of initiatives or programs seen in health care organizations that are known for successful diversity leadership, and use the list to determine whether your organization has such programs or initiatives in place.

Certain items from the Maryland Hospital Association's (1992) survey instrument would be appropriate in such a checklist, such as "The hospital has a task force/committee/advisory group to consider issues related to managing cultural diversity" and "The hospital requires recruitment firms to include minority candidates among those recommended for every position."

Checklists can be used to help internal or external assessors evaluate the health care organization's culture from the perspective of a diverse customer base. Checklists can guide the assessor in identifying the sometimes hidden messages that are given by factors such as the communication style of the admissions staff; artwork that appears in patient rooms, the cafeteria, or the health care organization's hallways; and images in the patient newsletter or marketing materials.

Checklists are successfully used to help the observer gather and interpret data and can be structured to help the assessor quantify impressions. A checklist item might, for example, require the assessor to count the number of men and women by role and function that appear in photographs in the patient newsletter or in the artwork and signage in the facility itself.

Checklists can help structure the generally informal assessment by wandering around (ABWA) process, resulting in a richer data base for discussion, analysis, and interpretation. The process of creating a checklist of key areas to look for can, in itself, encourage new insights.

The key disadvantages of checklists include the fact that checklists act as perceptual filters that may direct attention away from relevant observations not included on the checklist. In addition, although checklists tell the assessor what is or is not present in the organization, they provide no insight into the reasons why.

Focus Groups

This technique, often used in market research, has been successfully used by diversity consultants undertaking a cultural audit. Focus groups generally consist of small groups of individuals that are homogeneous with respect to the aspect of diversity that is of interest. For instance, if your health care organization is exploring concerns about women in management, your focus groups may be homogeneous with respect to gender.

Focus group participants are asked a series of open-ended questions, and results are recorded and subsequently analyzed. Analysis usually consists of looking for common threads in focus group members' responses in order to label or categorize them into major areas. Focus group information is qualitative in nature. Because it is a qualitative technique, the focus group technique is often employed early in the organizational assessment process.

The Maryland Hospital Association (1992), for example, used the focus group approach to discover and understand barriers that may impede the advancement of minority employees in Maryland hospitals. Responses from focus group participants assisted the task force in preparing the closed-response survey instrument "Assessing Your Organization's Diversity Quotient: A Self-Assessment Tool for Hospitals." Perceived barriers to advancement identified by MHA focus group participants clustered in four major areas—corporate culture, career development opportunities, mentoring/networking opportunities, and hospital personnel policies.

In the area of corporate culture, common threads such as the following were uncovered by the MHA task force: minority focus group members felt that they had to give up their own cultural identity in order to advance in their organization; participants also felt that others in their organization harbor negative stereotypes about them; and participants identified the need for multicultural training for middle and upper management.

In addition, participants commented that career development opportunities such as on-the-job training, tuition reimbursement, and continuing educational opportunities were perceived as valuable. Participants suggested hospital-sponsored training programs to assist African Americans with differences in dialect that they perceived as contributing to communication problems and to improve English as a second language for recent immigrants.

Participants also observed that "there are not enough minorities in leadership positions to help others progress" and suggested that mentoring/networking through participation in minority professional organizations needs to be encouraged by health care organizations. Focus groups' suggestions with respect to personnel policies included giving more credit for experiences, advertising jobs in minority publications, and routinely posting job opportunities. Focus groups, like those conducted by the Maryland Hospital Association (1992), can provide a wealth of ideas for organizational action planning.

GENERAL MEASUREMENT ISSUES · · · · · · · · · · ·

Sampling

Regardless of the data collection approach used, sampling issues must be addressed. If subjects are randomly selected, underrepresented groups such as African American managers or Japanese American patients, most often must be oversampled in order to produce statistically meaningful results and to ensure confidentiality of individual responses.

Convenience rather than random sampling is often employed to ensure appropriate representation of key individuals and constituencies. The lead custodian, for example, may not be the leader of the custodians. The key personality who galvanizes opinion in the medical staff may not be the vice president for medical affairs.

Reliability and Consistency

Regardless of whether the assessment approach consists of interviews, paper and pencil surveys, focus groups, cultural audit checklists, a review of documents, policies, and procedures, or other methods, results are less meaningful if they are inconsistent. Ask consultants how they ensure that different interviewers will elicit the same response from each interviewee, how they ensure that different auditors will fill out a checklist the same way, and how they ensure that the same respondent will give the same answer to a survey question at different times.

Training of interviewers and auditors is essential to ensure consistency. Clearly worded, specific, and unambiguous questions will help maintain consistency in response. Even customized surveys, created specifically for or modified to suit your health care organization, should be pretested on a group of respondents similar to those for whom the instrument is intended. This can help to identify design flaws that will bias results. Consistency can also be established by administering the same survey to the same respondent at two different times and correlating the results. A high positive correlation indicates that the instrument is reliable.

Validity

Validity is another key issue in assessment. Valid assessment tools and approaches measure what they were intended to measure, not any other problem or issue. **Face validity** is the most basic measure of validity and should be evaluated in all cultural assessment tools. Face validity can be assessed by answering questions like these: Which aspects of diversity culture does the tool assess? and Which aspects of diversity culture does the tool fail to assess? Content area experts in the field are most qualified to review your assessment tools to ensure face validity.

Clearly defining the scope and purpose of the cultural audit prior to its design can lead to the development, selection, and use of valid instruments. Statistical methods to assess the validity of data collection instruments are also available but are seldom used in practice other than for standardized, norm-referenced assessment instruments.

Asking the Right Questions!

The questions asked of a focus group or contained in a paper and pencil survey can be considered to be a sample from the universe of all possible questions that could be asked about the health care organization's culture and workforce diversity. Does the sample reflect the universe, or are some key areas missing while other areas are overemphasized? For example, are all of your questions about recruitment, and are there none about advancement? Do the questions imply that race or gender are the only dimensions of diversity, despite your health care organization's stated intention to frame the issue more broadly?

Asking the Questions in the Right Way!

Whether a checklist, survey instrument, or interviewer's question guide for focus groups or individual interviews is used, certain key design issues must be addressed by the consultant if results are to be meaningfully interpreted:

1. *Is the meaning of the question clear to the respondent? Do the questions use the appropriate terminology and vocabulary? Are the questions at an appropriate difficulty level?* Jargon should be avoided and replaced with simple, everyday language. Pretesting is an essential technique to determine whether the meaning of the question is clear to the respondent. Instruments designed for general business cannot always be used in health care organizations without some modification. Different terminology—for example, using the word customer instead of "client" or "patient"—can affect results and respondents' feelings about the survey.

2. *Does each question ask only about one thing?* Poorly worded questions sometimes combine two or more issues in the same question, confusing the respondent and making the meaning of the response unclear and open to multiple interpretations. For example, responses to the following survey item would be difficult to interpret: "Blacks, gays, women, and other people are given unfair advantage by the laws and the courts." A respondent who strongly agrees with this statement might think that blacks are given unfair advantage, but women are not. On the other hand, the respondent who answers in the affirmative may think that "other people" are given unfair advantage but blacks, gays, and women are not. An African American and a European American respondent may give the same answer but mean something totally different.

3. *Do the questions reflect the consultant's hidden (and, perhaps, unfounded) assumption about the respondent, the response, or the health care organization?* Questions of the "describe the last time you told a racist/sexist joke" variety reveal the survey developer's tacit assumption that you told one.

4. *Does the question "lead" the respondent to a response desired (by the questionnaire designer)?* For example, the question, "Due to the discrimination blacks experience in the workplace, should special support services be offered to blacks?" actually prompts the respondent to say "yes." Questions need to set the context, without biasing the response.

ANALYSIS OF ASSESSMENT RESULTS

The approach to results analysis can be key to obtaining diversity data from general climate or cultural assessments, equity studies, or other data collection efforts. Climate assessment instruments that are not specifically focused on diversity can also yield a rich database about diversity climate. The key is in analyzing and comparing response patterns along important dimensions of diversity such as gender, race, or age.

Psychometric instruments such as the popular Myers-Briggs Type Indicator (MBTI) (Briggs-Myers and McCaulley 1985) are also useful in initiating discussions about the diversity within groups—such as white males—that are often tacitly viewed as homogeneous and in this example can, consequently, feel estranged from the diversity leadership process. The MBTI assesses a respondent's temperament along four dimensions—**extraversion / introversion, sensing / intuition, thinking / feeling,** and **judging / perceiving**—using the responses to categorize the subject into one of 16 personality or temperament types. Discussion of MBTI results can produce insights into alternative dimensions of diversity and build bridges of understanding and similarity across gender, racial, age, sexual preference, or other differences.

Also providing insights into the different perceptions of the health care organization's culture and climate that can result when the organization is viewed from the vantage points of diverse respondents are general culture or climate assessment instruments such as the Work Environment Scale (WES) (Moos 1986) or the Organizational Culture Profile (OCP) (O'Reilly, Chatman, and Caldwell 1991). When general culture or climate assessment instruments are analyzed by key dimensions of diversity, such as race or gender, they can provide valuable insights into diversity climate.

The WES (Moos 1986), for example, is a climate assessment instrument that consists of ten subscales, nesting into three broad dimensions of the organization's work climate: relationship, personal growth, and system maintenance and system change. There are three forms of the WES: (1) the **real,** measuring perceptions of the current work environment; (2) the **ideal**, measuring characteristics of the preferred work environment; and (3) the **expectations**, measuring those characteristics the respondent expects to find in the work setting. Because the WES has been used in health care settings (Flarey 1991), the WES manual (Moos 1986) itself reports differences in perceptions of patient care and nonpatient care personnel that appear consistently across health care organizations. Comparing Form R or real profiles by race, gender, or ethnicity while controlling for factors known to affect respondents' profiles, such as management/staff position or clinical/nonclinical personnel, can add to the health care organization's understanding of its diversity climate.

An alternative survey, the Organizational Climate Index Survey, which appeared in the journal, *Management Solutions* (Nave 1986) is an instrument that consists of 29 items categorized into four major section headings—job, communication, management, and motivation and morale. Respondents are directed to rate each item on the following scale: 90–100, excellent; 80–89, good; 70–79, fair; 60–69, poor; and 0–59, very poor. Sample items follow.

1. Job expectations are realistic and clearly stated.
2. Two-way communication is encouraged and present in our organization.
3. Grievance situations are handled in a fair and unbiased manner.
4. There is tolerance for individual differences and dissent within our organization (Nave 1986, 16–17).

Another general assessment instrument cited in the health care literature (Thomas et al. 1990) is the Organizational Culture Inventory (OCI) whose results are graphically displayed as a figure. Respondents can compare their institutional profile to those of reference groups, or reference group profiles can be compared to one another. The OCI (Thomas et al. 1990, 20) categorizes organizations' cultural styles into three types: **aggressive/defensive** cultural styles, which "promote members' security needs" and "require them to approach tasks in forceful ways to protect their status and position"; **passive/defensive** styles, which "promote the security needs of members" and "implicitly require them to interact with people in self-protective ways to meet those needs"; and **constructive** styles, which "emphasize members' satisfaction needs" and "encourage them to interact with people and approach tasks in ways that will help them meet those needs."

In contrast, the Organization Culture Profile (OCP) was developed by Dr. Jennifer Chatman (1989) and her colleagues (O'Reilly, Chatman, and Caldwell 1991) to assess person-organization fit, which is defined "as the congruence between the norms and values of organizations and the values of persons" (Chatman 1989). The OCP uses a **Q-sort** methodology. Respondents generate a Q-sort profile by sorting 54 value statements into nine categories (Chatman 1989; O'Reilly, Chatman, and Caldwell 1991). Categories range from most to least desirable, for an individual's personal profile, or from most to least characteristic, for an organization's aggregate profile. Respondents may be asked to sort the deck of 54 value statements in a way that describes their own values or the value system of the organization. Examples of the 54 values to be sorted by respondents include the following: tolerance, being rule-oriented, being distinctive/different from others, being socially responsible, or being demanding (O'Reilly, Chatman, and Caldwell 1991). Person-organization fit scores then are calculated by correlating individual preference profiles with an organization profile developed through averaging responses of raters representative of the organization. The individual profile is generated when raters sort by keeping in mind the question, How important is it for this characteristic to be a part of the organization I work for? (Chatman 1989).

On the other hand, the key question for the organization profile is, How much does this attribute characterize your organization's values? (Chatman 1989). Here the rater sorts based on the extent each attribute reflects the organization's value system or culture. Typically, sorters are employees, referred to as members by the researchers (Chatman 1989; O'Reilly, Chatman, and Caldwell 1991), who have been with the organization for at least one or two years, and member profiles are combined by averaging each item to form an organization profile.

A strong organization value system would be indicated by a high inter-rater reliability coefficient, which the researchers (Chatman 1989) have operationally defined as anything above .70. A low-reliability coefficient may indicate a weak culture or the existence of many subcultures with different value profiles. A high correlation between the organization and an individual's profile indicates a good fit. The OCP has successfully predicted job satisfaction and organizational commitment a year after fit was measured and actual turnover after two years (O'Reilly, Chatman, and Caldwell 1991). Readers should note that applications of OCP cited in the general literature are not diversity-oriented, but profiles and person/organization correlation coefficients could easily be compared by key dimensions of diversity and used in this way.

The instruments discussed here and other psychometric and culture or climate assessment instruments can yield valuable insights into diversity-related issues when properly analyzed.

RESULTS REPORTING

Survey respondents have a right to review survey results. If the health care organization fails to disseminate the results and take action based on them in a timely fashion, the organization's credibility will be brought into question. If feedback is the goal, in order to "promote increased understanding of the client system by its members" (Alderfer 1980, 466), then the consultant must share results in a forum and a format that is palatable to the client organization. Failure to do so reflects poorly on the consultant's understanding of the client health care organization.

Health care organizations that value data should be given numerical results, while those organizations that are philosophically oriented or theory-based should have their feedback put in context within a theoretical framework. Organizations that value the process of questioning and open discovery could be presented with data that are more "raw" and participate in the process of summarizing, analyzing, and attaching meaning to the data.

There are basically two traditional feedback designs (Alderfer 1980).

1. The **family group model**, which is used when organizations are structured, as are many health care organizations, in a traditional hierarchy. Each functional area or department or unit is viewed as a family group, and feedback is given to the group. This model relies on trust between supervisor and subordinate and, according to Alderfer (1980), works best when subordinates feel free to openly disagree with the supervisor without fear of retribution, when the team is not interested in attacking or undermining the leader, and when the feedback is specific to the functional area or family group.

2. The **peer group–intergroup model**, on the other hand, is used when the feedback relates to the organization as a whole. People first meet in groups of peers of the same status level or identity group in the organization. Then, combinations of peer groups meet to discuss data about the relationship among their peer groups. Finally, groups representing different hierarchical levels—such as department heads and executive leadership, minority and nonminority workers, or physicians and nurses— meet to discuss results.

When using the peer group–intergroup feedback model, Alderfer (1980) gives the following advice:

> The effectiveness of the peer group–intergroup model depends on managing effectively the tendencies toward ethnocentrism that exist in all groups. Groups exhibiting ethnocentric patterns attribute primarily positive traits to their own group and mainly negative properties to other groups. If ethnocentric dynamics are set off by the feedback process, then the data analysis will be rejected and little learning will occur. The primary means to guard against heightening ethnocentrism during feedback are to be sure that the peer groups address their internal conflicts during the first phase of the process (thereby reducing the likelihood that internal conflicts will be projected onto outgroups) and to restrict the discussion of external group relations until the intergroup meeting (when both groups will be able to share their perceptions of the relationship between the groups). A further step in managing these intergroup dynamics is to intervene in the interpersonal relationship between the leaders of the peer groups, whose behavior in the feedback sessions will have a significant impact on the degree of ethnocentrism demonstrated in the joint meeting (p. 467).

In reporting data, confidentiality of the responses of underrepresented groups must be considered. If your health care organization has only two executive-level women managers, for instance, executive-level responses cannot be publicly reported by gender without compromising confidentiality. Questions about sexual preference or orientation can be particularly sensitive in this regard. Failure to build respondents' confidence in the confidentiality of their results prior to the interview can result in invalid information because respondents will mask their true opinions as a self-protective measure.

ASSESSMENT AND TRAINING · · · · · · · · · · ·

Finally, assessment is of critical importance in identifying the diversity issues that are specific to your health care organization's context. Assessment results provide focus to your training initiative and serve to connect training to the process of organizational change. This connection is discussed further in chapter six.

REFERENCES · · · · · · · · · · · ·

Alderfer, C. P. 1980. "The Methodology of Organizational Diagnosis," *Professional Psychology* 11 (3): 459–68.

Briggs-Myers, I., and M. H. McCaulley. 1985. *Manual: A Guide to the Development and Use of the Myers-Briggs Type Indicator (A).* Palo Alto, CA: Consulting Psychologists Press.

Chatman, J. A. 1989. "Improving Interactional Organizational Research: A Model of Person-Organization Fit." *Academy of Management Review* 14 (3): 333–49.

Cooper, S. E., and R. M. O'Connor, Jr. 1993. "Standards for Organizational Consultation Assessment and Evaluation Instruments." *Journal of Counseling and Development* 71 (6): 651–60.

Flarey, D. L. 1991. "The Social Climate Scale: A Tool for Organizational Change and Development." *Journal of Nursing Administration* 21 (4): 37–44.

Maryland Hospital Association. 1992. *Work Force 2000: Valuing Cultural Diversity: Report of Minorities in the Workplace Task Force.* Lutherville, MD: Maryland Hospital Association.

Moos, R. H. 1986. *Work Environment Scale Manual,* 2d ed. Palo Alto, CA: Consulting Psychologists Press.

Nave, J. 1986. "Gauging Organizational Climate." *Management Solutions* 31 (6): 14–18.

O'Reilly, C. A., J. Chatman, and D. F. Caldwell. 1991. "People and Organizational Culture: A Profile Comparison Approach to Assessing Person-Organization Fit." *Academy of Management Journal* 34 (3): 487–516.

Shortell, S. M., and A. D. Kaluzny. 1987. *Healthcare Management: A Text in Organization Theory and Behavior.* New York: John Wiley & Sons.

Thomas, C., M. Ward, C. Chorba, and A. Kumiega. 1990. "Measuring and Interpreting Organizational Culture." *Journal of Nursing Administration* 20 (6): 17–24.

PART III

Exploration

CEO Bryant has some decisions to make. Results of the assessment are in and, as he expected, are mixed. Community and employee concerns were surfaced that pique his interest and demand his attention. The level of diversity awareness is, apparently, quite varied within Urban Medical Center. The seeds of backlash and resistance exist within the center and, he suspects, would be unleashed with a vengeance if training were mishandled.

Bryant has heard some horror stories about diversity training from friends and colleagues. He is simultaneously tempted to bury the assessment results and to forge ahead, embracing the training process wholeheartedly. He rolls up his sleeves. Bryant is poised to take the next step in diversity leadership—training design and implementation.

CHAPTER 6

The Training Process

JUST AS diversity consultants use different tools to assess organizational culture and climate, they also have a variety of training approaches at their disposal: "Because every corporate culture is unique, it's understandable that work force diversity training programs vary between companies. The number of employees, the type of product or service and the origins of the multicultural movement within the organization dictate some of the training program parameters" (Solomon 1989, 45). The methods and approaches consultants use are determined, in part, by the results of the assessment. This chapter will discuss how assessment directs training and will evaluate different training approaches within the context of group composition and organizational needs.

THE LINK BETWEEN ASSESSMENT AND TRAINING

Regardless of the type of assessment used, the results are crucial in directing the consultant in the design of a training process that will meet the needs of the health care organization. The assessment is a diagnostic tool that provides the consultant with information about power relationships, decision making, group dynamics, and diversity hot buttons. The consultant can gain insight into the personnel practices and group-specific attitudes and values that are operative at different levels of the organization and within departments. Consultants can also gain insight into regional and local issues that affect how the health care organization does business within the larger context of the community. The assessment results are a snapshot of the organization taken in real time. Once data are analyzed, the consultant uses the results to design the training approach and to determine which training issues should be addressed first.

External and Internal Issues Affecting Training

There are many indirect factors that could affect participants' receptivity to diversity training. A well-conducted assessment will make the consultant aware of such factors so that any potentially negative impact on the process and outcome of training can be minimized. Some of these factors are external in nature—for example, managed care requirements or changes in patient mix driven by trends in the local economy or service area demographics—while others may be internal—for example, restructuring, downsizing, cost-cutting efforts, and union negotiations. Conflicts between professional and support staff, nurses and doctors, or social work and psychiatry staffs that reflect competition between departments with related areas of responsibility will also affect receptivity to diversity training.

If an organization is or has undergone reengineering efforts, the impact of associated cost-cutting moves may heavily influence workers' attitudes toward any training, but especially toward diversity training (more about this will be discussed in the next chapter, "Backlash"). Suffice it to say that morale issues may need to be addressed early on in the training.

Since diversity has many dimensions and since health care agencies vary in employee and patient mix, the training focus will also vary. For example, if there are few or no minorities in the training group, the consultant may want to begin training by looking at gender issues. If training is for woman-dominated support staff, the key diversity dimensions may be ethnicity, race, or social class. If there are large numbers of single-parent families, the focus could be on family–work life issues. The assessment should identify those dimensions of diversity that are most relevant, based on employee and service area demographics.

The trainer can also use the assessment to determine the specific issues that need to be addressed. For example, if the organization is plagued with litigation, the trainer may want to focus on "safer" issues earlier in the process and introduce potentially explosive topics later because it is important that the training group develop a sense of cohesion prior to working on potentially volatile issues. Or, conversely, if management has been minimizing problems involving the treatment of diverse groups, the trainer may need to help the organization explore these issues early on in the process. A good rule of thumb is to select an issue that allows the group first to create safety and then to move and work through increasing levels of conflict.

Effect of Assessment on Group Composition

Consultants also use assessment data to make decisions about training group composition, and they should make them co-operatively with their internal organizational liaison system. If at all possible, training groups should be heterogeneous along key dimensions of diversity, but homogeneous by level in the organization. Including participants from several racial or ethnic groups, varied age groups, and balance in terms of gender in the same training cohort is considered ideal. When training groups are diverse, both majority and minority perspectives can surface and difficult intergroup issues can be identified and addressed. If it is not possible to form groups that are homogeneous by level but are heterogeneous along key dimensions of diversity, the consultants and members of their internal organizational liaison system can determine how to ensure a heterogeneous training group without destabilizing the supervisory relationship.

Some health care organizations have achieved diversity in their training groups by training minority support staff with white supervisors. It must be noted that, if not done carefully, the training could fail if support staff do not feel free to talk candidly about their work experiences. Consultants are aware that better training results if workers at the same level are able to discuss diversity issues with other service workers than if they are forced to discuss them with those who have supervisory power over them. On the other hand, some health care organizations, departments, or teams have flatter organization designs where position does not hamper candid discussion.

Disclosure of Assessment Results during Training

The training sessions may be used to deliver assessment results. In doing so, decisions about who receives what feedback during training are crucial. Prior to public disclosure, the organization's leadership needs to receive a comprehensive report of assessment results. But, in the training itself, only highlights of the results should be presented to each training group, and *only* information pertinent to that specific group is presented during the training.

Special attention needs to be paid to protecting the confidentiality of individual responses as well as the identity of individuals who may somehow be singled out in the assessment results. Consultant judgment about what to share and with whom is very important, as is determining how much the group can handle prior to and during the training. If the organization is polarized around other work-related issues, the manner in which diversity assessment results are presented can potentially galvanize the group to resist the diversity training process or embrace it.

While assessment results are used strategically to provide the organization with clear feedback about itself, the consultant needs to be aware that boundaries of supervisor/subordinate relationships must be respected. It's essential that confidentiality and openness be balanced so that problems are not hidden and so that employees' rights to anonymity are protected. Because the relationship between the consultant and the organization is founded on trust, the consultant's audit must reflect a candid view of the organizational dynamics without destabilizing structural relationships.

Effect of Assessment on Training Design

Finally, assessment results are useful in helping consultants select the most appropriate training methods and materials. Training design is influenced by several factors, including the participants' educational background, intellectual astuteness, occupational level, and the critical issues identified through the assessment. If the participants are direct service providers, a hands-on approach with less emphasis on theory can be most effective. Academic professionals, on the other hand, tend to respond more favorably to theory tied to experience, while managers prefer that training ties work-related experiences to concrete strategies for changing behavior.

If a mixed data collection model was used, the consultants should have a rich information base gleaned from interviews, survey data, and other data collection methods that provides insights into the way participants process information and view diversity.

TRAINING APPROACHES

In diversity training, there are three major approaches consultants use—the consultant-centered approach, the group process–centered approach, and the organizational systems change approach. Each approach has distinct advantages and disadvantages, which are discussed below. Consultants, along with members of their organizational liaison system, must select the approach that best fits the health care organization's needs.

Consultant-Centered Approach

To be successful, the **consultant-centered approach** requires a charismatic leader who is able to motivate decision makers to action. Consultant-centered leaders have strong presentation skills and use speeches or lectures as the primary training tool. In this approach, participants are motivated by the consultant's personality and knowledge base. Consultant-centered presenters are usually dramatic, personable, and high-powered, and they can influence large numbers of people; their approach is provocative, forceful, and intense, and they stimulate participants into thinking about the ways in which culture shapes attitudes, biases, and behaviors in a historical, socio-political context.

The techniques consultant-centered leaders use are personal stories, thought-provoking questions, confrontation, metaphors, and small group demonstrations. Once the group is stimulated, the consultant interprets the audience's responses for the large group. This approach is particularly beneficial when upper-level management needs to be convinced about the importance of diversity leadership. When upper-management is in denial, complacent, or resistant to the diversity imperative, a consultant-centered approach can be the boost that is needed to engage management's interest. The consultant-centered approach provides management with a wake-up call. If consultant-centered leaders are persuasive, knowledgeable about the health care industry, and able to interpret the organization's group dynamics for training participants, this approach can be a powerful force for organizational change.

The consultant-centered approach provides the biggest "bang for the buck" and requires the least amount of commitment on the part of management. If the goal is to show your staff and the public that your organization recognizes that the workforce is changing and if you want to expose other areas of the organization to the need for diversity initiatives, then this approach is a good introduction because it is short-term, high-energy, and engaging. Executives will usually buy into consultant-centered training as a first step.

One disadvantage of the consultant-centered approach is that it can be heavy-handed and may polarize groups if the issues raised in the training are not subsequently worked through. Participants may feel confronted, inspired, and more aware of the institutionalized "isms," yet they may not see the importance of diversity as a process that involves personal *and* organizational change. The consultant-centered approach can leave participants wondering about what to do next.

Another disadvantage is that this approach is usually centered on the consultant's personality rather than on the health care organization's commitment to change. Often executives will endorse training if and only if the charismatic consultant does all the work. The charismatic consultant may not possess the group process skills needed to help the organization change its practices, procedures, and behaviors. As a result, consultant-centered training becomes a one-time media event rather than a step in the organizational change process.

Commitment to changing the organization's culture is critical to effective diversity leadership and is discussed extensively in Part 4. Often when executives endorse short-term training initiatives, they want to impress large numbers of staff while postponing real organizational change. While consultant-centered training may be a good first step, it does not help the health care organization to navigate through the process of organizational transformation and change.

Group Process–Centered Approach

A **group process-centered approach** requires that consultants work as facilitators with selected groups within the organization. This approach is experiential in nature, with a heavy emphasis placed on structuring participatory activities so that groups can study themselves in process. Activities include role playing, simulations, small and large group discussions, and other structured experiences. Participants, with the help of facilitators, then interpret what they learned about themselves in the context of diversity. The facilitators also assist participants in linking the experiential activity to the workplace.

Attitudes and behaviors are contrasted by race, ethnicity, gender, or other key dimensions of diversity and are explored in the training. Solomon (1989) describes one such training exercise.

> A group of managers face a trainer. The instructor asks the group to complete this phrase: "A woman is. . . ." The managers brainstorm about what comes to mind. Later, they replace woman with "white male," "black," "Hispanic," "Asian," and "disabled." Then the trainer helps them understand the assumptions behind the stereotypes they voiced. (p. 45)

The group process consultant's role is not only to help participants understand how assumptions work, but also to help the group learn how to communicate effectively with a wide range of employees from different backgrounds. In addition, the participants learn to identify and address barriers that may influence an employee's receptivity to supervision or mentoring (Delatte and Baytos 1993; Farr 1992; Solomon 1989).

Effective group process–centered facilitators rely on assessment results to determine the focus of training activities. Assume, for instance, that a hypothetical health care organization's assessment results indicated that men in the organization are stereotyped as being rigid and incapable of listening to others' opinions. The group process–focused consultant in this case would structure activities to bring out these beliefs in the training, and women participants might be asked to form small groups and discuss the advantages and disadvantages of being a man at work. Once the beliefs about men emerge in the training, the consultant can help the group process its feelings. This activity would likely be reversed so that the men participating also get to discuss their beliefs about women.

The consultant would then facilitate a constructive dialogue between the men and women training participants with the goal of helping each group understand the other's reality. Eventually the training group would explore the relationship between scape-goating or stereotyping and the quality of communication between men and women within the health care organization. This kind of processing can help employees reframe diversity-related problems and develop constructive strategies to improve intraorganizational communication.

The group process–centered approach has several important advantages over the consultant-centered approach. First, since group process–centered consultants focus on encouraging training participants to voice and explore their own attitudes, beliefs, and behaviors, training groups are likely to be more involved and to acknowledge ownership of diversity problems and solutions.

In addition, the group process–centered approach requires that employees invest in each other to work out organizational problems. Training participants have the opportunity to distin-guish between issues that affect groups of people who share a key dimension of diversity and issues that affect one or two individuals. When groups recognize the magnitude of diversity-related issues in the health care organization and accept owner-ship for the culture and climate, they are able to invest energy into continuous improvement. Group process–centered training can help employees learn to support one another through the change process.

The group process–centered approach also offers a very real opportunity to help small groups of employees develop true working alliances across preexisting boundaries, and interpersonal issues affecting work can be identified and explored in depth. The consultant can assist the group in developing its own solutions.

The group process–centered approach is very effective in enabling racial or ethnic groups to identify and confront culturally based behavioral styles that may inadvertently provoke distrust on the part of others. For example, supervisors may believe that repeatedly using "why" questions is appropriate and an expression of their prerogative to know how an employee implements a job directive, and if employees are members of the same racial or ethnic group as the supervisor, they may interpret the questioning behavior as appropriate and supportive or possibly somewhat annoying. But if the supervisor is white and the subordinate is black, the same questioning behavior may be interpreted as a sign of hostility and distrust. Employees' reactions are influenced by their cultural expectations.

Several key disadvantages to the group process–centered approach must be considered by health care organizations in selecting a training approach. If the organization is large, the group process–centered approach can be slow, inefficient, and expensive. Facilitators need a lot of time to help a group move from casual conversation to an in-depth and candid exploration of emotionally charged issues such as race, gender, disability, or sexual orientation. The organization may not be willing or able to make the requisite investment of time and resources; such an investment can be particularly problematic to the health care organization if reengineering or a similar program has resulted in downsizing and a concomitant feeling of overload.

If the diversity consultants selected by the health care organization are not skilled at group process work, this approach can easily backfire. Training participants may blame organizational problems on the consultants, and it's not unlikely for the staff to think that the diversity consultant could be an organizational spy for management. If consultants do not know how group processes unfold, they may personalize participants' reactions and derail the group's development by trying to control conflict.

Nevertheless, the group process–centered approach can be one of the most effective training models, particularly for organizations with employee morale problems. It requires, however, a skillful facilitator, a commitment of time and resources on the part of the health care organization, and executive leadership that understands and appreciates how groups work.

Organizational Systems Change Approach

The last approach, **organizational systems change**, is comprehensive in scope and long-term in focus. In this case, the consultant works as a team member with an internal organizational liaison system whose mission is to transform organizational culture by developing and implementing planned change. The organization's mission, goals, productivity, procedures, and work practices are revisited to determine where barriers exist and how the health care organization can redesign to meet the needs of the changing workforce and patient mix.

The organizational systems change approach views training as one component of a multifaceted process that may include a realignment of mission and goals, revision of personnel policies and practices, assessment of purchasing policies with vendors, evaluation of patient services, and exploration of community utilization patterns. The organization may engage in studying its reputation with customers, employees, and the community it serves, as well as its relationships with other health care institutions.

The organizational systems change approach moves beyond just training employees to value and manage diversity; it requires a paradigm shift. The multifaceted diversity initiative will include components such as process consultation with leadership, ongoing training of staff, integrating diversity values in the orientation of new employees, strategic planning for diversity, and supervisory training for managers. These components are followed by evaluation of success in timed intervals after each component of the change process is completed. Health care organizations that select the organizational change approach typically make a three- to five-year commitment to the change process.

Health care executives who commit to the organizational systems change approach envision diversity leadership as an essential and comprehensive effort to prepare the organization to meet the demands of the future. In the long run, the organizational change approach is an investment in the future survival of the health care institution. The amount of time spent recruiting and training new employees, for instance, is often considerable, and if new employees leave because of institutional barriers, the cost to the health care organization from this dimension alone can be exorbitant (Cox 1993). Proponents of the organizational systems change approach contend that training alone is not sufficient to address institutional barriers.

An important aspect of this approach is aimed at creating a culture that takes into account how policies, procedures, and practices that serve as rewards for some may serve as barriers for others who do not fit traditional worker profiles. In some companies, for instance, managers have used sports tickets as perks for employees. While sports tickets may be a reward for some employees, they may not be viewed as a reward for a single parent, for instance, who may prefer coupons for use at a fast food restaurant. This approach can make it clear that the "one size fits all" approach to managing people is passé (Jamison and O'Mara 1991).

Systems change, if planned and implemented cooperatively by employees and leadership, can positively affect retention, morale, and productivity. The organizational systems change approach involves management and staff in the planning process at every level within the organization, and the desired outcome is a work environment that is economically sound, open to change, flexible, and responsive to the needs of employees and consumers.

Despite its strengths, there are several key disadvantages to this comprehensive approach that views training as only one tool in the consultant's portfolio. The length of time required for the process to unfold is extensive, and the commitment required for successful implementation is great. To engage in this process, the health care organization has to make a considerable investment of its financial and human resources. Because the organizational systems change approach usually takes one to five years from assessment through training, design, and implementation, ongoing adjustments to the design are needed to address changing circumstances.

When using this approach, remember that cultural change is slow. Beyond an initial honeymoon period, intergroup conflict will increase in early stages of the change process. The hard work of managing conflict and struggling with ambiguity is unpredictable, and problems that may have been hidden for years are often uncovered. Early on in the organizational systems change approach, executives struggle with wanting to stop the diversity training because the conflict feels unmanageable. Recognizing that escalating conflict is part of the change process can be difficult and may cause the organization to derail the diversity leadership process before it has reached its destination.

THE IMPETUS FOR DIVERSITY TRAINING

Health care organizations identify the need to invest in diversity training for a variety of reasons. Clearly, training design must take into account the force that spurred the organization's interest in diversity leadership in the first place, and it generally stems from one of the following four sources—executive leadership, internal crisis, consumer pressure, or middle management. Each impetus for training and its implications for the organization and its diversity consultants are discussed below.

Driven by Executive Leadership

There are a few pioneers in health care leadership who see the trends of the future and understand the business rationale for diversity initiatives; these pioneers realize the need to be proactive. To stay on the competitive edge, these leaders see the need to prepare a diverse workforce to meet the challenges of the future. Health care organizations whose leaders have this vision of diversity leadership are ready to embrace the organizational systems change approach previously described. Leadership's role is to inspire staff and encourage others within the organization to embrace the process of diversity leadership, while the consultant's role is to design and implement the process over the long term.

Health care organizations with leadership-driven training initiatives often begin the training with executive management staff. Engaging upper-management staff early in the change process is a key strategy, and in some cases this introductory training may be intense and, perhaps, confrontational. Such an approach allows senior management to see how cultural bias influences the organization's selection, promotion, and evaluation practices. Management training should also incorporate strategies to help executives understand the business rationale for diversity leadership.

Driven by Internal Crisis

If the health care organization's interest in diversity training is litigation-driven, leadership and staff are likely to be in a crisis-focused, reactive mode. As a result, the diversity training will be expected to put out forest fires. When a health care organization is in this state, it typically wants consultants to conduct half-day workshops with large numbers of people, while the executive handles damage control. The organization that is crisis-driven sees training as a way to manage its current situation and to prevent further legal problems. The consultant's task in these cases is to move leadership toward adoption of a longer-term focus.

Driven by Consumer Pressure

When diversity initiatives are consumer-driven, the leadership's reason for follow-through may be cosmetic. Typically, health care executives will allow a few staff members to be trained and may change some aspects of clinical practice or customer relations, but, once the pressure subsides, the work stops. As with training driven by internal crisis, consultants will have to engage in short-term interventions while trying to convince leaders of the need to adopt a longer-term focus. Often health care executives will not recognize the need to be proactive until the organization's consumer base has taken its business elsewhere.

The difficulty that health care organizations can experience in responding to pressure from their customer base is multifaceted. The organization has to make decisions about addressing the special needs of the community given the constraints presented by limited resources. For instance, finding trained staff with specific language skills, if the customer base consists of new immigrant or refugee groups, can be challenging. Conflict between established racial and ethnic groups and new immigrants can provoke charges of reverse discrimination and create a new crisis for leadership to address.

Consultants must work effectively with their internal organizational liaison system to sort out the situation and design a training approach that addresses complex, interconnected diversity dilemmas without creating new crises to be managed. The ultimate goal is to maintain the customer base and strengthen community relations while creating a future labor resource from the community itself (Hunt 1994).

Driven by Middle Management

Often middle management recognizes the need for diversity training before executive leadership. If these middle managers are de facto leaders, they will have the ability to influence others and may have the power to begin diversity training within their own unit without executive involvement. These diversity pioneers can function as catalysts for change among other middle managers and may also influence executive management. When executive management does not initially recognize the need for diversity leadership, the internal pioneer's role as a catalyst becomes vital.

If middle management recognizes the need for diversity leadership but executive management does not, the consultant's first order of business should be to obtain executive management's endorsement of and participation in the training. If this is not accomplished, the diversity change process will ultimately derail.

CONSULTANT SELECTION AND COMPETENCIES

Once the health care organization has clarified its motives for undertaking diversity training, the process of selecting a consultant to design and conduct the training begins. The approach to training, the cost of services, and the skills and experience of diversity consultants vary widely. Because diversity consulting is an unregulated industry, the health care organization must proceed cautiously and heed the maxim: *caveat emptor* (let the buyer beware).

How do executive leaders determine which diversity consultant is best suited for their organization? Taking the time to gather the data needed to make an informed decision is essential. Ask consultants to submit evaluations from previous consulting engagements. Contact former clients to discuss their work and clients' satisfaction with the results. Meet the consultants personally before signing a contract, and request a detailed written proposal that describes how the consultant intends to address your organization's unique needs.

If a cadre of consultants are employed under the aegis of one firm, be sure that the evaluations you have gathered pertain to the particular consultants who will be working with your organization. The evaluations should include both positive and negative reactions to the consultants' work. Results should indicate that the consultants have demonstrated competence in these areas:

- processing of group interactions;
- presentations;
- conducting training that stimulates the cognitive, emotional, and behavioral dimensions of training participants;
- key dimensions of diversity, including race, ethnicity, gender, sexual orientation, and physical ability;
- customizing training based on group composition; and
- conducting cultural audits and climate assessments, as well as reporting assessment results.

Group Process and Presentation Skills

Group process skills for consultants go beyond the prerequisite of a thought-provoking presentation style to focus on the consultant's ability to stimulate group interaction, manage conflict, and lead groups to explore controversial issues and their own group dynamics. These skills are especially important as training moves from consultant-centered to group process–focused approaches.

The first task for the consultant is, of course, to command participants' attention by presenting the material in an interesting way. Presentation style should be engaging, empathic, and powerful. It is important for the consultant to model relevant self-disclosure for the group, particularly in early stages of the diversity training process. The consultant needs to demonstrate that it is safe to take risks and that openness and honesty within the group is expected and desired.

The ability to interweave didactic presentations with both small and large group activities in diversity training is also important in the successful consultant. Most diversity training begins with a focus on awareness building because it achieves two goals: (1) it allows participants to become more familiar and comfortable with each other, and (2) it encourages participants to explore and discuss work experiences that touch on dimensions of diversity that are emotionally loaded. Awareness is the bedrock of diversity training. Therefore, the consultant's role is to start the awareness process by (1) modeling openness, (2) listening to others' experiences, and (3) facilitating the group's exploration of its own history within the context of the diversity issues at hand.

It should be noted that employing awareness activities in the beginning phase of training is often viewed by hard-line behaviorists and business managers as too "touchy-feely" (Geber 1990) and by some managers as being too personal and not work-related. However, without an awareness component, diversity training can become nothing more than an intellectual exercise and, consequently, will not result in cultural change. The consultant must be able to establish credibility quickly and help the group manage its initial anxiety about exploring the affective and behavioral ramifications of diversity.

Strong group process skills are imperative for diversity consultants because diversity training will, inevitably, cause conflicts to surface. Conflict is a natural part of a group's life and is vital to the growth and productivity of healthy teams. If conflict is not well managed, however, it can be divisive and destructive. Conflict management is a "sink or swim" issue for consultants, as well as for the health care organization. Health care executives must be able to tolerate conflict in training in order to develop a corporate culture that values the ideas and opinions of employees, even if those opinions are controversial or unpopular.

The consultant's role is to stimulate organizations to face interpersonal problems that have inhibited the full participation of all staff. Such stimulation should surface latent discord in the group. The group, when facilitated by a skilled diversity consultant, can learn to tolerate conflict and work through it productively. Diversity consultants can employ a variety of communication tools to help groups learn how to resolve conflicts in healthy ways.

Mastery of Key Dimensions of Diversity

The next area of competency is mastery of content and the ability to convey complex information about a particular dimension of diversity. Some diversity consultants specialize in particular dimensions of diversity while others have broad-based knowledge and experience. The match between the consultant's specialization and your organization's needs is critical because a consultant whose experience is focused on gender diversity, for instance, may not possess the requisite knowledge to conduct training for a health care organization whose salient diversity issues are race, age, ethnicity, or sexual orientation.

If your health care organization is struggling to redefine its relationship with the Latino community, choose a consultant whose knowledge and experience are appropriate. Don't assume, for instance, that consultants who are knowledgeable about black/white race relations are able to effectively address the relationship between other racial and ethnic groups as well. Consultants who specialize in racial and ethnic diversity need to be knowledgeable about the sociopolitical history of racial and ethnic group relations.

A very important aspect of diversity training is explaining how communication styles differ within and between groups. The ability to articulate key differences in communication style across gender, age, or race and ethnicity constitutes a critical competency for diversity consultants.

In addition, consultants must be able to convey the complexity of interracial or cross-gender communication and assist participants in moving beyond the dichotomous thinking that participants too often embrace using convenient labels (liberal, racist, feminist, sexist, etc.).

Ask consultants to demonstrate their ability to describe the assumptions, beliefs, and communication styles of different groups and to explain how differences in communication style can influence how information gets interpreted in a cross-cultural context. There is a fine line between describing communication differences and reinforcing prejudicial stereotypes, however. Remember that archetypes are not stereotypes. Your goal is to select consultants who can help participants understand how culture influences our interpretation of other groups' behavior, while reminding participants that the ultimate objective of diversity leadership is to understand and value the individual.

Detailed knowledge of cultural archetypes allows consultants to make valid cross-cultural comparisons that express the commonalties of the group while giving voice to the unique characteristics of each member. The consultant's goal should be to create a context for exploring the notion that differences are neither good nor bad, but they exist, and they direct behavior and have a major impact on how individuals interpret behavior within and outside of their identity groups. For example, the conversational space or physical distance between two individuals may be interpreted differently depending on their cultural backgrounds. Some Latinos stand close in proximity when talking to each other. For them, conversational space for casual talk among business acquaintances varies little from the physical distance for private talk among friends. Conversely, European Americans tend to stand farther apart when engaging in talk with business acquaintances and closer in private talk. European Americans may interpret Latinos' behavior as invasive or intrusive. Latinos, on the other hand, may interpret European Americans' conversational space as cold and distant.

Acknowledgment of communication style differences between the genders and among racial and ethnic groups are important in the workplace. Comfort levels and trust between coworkers can be strengthened or diminished based on the way individuals respond in social situations. Diversity consultants should be able to help training participants learn about culturally based behavioral patterns that can influence workplace interactions without re-creating prejudicial stereotypes.

Consultants should also be able to convey knowledge about identity formation as it affects work performance. How do individuals come to think of themselves as members of racial, ethnic, or other identity groups? What happens to individuals who are biracial or bicultural? How do these individuals address the issue of belonging to two racial or ethnic groups? The consultant's role is to help training participants explore the boundaries among loyalty to self, to the racial/ethnic group, and to the work group. In an integrated health care setting, racial and ethnic group loyalties may be a source of conflict for individuals, especially as racial or ethnic minorities move into managerial roles. Therefore, the consultant must have the knowledge to facilitate a process where issues such as these are surfaced and resolved.

Group Composition and Customization of Training

The consultant needs to take into account the racial, ethnic, and gender composition of your organization prior to designing the training. If your organizational hierarchy reflects stratification by race and gender, consultants should be able to design appropriate training for each level. In many health care organizations, leaders are white men, nurses and administration staff are mostly women, and service workers are disproportionately Latino and African American. An important aspect of diversity training is responding to disparate training needs. Diversity training for all-white groups, for example, should be different from training designed for racially mixed groups.

Homogeneous Training Groups

When training groups share a common dimension of diversity, such as age or gender, individual members of the group are more likely to be comfortable around each other and, consequently, more open to talking about their shared perceptions of other groups. For example, men in a gender-segregated group may feel freer to joke about women than they would in a group that includes women, and whites are generally more comfortable revealing negative thoughts about other racial groups around other whites than they would be in a racially integrated group. This same principle applies if African Americans or women comprise the homogeneous group, or if the group is defined by professional affiliation. Doctors, nurses, or administrators are freer to express frustrations, stereotypes, and anger directed at other professional groups when they are in a group that is homogeneous by professional affiliation. Homogeneous training groups present both challenges and opportunities to the diversity consultant.

Homogeneous training groups clearly present the consultant with different challenges than do heterogeneous groups. Homogeneous groups are generally more insulated than heterogeneous groups, and they usually develop stronger bonds of loyalty within the group; in particular, in groups that are racially homogeneous, members will often defend against the need for diversity training. Racially homogeneous groups often express the belief that, while other racial groups need diversity training, their group does not.

From the majority group perspective, which is generally white and generally men, minorities need the training. However, the reverse is true from the minority perspective. White training groups, for example, will sometimes contend that blacks need training, and responses such as these are not atypical: "They don't know how to get along with us. This is our institution. They need to learn how to do things our way." Majority group members generally want the focus on minorities, believing that minorities need to change, not them. Minority groups, on the other hand, will emphasize the need for the majority group to change its attitudes, beliefs, and behaviors.

Whites in homogeneous groups often explain communication problems between members of different racial groups as individual personality conflicts, unrelated to cultural differences. In one health care facility, several white employees told a diversity consultant that "there are no racial problems in our health care facility, only people problems. The reason minorities have not excelled is that they don't meet minimal standards for managerial positions. Minorities need diversity training so that they can develop the proper attitudes and stop complaining about racism. It doesn't exist here." For some majority group employees, the focus is on "them," the minority group.

A similar comment from the minority perspective was put forth from a black male focus group participant in reference to his white male colleagues. He explained to the consultant, "We don't need diversity training, the white managers need it. Racism is a problem here because there are no people of color in upper management. The top is all white and the bottom is all black and Latino." Because loyalty and isolation are more prominent in homogeneous groups, diversity consultants need to use strategies that will stimulate introspection.

Consultants who are skilled at working with homogeneous groups will employ techniques that help participants identify and confront diversity within the homogeneous training group. Diversity always exists in spite of perceived similarities among training group members; participants, for instance, might be asked to describe behavioral norms in their health care organization and discuss the consequences experienced by individuals who violate the norms. Insights from diversity training often take more time to occur in homogeneous training groups, and this is due to several factors. Following are the key explanations for this phenomenon:

- Homogeneous groups can more easily deny that barriers to full participation exist for underrepresented groups in their workplace.

- More training time is generally needed to convince participants that other perspectives do exist.

- Within-group pressure may serve to inhibit discussion of the range of diversity within a homogeneous group.

- It is more difficult for the consultant to illustrate some of the consequences of ignoring intergroup problems when training participants are homogeneous on key dimensions of diversity.

- The group can easily conspire to keep discussion focused on the ills of society at large, thus avoiding workforce issues confronting the organization.

Therefore, the consultant must employ creative strategies that enable homogeneous groups to identify and explore the consequences of being different. For example, if the organization's unspoken rule is that managers come in early and stay late, then those who arrive and leave within regular office hours may be stereotyped as lazy and unproductive. Skilled consultants can invariably uncover diversity in seemingly homogeneous training groups, such as exploring how managers, who do share a common experience as supervisors, represent different divisions in the health care organization.

Once the group begins to discuss how differences among their seemingly homogeneous peers are dealt with, then the consultant can begin to help the group transfer this knowledge to key dimensions of diversity such as race, ethnicity, and gender. The consultant's design might include assignments in which participants are asked to conduct interviews with people from racial, ethnic, or gender groups different from their own.

Diversity can be explored effectively in homogenous groups, but heterogeneous training groups clearly present a more fruitful learning environment. The skills that diversity consultants need in working with heterogeneous training groups, while different, are equally demanding.

Heterogeneous Training Groups

While on the surface heterogeneous groups appear to be easier, they do present some interesting challenges for the diversity consultant. Since the group is mixed, it is not difficult for the consultant to design the training to bring out diverse perspectives. Minority and majority group members' interpersonal experiences at work can be discussed so that significant aspects of each group's work life that were previously invisible to the other group can be explored. However, once these previously invisible experiences have been made visible, the consultant must be able to facilitate and manage conflict between and within identity groups.

The potential for polarization and split loyalty is greater in heterogeneous groups. If conflict occurs too early in the training, then participants may feel attacked. If and when this happens, the participants may feel they have to protect themselves and other members of their identity group. If no conflict occurs at all, participants may summarily dismiss the training as superficial or a waste of time. On the other hand, if the consultant forces conflict rather than facilitating expression of the group's feelings, participants may band together to prove to the consultant that there are no organizational issues. Several potential sources of conflict the consultant must be able to manage in heterogeneous diversity training groups are discussed here:

- **Conflicts within society that are projected onto work relationships.** Conflict between blacks and whites, conflict between men and women, as well as conflicts between heterosexuals and homosexuals, the able-bodied and the physically challenged, the young and the old happen daily in our society. Attitudes and stereotypes prevalent in society at large will be expressed at work and in diversity training. As participating members of a culture, we all bring preconceived attitudes, values, and beliefs to the workplace. It is the consultant who must guide participants' growing awareness of the influence of their own culturally based attitudes, values, and beliefs on their workplace behavior without making participants feel judged, threatened, or defensive.

- **Conflicts generated from the internal organizational structure.** Conflict often results from the differential status sometimes given to individuals due to their profession or their position in the health care organization's hierarchy. In every organization, certain professions receive more perks and are allowed wider latitude: in terms of behavior, physicians, for instance, usually receive preferential parking and are freer to move throughout the hospital; due to their social status, physicians are allowed more latitude in how they talk to nurses and support staff. During training, resentment about position may be compounded by racial, ethnic, gender, or age conflicts. As a result, the consultant must be able to help training participants understand the subtle similarities and differences between entitlement due to position and entitlement due to racial, ethnic, gender, or other differences. The consultant must be proficient in both content area knowledge and group process skills to manage successfully this volatile source of conflict in health care organizations because positions and roles are often segregated by race, gender, or ethnicity.

- **Conflicts generated by group dynamics during training.** In the beginning phase of training, participants will test the credibility of the consultant and each other in order to determine if it is safe to reveal their personal work experiences. Participants in the group may express a range of emotions toward the consultant, other participants, or toward leadership. If participants are required to attend training, diversity consultants must move slowly so that participants' reactions can be worked through before diving into diversity issues. Often the consultants or the health care organization's leadership will be the target of participant resentment when there is mandatory training. If consultants understand group dynamics, then they will be able to help participants express their resentment and participate fully in the business of diversity training.

After initial reactions are worked through, the consultant may notice a shift from blaming leadership for workplace problems to studying interactions with each other. Member-to-member conflict could surface prematurely if any participant expresses strong controversial attitudes or stereotypes early on in the process before the training group has had a chance to establish safety boundaries. Sometimes participants inadvertently push one another's "hot buttons." The consultant must find a way to make it safe for controversial feelings to be aired, while simultaneously facilitating the group's ability to deal with conflict in a constructive manner. The diversity consultant's goals should be to create safety, model risk-taking, and demonstrate active listening.

Consultants may purposively stimulate conflict between themselves and participants early on in training. Confrontation can be used as a training tool to help participants to recognize how ingrained institutionalized racism, sexism, or other "isms" function subconsciously. When a confrontational style is used, the diversity consultant must be able to stimulate and direct conflict so that the group's learning moves beyond the initial shock and trauma. And, it is the consultant's responsibility to debrief participants before the training ends.

• **Conflict generated by individual personality styles.** Like groups, individual personalities in training must also be managed. The way participants communicate within the training group is a function of variables such as their personal style, workload, status needs, trust and anxiety level, and confidence in the consultant. Participants will act out both constructive and destructive roles depending on their need for recognition and attention or other factors specific to each individual, and they play many roles in groups. The consultant's role is to help participants who exhibit unproductive styles to survive the initial stages of the group process so that their contributions can be received by the group.

Certain interpersonal styles are likely to interrupt the group's development and, if not well managed by the consultant, may derail the training. Individuals who monopolize conversations, are extremely critical or hostile, passive-aggressive, or openly bored tend to derail the group process. The consultant must help the group manage disruptive individuals without discounting their experiences or perceptions. It is the consultant who must guide the training group's growth and development, supported unwaveringly by the executive leadership when interpersonal conflicts begin to emerge. Confidence by all in the consultant's skills is essential.

SHORT-TERM VERSUS LONG-TERM DIVERSITY TRAINING

Health care executives must make decisions about their organization's commitment of financial and human resources to the diversity training process, and they and the diversity consultant must be in agreement on the goals and objectives of training. Clearly, certain goals and objectives can be achieved through a short-term commitment to diversity training, while others require a longer-term commitment.

Unlike other management training programs, diversity training is often emotionally loaded and interpersonally compelling for participants. So when a health care organization's impetus to conduct diversity training is driven by internal crisis or consumer pressure, leadership often initiates short-term training with unrealistic expectations, limited financial resources, and poorly articulated goals and objectives.

Both short-term and long-term training are potentially valuable. Health care executives must ensure that the approach they select can deliver the outcome desired. The strengths and drawbacks of three commonly used timeframes for diversity training—half-day workshops, one- or two-day trainings, and spaced-interval training—are discussed.

Half-Day Workshops

The first wave of diversity training in many organizations is the **half-day workshop**. Diversity consultants are invited in, given a list of complaints made by staff, and asked to resolve conflicts among groups in a three- or four-hour workshop. The task may involve training large numbers of employees in short periods of time. Consultant-centered training or basic awareness training using a group process–focused approach are commonly used in half-day workshops.

Logistical concerns, the need to respond quickly to a crisis, limited financial resources, and misconceptions about diversity training often lead to the decision to invest in half-day training that is conducted in an intense, abbreviated timeframe. The time, opportunity, and productivity costs associated with releasing employees from their regular responsibilities to attend a diversity workshop can be considerable. The health care organization may have to hire temporary help or pay overtime to keep operations running while employees are in training. Shift workers further complicate the process of scheduling diversity training. Due to these factors, it may seem reasonable to conduct mass training of large groups in a compressed timeframe. On the surface, this option can appear to give the organization "the biggest bang for its buck," but, in reality, it may frustrate staff by opening up complex issues in training sessions where there are too many people and too little time to deal with them.

Once the workshops are underway, the leadership may quickly learn that diversity training can be volatile. Short-term diversity training undertaken as a reaction to employee or customer complaints may uncover more fundamental, longstanding personnel or community relations issues. The training may precipitate an escalation of conflict, especially if the leadership's operative goal was to engage in damage control instead of dealing with longstanding personnel or community relations problems.

There are some advantages, however, to half-day diversity workshops conducted in an abbreviated timeframe. Half-day workshops can be very effective in building awareness. Participants can become familiar with the diversity imperative and its implications for the health care industry, and awareness is the foundation for more in-depth exploration of diversity and its ramifications. In a half-day workshop it is possible to explore one dimension of diversity, conduct no more than two experiential activities, and still allow the participants time to discuss their reactions and begin to develop a framework for understanding diversity.

However, it is not advisable to use half-day workshops with large numbers of participants in an attempt to address employee conflicts about race, gender, or other dimensions of diversity. Half-day workshops are not sufficient to change participants' behaviors or to work through emotionally loaded issues that have been longstanding in the organization, and trying to do so will only frustrate participants and open up issues that cannot be resolved in the training session. Even highly skilled diversity consultants are hard put to lead groups in an honest dialogue about organizational climate or interpersonal conflict in a safe setting, given such an abbreviated timeframe.

One- or Two-Day Training

One- or two-day training sessions are often conducted in a conference or retreat setting. Participants may represent different health care organizations or separate units within a single health care organization. One- or two-day training sessions can effectively introduce several diversity concepts as well as provide interactive activities that allow participants to explore the impact of diversity in the workplace.

The primary advantage of this type of training is that the group is able to delve into some topics with more depth than in a half-day session. Now, basic concepts can be introduced, as can a beginning awareness of cultural archetypes. It's possible for participants' interest in the topic to move from denial to curiosity and from curiosity to acceptance.

This somewhat longer timeframe gives participants the opportunity to coalesce as a group. In a two-day format, for instance, the group can move through the initial stage of team building into later stages where participants can risk talking about volatile topics with one another. The consultant has sufficient time to facilitate the group through its initial anxiety about training; constructive conflict can surface and be worked through in the context of the group.

The main disadvantage of one- or two-day trainings is cost and loss of work time for employees. Participants may initially express resentment about losing time from work, especially if they anticipate that a backlog of tasks awaits their return. If successful, one- or two-day training may leave the group wanting more because participants can become energized by the group's richness and difference. However, one or two days is not sufficient time to learn new behaviors for subsequent practice in the workplace.

Spaced Interval Training

Spaced interval training is usually the timeframe chosen by health care organizations engaged in the organizational systems change approach previously described. Training is conducted in a one- or two-day format and is scheduled in two- or three-month intervals over a 12-month period. The training modules are first, awareness building, then behavioral change, and last, alliance building. During the interval between each training module, participants complete assignments consisting of readings or tasks. These assignments ensure that key concepts are understood, applied, and reinforced between trainings.

Spaced interval training is more likely to produce fundamental changes in the health care organization's beliefs, values, and behaviors for these reasons:

- Participants can learn diversity concepts, practice and apply them in the workplace, and discuss the results at a subsequent training session.

- Participants can work through conflicts directly with other staff in the training session and receive timely, specific feedback about their behavior in a controlled setting.

- Participants can receive support from one another as they strive to exchange ineffective for effective interpersonal behavior in the intervals between training sessions.

Despite its strengths, spaced interval training also has potential limitations: leadership is challenged to maintain a clear focus as training groups move through conflict and stagnation; learning to respect and manage differences between people can be frustrating; leadership may be tempted to abandon the diversity initiative when training participants begin to uncover organizational problems or air longstanding complaints, and leadership may feel as if the organization is out of control.

Additional limitations are that minority participants may direct anger toward leadership and power-brokers: white men, middle managers, and supervisors are often the first targets of minority training participants' complaints. As a result, participants from majority groups may respond in kind, answering anger with more anger, producing the phenomenon known as **backlash.**

Acknowledging and expressing anger is prerequisite to the resolution of differences and establishment of a new order. However, this chaotic phase in the spaced interval training process tends to produce considerable discomfort for leadership and, again, results in the temptation to end the conflict by dropping the training. The diversity consultant must know how to help the organization work through these difficult periods without jeopardizing the training program or the organizational change process as a whole.

For the health care organization, the advantages of spaced interval training far outweigh the disadvantages. Leadership sends a message that understanding and managing diversity is more than just "window dressing" and constitutes a long-term commitment to the organization, its employees, and the community it serves. A long-term commitment to diversity training signals the health care organization's sincere commitment to the organizational change process.

Some organizations combine spaced interval training for all staff with an intense, focused, and long-term investment in diversity training for selected individuals within the organization. Those selected are generally carefully chosen from a pool of volunteers, represent management and staff, and reflect key dimensions of diversity within the health care organization. This is an opportunity for the organization's leadership to seed the organization with change agents who are trained in diversity, conflict resolution, and small group facilitation, which can lift the organization out of crisis mode and build an infrastructure to support long-term organizational transformation and change.

Regardless of the training approach selected, the skill of consultants, the composition of the training groups, or the length of time invested in the process, diversity training generates reactions from individuals and groups within the organization, as will be discussed in the next chapter, "Backlash."

REFERENCES

Cox, T. 1993. *Cultural Diversity in Organizations: Theory, Research, and Practice.* San Francisco: Berrett-Koehler.

Delatte, A., and L. Baytos. 1993. "8 Guidelines for Successful Diversity Training." *Training* 30 (1): 55–60.

Farr, C. 1992. "Building and Supporting a Multicultural Workforce." *Public Management* 74 (2): 20–26.

Geber, B. 1990. "Managing Diversity." *Training* 27 (7): 23–30.

Hunt, P. 1994. "Leadership in Diversity." *Health Progress* 75 (10): 26–29.

Jamison, D., and J. O'Mara. 1991. *Managing Workforce 2000: Gaining the Diversity Advantage.* San Francisco: Jossey-Bass.

Solomon, C. 1989. "The Corporate Response to Work Force Diversity." *Personnel Journal* 68 (8): 43–54.

CHAPTER 7

Backlash

BACKLASH IS a natural human response to changing or challenging the status quo, and diversity training is designed to do just that. When viewed in this context, it isn't surprising that backlash is among the reactions that diversity training produces in organizational stakeholders. Change inevitably elicits both champions and resistors because it alters the status quo.

Sometimes, the threat or anticipation of change can be enough to produce backlash as a reaction. **Backlash** is defined by the American Heritage Dictionary as "a sudden or violent backward whipping motion" and as "an antagonistic reaction to some prior action construed as a threat, as in the context of social or racial relations."

BACKLASH AS A REACTION TO DIVERSITY TRAINING

Diversity training requires that participants question both organizational and personal assumptions, values, beliefs, policies, and practices. Even skillfully facilitated diversity training can leave white participants who are men feeling unfairly targeted as perpetrators of injustice and beneficiaries of entitlement rules that, by their nature, exclude others. Tales of diversity training gone awry, resulting in civil suits, antagonistic post-training working relationships, and other forms of backlash abound in both trade journals and the popular press (Morrison 1994; Kane 1994; Murray 1993; Mobley 1992; Galen and Palmer 1994; Hirshey 1995).

How backlash is expressed will vary from organization to organization and from situation to situation. The way in which backlash will be expressed depends on factors such as

- cultural norms in the health care organization;
- economic and social trends in the nation, the service area, and the health care organization; and
- the manner in which diversity training and the change process are handled by external consultants and by organizational leadership.

The first factor, **cultural norms**, will profoundly affect the expression of backlash. In some health care organizations, disagreements are discussed openly and directly through face-to-face dialogue among the individuals or groups that are involved. In others, resistance goes underground and is expressed through whispered conversations in the cafeteria or passive-aggressive behavior: white administrators who are men may cluster around the water cooler and discuss the latest "affirmative action" hire; the lone, white male nurse may be excluded from social functions by his white female colleagues; or the male physician may sarcastically refer to the female nurse as "Ms." Jones. In its extreme, backlash can be expressed through overt bigotry: lockers are spray-painted with racist slogans, "girlie" calendars are openly displayed, or a makeup kit is placed on the gay occupational therapist's desk.

The second factor—**economic and social trends in the nation, the community, and the health care organization**—can also have a profound effect on the intensity with which backlash reactions are felt and expressed. When resources and opportunities are abundant, those who benefit from the status quo—as evidenced by salary, status, position, education, or other external indicators of power—are more willing to explore ways to extend opportunity to others. On the other hand, in a era of downsizing, reengineering, and flattening of the organizational hierarchy, people are more likely to feel threatened and vulnerable. A white specialist physician who sees his referrals and revenue dwindling as a consequence of managed care is less likely to see the need to change entitlement rules in order to increase the proportion of minority physicians in the specialty. A white service worker who is a man in a health care organization that anticipates layoffs in conjunction with the movement to patient-focused care isn't likely to feel like a member of a privileged and entitled white men's club. Within such a context, majority group members are less likely to want to openly explore and change entitlement rules in order to share what they perceive as a smaller and smaller pool of resources.

The third factor—**the manner in which training and the change process are handled by leadership and by external consultants**—can often be a determining factor in the expression and consequences of backlash. If diversity is framed narrowly as an issue of race and gender rather than broadly across additional dimensions such as age, family and marital status, personality or temperament, social class, or physical ability, backlash from white men is more likely to occur. If trainers implicitly or explicitly present white men as a homogeneous group of unjustly entitled oppressors, backlash is more likely to occur.

The reaction of leadership to expressions of backlash is also pivotal. The leadership must demonstrate through its actions that, while overt bigotry or passive-aggressive acts will not be permitted or condoned, the open expression of a wide range of feelings, including anger and backlash, are expected and accepted as part of the diversity training and change process. The effect of these and other factors in training design and delivery and the change process are discussed in greater detail in a later section of this chapter.

When power dynamics between groups are threatened or changed, denial, anger, resistance, acceptance, and residual reactions are always expressed. The organization and its stakeholders long for a return to some form of homeostasis, or balance, and health care organizations are no exception.

As previously discussed in Chapter 3, people use identity groups as a reference for personal behavior in work situations. But when the status quo is questioned or changed, old ways of relating are no longer safe or predictable, and uncertainty replaces comfort and clarity. Consequently, people experience loss and may express resentment toward those who initiated the change and upset the balance.

THE FOUNDATION FOR BACKLASH

Current and historical discrimination, prejudice, and stereotyping combined with selective perception lay the foundation for backlash as a response to training and other diversity initiatives. The role of each in enabling backlash will be discussed.

Discrimination

Discrimination is behavior that favors one identity group over another. Whether de facto or de jure, the legacy of past discriminatory behavior is reflected in today's workforce. As the statistics presented in Chapter 1 attest, race and gender are highly correlated with power and status in health care and other organizations; census data confirm that African Americans and Latinos are disproportionately represented among the ranks of the poor; and the "skills gap" for African Americans, Latinos, and women exceeds that of white men.

Affirmative action programs, which were instituted in response to historic discriminatory behavior, may provoke charges of reverse discrimination, and it may not be surprising for white men during training to express the opinion that they are the new disenfranchised. The legacy of discrimination perpetuates deep divisions by race and gender such that remedies for past acts may appear to some to produce new forms of discrimination in the present.

Prejudice

Because, literally translated, **prejudice** means "pre-judgment," prejudice means harboring unfavorable feelings about an identity group and its members—feelings that were formed without knowledge, thought, or reason.

Three major social science theories attempt to explain the roots of prejudice.

1. **Cultural transmission theory** contends that prejudicial feelings are taught by one generation to the next and are reinforced through maintaining social distance from the stigmatized group (McLemore 1991).

2. **Frustration/aggression theory** explains prejudice using the lens of personality theory (Allport 1958). Certain personality types, the theory contends, are more prone to prejudicial attitudes, and scapegoats are chosen as the target of negative prejudicial feelings. **Scapegoating**, the theory contends, allows members of an identity group to express feelings of frustration and aggression that stem from their own personal circumstance and, in fact, have nothing to do with the group being scapegoated. "In this way, prejudice," contends McLemore (1991, 143), "serves to assist the majority-group members to displace (and possibly to 'drain off') their accumulated feelings without exposing themselves to a high risk of retaliation."

3. The third major theory contends that prejudice is an expression of **ethnocentrism**, whereby one's own reference group is believed to be superior to all others and is used as the yardstick by which the worth of all other groups is measured. Prejudice, this theory contends, is an expression of identity group belonging and affiliation. Prejudicial feelings are generally strongest for identity group members in the third stage of the racial and ethnic identity models discussed in Chapter 3.

Regardless of its origin, prejudice creates a fertile backdrop for the expression of backlash. It justifies and supports antagonistic reactions to the expression of attitudes, beliefs, or behaviors that contradict the prejudicial feeling. When viewed through the lens of prejudice, for example, changing standards to value diversity can be seen as lowering standards to admit the unqualified. If women, for instance, are prejudged as inferior, then job redesign for the stated purpose of enabling more women to perform the functions of a building engineer will be viewed as unacceptable.

Stereotypes

Stereotypes are generalizations about individuals based on their identity group membership or affiliation. Prejudices, as Cox (1993) explains, are attitudes and emotional reactions, while stereotypes are beliefs about an identity group that are applied indiscriminately to all individual members of that group. Stereotyping is a natural, perceptual process that simplifies decision making and makes the world more manageable. Cox's (1993) review of the literature on stereotyping demonstrates that stereotyping is widespread and that it affects interpersonal relationships and career opportunities.

Is there a difference between stereotyping and acknowledging group differences? Cox (1993) contends that, unlike stereotyping, acknowledging group differences "(1) bases beliefs about characteristics of culture groups on systematic study of reliable sources of data, and (2) acknowledges that intragroup variation exists." An additional distinction, explains Cox (1993, 91), "is that contrary to valuing diversity, stereotypes represent not merely an acknowledgment of differences but also an evaluation of them. Thus many common stereotypes are words or phrases with built-in negative connotations."

Because stereotypes act as perceptual filters—screening in data that support the stereotype while screening out data that do not—they often lead to selective perception. If a white nurse believes that all blacks are lazy, for instance, then when she sees two black nurses aides standing in the hallway talking, she may assume that they are socializing when they may, in fact, be discussing a patient. Stereotypes can limit our vision, allowing us to see only that which conforms to our stereotype, interfering with our ability to respond to people as individuals and see them as they really are. This phenomenon is known as **selective perception**.

Stereotypes and selective perception create a strong foundation for backlash. When people see only that which reinforces their belief system, they naturally react with anger when beliefs that are supported by what they see every day in the workplace are challenged by training and other diversity initiatives.

BACKLASH: ACTION AND REACTION

Diversity training and the organizational change process uncover institutional and individual expressions of discrimination, prejudice, stereotyping, and selective perception. The action of exploring these often unacknowledged dimensions of organizations and individuals produces backlash reactions that reflect underlying beliefs and assumptions, eliciting comments such as,

- "We earned our positions solely on the basis of merit."
- "We have a black administrator. That proves we're not prejudiced."
- "We are the victims of reverse discrimination."

There are three strong beliefs that produce backlash—faith in the meritocracy, belief in fair rules, and the concept of reverse discimination.

Faith in the Meritocracy

Diversity training challenges the belief that merit alone explains the strong correlation between key dimensions of diversity such as race or gender and measures of success such as salary, professional status, or position in the organizational hierarchy. No one welcomes the implication that one's race or sex, in whole or in part, explains one's achievements. When white men are asked to acknowledge that discrimination, prejudice, and stereotypes limit opportunities for women and other racial/ethnic groups, they are implicitly being asked to also acknowledge that being white men provides them with an unfair advantage. That done, their belief that "we earned our positions solely on the basis of merit" is no longer secure.

Belief in Fair Rules

Diversity training also challenges the belief that the standards and rules by which organizational rewards are distributed are fair and unbiased. Selective perception, as discussed previously, can operate to support this belief; the solitary black or woman manager is pointed to as evidence of the organization's fairness, and wheelchair accessibility is offered as proof that the disabled have equal opportunity. Prejudice and stereotypes can serve to reinforce the belief that more blacks and women would be promoted if they were as qualified and as hard working as the incumbents.

Diversity training requires that participants uncover and explore prejudices and stereotypes, which can call into question deeply held assumptions and beliefs. Again, asking white men to acknowledge that stereotypes and assumptions limit opportunities for members of other identity groups is tantamount to asking them to acknowledge that they benefit from the injustice. As a result, guilt and shame may be masked by anger and denial, unleashing strong backlash responses.

Concept of Reverse Discrimination

Participants in diversity training may also express the belief that they or their colleagues are victims of reverse discrimination: a white nurse describes how she was passed over for promotion to supervisor while a black nurse with less experience was given the promotion instead; a white associate administrator who is a man expresses the feeling that his career options are limited by his race and gender, believing direct affirmative action goals will ensure that he never becomes a vice president.

It is true that there are occasions when white applicants have been denied employment or promotion in favor of black applicants or seemingly underqualified women have been promoted over men. Anecdotes abound that support the contention that white men are victims of discrimination, rather than beneficiaries or perpetrators. Selective perception reinforces the belief that reverse discrimination has now surpassed discrimination as a principle cause of injustice in the workplace because people see that which supports their belief system and either fail to see or question the validity of contradictory information. Perceptions are again polarized by race, gender, and other dimensions of diversity; conflict ensues; and backlash is among the responses of diversity training participants struggling to reconcile new information with old paradigms.

RESPONDING TO BACKLASH · · · · · · · · · · ·

Backlash, because it is a natural and understandable response, should not be left unexpressed by training participants or unanswered by trainers and the health care organization's leadership. It must be expressed before it can be explored; differences cannot be resolved and balance cannot be restored when organizations fail to encourage the open expression of conflicting points of view. Here are some suggestions for managing the expression of backlash in health care organizations.

Backlash During Training Design and Delivery

Diversity trainers walk a tightrope between two dangerous extremes —avoiding the emotionally charged issues of race and gender and risking alienating women and people of color, or focusing exclusively on race and gender and risking backlash from white males. Some suggestions for designing and delivering diversity training that should help maintain that necessary, but delicate, balance follow:

1. **Define diversity broadly, not narrowly.** Trainers who focus exclusively on gender and race as the only salient dimensions of diversity are more likely to produce backlash reactions from participants who are white or men. Make the point that anyone can be the victim or the perpetrator of discrimination, prejudice, stereotyping, or selective perception, including white males. Failure to broadly define diversity for participants can inappropriately target all white men as perpetrators or beneficiaries of injustice and may encourage other participants to stereotype white males. Remember that the purpose of diversity training is to enhance, not detract from, mutual respect, understanding, and collaboration in the workplace. Diversity trainers must heed CEO Michael Jhin's maxim, discussed in Chapter 12: "The ultimate diversity is the diversity of one."

2. **Watch out for inappropriate activities that target white males.** It is inevitable that training participants will experience some discomfort with experiential activities, which create a forum for the exploration of feelings, beliefs, values, and behaviors about very sensitive issues. Some diversity trainers use approaches that, effectively, "turn the table" on majority group members, allowing them to experience minority status firsthand. Some trainers have been accused of crossing the line of propriety in the interest of "table turning," producing strong backlash reactions. The FAA gauntlet case that resulted in a civil suit is an example of one such activity which produced a strong, and potentially expensive, backlash reaction (Hirshey 1995; Kane 1994). Health care executives must ensure that trainers will use activities that provoke serious self-reflection on the part of all participants without unfairly targeting particular groups or crossing the boundary into social impropriety.

3. **Don't screen out white male trainers.** When only women and minorities are trainers, participants perceive that diversity excludes white men, creating an environment in which white men's backlash is likely to flourish. As Mobley (1992) explains, "A lack of white males on the diversity team can send participants the wrong message—that diversity work is still only about women and minorities" (47).

4. **Validate feelings; manage their expression.** Training participants must be permitted to give voice to their perceptions,

even if they run contrary to the dogma of diversity leadership. The following advice is offered to trainers in this regard:

> Acknowledge resistance. Do not downplay or ignore it. If you do, it can trip you up or sabotage the outcomes of training later on. Allow people to respond and express their feelings, including hostility, skepticism, and enthusiasm. Avoid becoming defensive. A good trainer is adept enough to use the resistance as a vehicle for learning. . . . Affirm the value of each person's experience and viewpoint. Acknowledge good intentions even while pointing out behaviors that create problems. . . . Put an end to the PC [politically correct] police. Encouraging people to pay lip service to a politically correct agenda does not qualify as effective diversity work. Such an approach only increases cynicism and backlash toward diversity work and creates distrust between groups (Mobley 1992, 51).

The trainer's role is to facilitate dialogue between individuals and groups so that participants can question their own perceptions. If, for instance, white men participants see themselves as being passed over for promotion in favor of women and minorities, the trainer must help participants explore this perception, both within and between identity groups.

The trainer must skillfully guide participants in the exploration of hidden bias that may provide the groundwork for certain commonly voiced perceptions. The perception that unqualified women are being promoted to management positions may, in fact, stem from an underlying assumption about women's inferiority. The perception that racial and ethnic minorities are being selected over equally qualified white males may stem from an unacknowledged assumption that jobs belong to white men who have the right to decide when, how, and how much they are willing to share.

Identity groups are sometimes more comfortable discussing reactive fears and backlash reactions in homogeneous groups before moving the dialogue to a heterogeneous, intergroup context. Skilled trainers will not confuse their own personal issues or agenda with those of the training participants, uncovering "hidden bias" where there is none. The trainer's job is to facilitate, not to judge, participants.

5. **Use data to address selective perception.** Selective perception can work in tandem with overgeneralization to reinforce backlash reactions. Trainers must be able to use quantitative data effectively in order to help participants explore their own perceptions and pursue the truth of the matter. Studies such

as the hiring audit conducted by the Urban Institute (Turner, Fix, and Struyk 1991), the latest report from the Federal Glass Ceiling Commission (1995), and statistics that describe patterns of employment and promotion within the health care organization's own workforce can be used to inform discussions about potentially divisive topics such as reverse discrimination.

6. **Conduct and use a pretraining assessment.** Assessment data can help trainers anticipate backlash and design training sessions with the health care organization's "hot buttons" in mind. Training must reflect knowledge of the organization's key diversity issues. The assessment should include questions that will uncover backlash reactions.

7. **Differentiate affirmative action from valuing diversity.** Cox (1993, 256) suggests that "affirmative action in practice fundamentally means the explicit use of a person's group identity as a criterion in making selection decisions. Usually this means that among candidates who are qualified on other criteria, candidates of underrepresented groups are selected in preference to those from overrepresented groups." A white man who applies for a secretarial position might, for instance, be given preference over an equally qualified white woman under affirmative action guidelines. Valuing diversity, on the other hand, stems from two fundamental assumptions: (1) diversity provides a strategic advantage, and (2) diverse workers respond to diverse management styles and reward structures. Managing a diverse workforce, explains R. Roosevelt Thomas (1990, 112), "does not mean controlling or containing diversity; it means enabling every member of your work force to perform to his or her potential. It means getting from employees, first, everything we have a right to expect, and, second—if we do it well—everything they have to give."

Trainers must know the difference between affirmative action and valuing diversity and impart that understanding to participants. Doing so can help move participants from divisive conflict about quotas and reverse discrimination to inclusive dialogue about valuing differences and discovering commonalities.

By Leadership

The role of leadership in framing training and in modeling the heart, head, and hand of diversity leadership is key to managing the expression of backlash and other reactions to diversity training.

Here are some suggestions for diversity leaders who are striving to turn backlash into a catalyst for positive organizational change.

1. **Model the treatment of women and minorities as serious competitors, not tokens.** Leadership sets the tone for inclusivity or exclusivity. If leadership operates from the tacit assumption that the differences that women and minorities bring to the table are, in fact, deficits, the organization cannot move from affirmative action to valuing diversity. When women and minorities are viewed as serious and legitimate competitors, backlash reactions are less likely to occur.

2. **Frame diversity as a bottom-line issue, as a business imperative.** Leadership must recognize and give voice to the bottom-line implications of diversity leadership and ensure that diversity training moves beyond theory to practice. The practice of diversity leadership must be tied to the health care organization's effectiveness in meeting the needs of an increasingly diverse marketplace. Be specific; measure and publicize the ways in which effective diversity leadership has reduced costs and increased revenue. Diversity training and associated change efforts must be subjected to the same scrutiny as any other business investment. Quantifying the impact of diversity leadership reduces backlash by countering the perception that diversity training is just another "feel good" or damage control initiative.

3. **Don't separate diversity training from a real commitment to change.** Diversity training is not a solution to employee, patient, or community discontent—organizational change is. Training can provide the opportunities for self-exploration and the avenues for learning about diversity that are prerequisite to organizational transformation and change. Diversity awareness that stops at the classroom door will only fuel backlash reactions. Window-dressing style training will anger all organizational stakeholders. Training should not be viewed as a panacea.

4. **Prequalify consultants' skills in handling backlash.** Ascertain how the trainer views backlash and inquire as to how he or she addresses it in the assessment and training phases of work. Talk personally with leadership from other organizations that have used the trainer's services. Ask about the trainer's success in handling backlash and other reactions. Request that prospective trainers demonstrate their approach through a short sample presentation. Don't judge the sample presentation

on content alone, but assess the trainer's ability to manage group process while discussing potentially volatile topics.

5. **Ensure that you and senior management personally participate in diversity training initiatives.** Leadership's commitment to valuing diversity will be seen as superficial if training is mandatory for staff, but management and executive leadership do not participate. If management is ambivalent about diversity training and if longstanding organizational problems are ignored, training participants will be more likely to project their resentment toward leadership onto the diversity trainers.

6. **Answer backlash responses with organization-specific data.** Downsizing and flattening of health care and other organizations have resulted in stalled careers. White men training participants may express the opinion that their career opportunities are limited in direct proportion to increased opportunities for women and minorities. Leadership must be prepared to counter selective perception with quantitative data. Share employment statistics to address such perceptions and provide a forum for white men to express their concerns without fear of judgment or retribution.

7. **Remove the double bind from white male managers.** White men managers who support diversity initiatives may feel that they are in a double bind. If they fail to support, or actively lobby against, diversity initiatives, they may be accused of backlash. If they lend active support to diversity initiatives, they may be the object of backlash reactions from within their own identity group and be viewed as encouraging a movement that is contrary to their own self-interest. Organizations such as AT&T and Amoco have instituted training or focus groups specifically for white men, according to Galen and Palmer (1994) in their article, "White, Male, and Worried."

8. **Reward champions of diversity.** Leadership must provide meaningful rewards to those who support diversity training and the change process, including white men. Include diversity goals in the formal management appraisal process. Use positive reinforcement to encourage active participation in training and in change initiatives that reflect the value of diversity.

FROM EXPLORATION TO TRANSFORMATION AND CHANGE

Engaging in training and addressing backlash are key steps on the journey of diversity leadership. The next steps, transformation and change, are designed to move organizations and individuals to new levels of awareness and performance.

REFERENCES

Allport, G. 1958. *The Nature of Prejudice.* Garden City, NJ: Doubleday.

Cox, T. 1993. *Cultural Diversity in Organizations: Theory, Research, and Practice.* San Francisco: Berrett-Koehler.

Federal Glass Ceiling Commission. 1995. *Good for Business: Making Full Use of the Nation's Human Capital.* Washington, DC: U.S. Government Printing Office.

Galen, M., and A. T. Palmer. 1994. "White, Male and Worried." *Business Week* 3356: 50–55.

Geber, B. 1990. "Managing Diversity." *Training* 27 (7): 23–30.

Hirshey G. 1995. "You Will Feel Their Pain." *Gentleman's Quarterly* 65 (3): 212–17, 256–58.

Kane, M. 1994. "Sensitivity Training Backlash Hitting Companies." *The Times-Picayune,* 4 December.

McLemore, S. D. 1991. *Racial and Ethnic Relations in America.* Boston: Allyn & Bacon.

Mobley, M. 1992. "Backlash! The Challenge to Diversity Training." *Training and Development* 46 (12): 45–52.

Morrison, A. 1994. "Building Diversity." *Executive Excellence* 11 (10): 17–18.

Murray, K. 1993. "Companies Encounter Pitfalls in Diversity Training." *Star Tribune,* 8 August.

Thomas, R. R. 1990. "From Affirmative Action to Affirming Diversity." *Harvard Business Review* 68 (2): 107–17.

Turner, M. A., M. Fix, and R. J. Struyk. 1991. *Opportunities Denied, Opportunities Diminished: Racial Discrimination in Hiring.* Washington, DC: Urban Institute.

PART **IV**

Transformation

President Bryant remembered the experience vividly—that
flash of insight about diversity. It was on the second day
of the awareness seminar. The trigger was a random comment
by a coparticipant and occurred in the course of a heated
discussion about the difference between affirmative action and
valuing diversity.

Ralph Bryant and Urban Medical Center would never
be the same. The old pattern of recycling programs to help
the "disadvantaged" or hiring underqualified minorities to fill
quotas was over. Bryant had a vision, and this new insight
would transform not only him, but also the medical center.
Now he saw what the corporate vice president for human
resources had been trying to show him over the past few years,
and now CEO Bryant was ready to change!

CHAPTER 8

Discovery of a New Context

IS CHANGE ENOUGH?

INSIGHTS FROM assessment and training are, potentially, the harbingers of a new organizational identity. All too often, however, those insights result only in surface changes—the health care organization's recruitment advertising stating that it values diversity, customer relations materials suddenly including people of color, or an Asian woman joining the Board of Directors. These changes are viewed as "window dressing" by some and as "preferential treatment for minorities" by others. Although the organization, on the surface, may look different, below the surface, the same attitudes, beliefs, and values are in operation. Different is still viewed as deficient. The adage, "The more things change, the more they remain the same," is alive and well in many health care organizations that appear to value diversity.

Health care organizations that truly value diversity have not just changed systems and procedures, they have transformed their organization's vision and adopted a new paradigm. As Alva Wheatley, vice president and manager of Kaiser Permanente's Cultural Diversity Project, says, "Diversity is not a program. Diversity is a way of dealing with people that determines how we live our lives—as individuals and as an organization." Surface change is not sufficient.

Consultant and theorist Stanley M. Davis (1982) has defined a three-step process in organization development that has special relevance to the diversity leader who wants to move beyond surface changes to organizational transformation:

1. Not knowing that you don't know.

2. Knowing that you don't know.

3. Knowing.

Davis calls movement from step 1 to step 2 **transformation**, while movement from step 2 to step 3 is **change**. Movement from step 1 to step 2 transforms the context within which the organization views diversity. Contextual transformation alters the organization's perspective and results in changed content that reflects the organization's new reality. This changed content, because it derives from a transformed context, is more than just "window dressing."

Diversity leadership is not possible without transformation of the context within which the organization views diversity. The responses to change chronicled in Chapter 7 are an inevitable consequence of experiencing change without transformation and a constant reminder of the leader's responsibility to create an organizational context in which diversity can thrive and in which individual and collective transformation can occur.

Contexts, says Davis (1982, 65), "are the unquestioned assumptions through which all experience is filtered." A health care organization's diversity context creates the reality within which the organization's diversity efforts will be designed, implemented, and perceived by its constituencies.

R. Roosevelt Thomas Jr. (1990) describes the diversity leader's task as follows:

> So long as racial and gender equality is something we grant to minorities and women, there will be no racial and gender equality. What we must do is create an environment where no one is advantaged or disadvantaged, an environment where "we" is everyone (p. 109).

BOUNDARY MANAGEMENT AND THE DIVERSITY LEADER

Most fundamentally, diversity leadership requires boundary spanning. **Boundaries** are neither inherently positive or negative. Their purpose is to separate, delineate, and define. Boundaries reflect history and tradition and are closely guarded because of the key role they play in defining our options, roles, and identities. Boundaries create security in an uncertain and often chaotic world. "Therefore," as Bruhn, Levine, and Levine (1993, 13) explain, "every boundary line is a potential battle line." This means the diversity leader must consider boundary management in order to facilitate achievement of Thomas' (1990, 109) goal of having "an environment where 'we' is everyone."

Bruhn, Levine, and Levine (1993) have explained the role and evolution of boundaries in the health professions. They identify as boundaries those based on gender, ethnic difference, class and hierarchy, monopolies such as those granted through licensure and certification, and those developed due to differences in history and tradition, such as those of psychologists and psychiatrists, all of which are reflected in today's health care organizations.

Some boundaries have outlived their usefulness and now serve as **barriers** to the optimal performance of the health care organization. The barrier boundaries that create divisions between people from different professions, races, functional areas, customers/caregivers, sexual preferences, genders, and abilities must be envisioned anew by the diversity leader.

Why not just tear down all of the barrier boundaries and create a boundaryless organization? Why not envision the health care organization as one boundaryless melting pot of race, gender, professional roles, and departments? Why not? Because, like the melting pot metaphor, the "boundaryless organization" does not ring true. Boundaries exist, whether or not the manager sees them (Bruhn, Levine, and Levine 1993), and they must be managed by the diversity leader so that boundary lines don't become battle lines.

Just as the salad bowl or vegetable stew metaphor transformed diversity leadership, a new metaphor for organizational boundaries allows the diversity leader to perceive boundaries as **paths of exchange** (Dreachslin, Kobrinski, and Passen 1994), not as barriers. Treating everyone the same, a guiding principle under the melting pot metaphor, is replaced with a new axiom consistent with the salad bowl or vegetable stew metaphor: "Treat everyone equitably." Equitable treatment may very well require different treatment. A reward for one worker may be seen as punishment by another. Criticism that is perceived as excessive by an Asian American worker may be viewed as mild enough to be discounted by a European American male.

When perceived as impermeable barriers, boundaries serve as obstacles to change. But when perceived as paths of exchange, boundaries facilitate change and organizational adaptation because they are permeable and ever changing. (Dreachslin, Kobrinski, and Passen 1994). The diversity leader walks the boundary path that distinguishes among divisions, roles, ages, professions, races, and genders, seeing the boundary path as movable and changeable, not fixed and insurmountable. The role of the boundary manager has been described by Bruhn, Levine, and Levine (1993) as follows:

The major function of boundary managers is to maintain the relative autonomy of all boundary parties while orchestrating their different talents to successfully accomplish common goals. A boundary manager is a gatekeeper, a person who possesses much of the magic that makes collaboration and the crossing of boundaries work. The boundary manager orchestrates the precise mixture of roles needed to bring about a desired outcome. . . . Boundary managers cannot have vested interests. . . . Boundary management is not a state or a trait, it is a process of perfecting the interrelationships between perceptions, personal values, and management style, which are changed and modified by intervention and experience (pp. 189–191).

The boundary manager who subscribes to the exchange path metaphor relies on three things to identify and facilitate fruitful exchanges among diverse groups—context, perspective, and continuity (Dreachslin, Kobrinski, and Passen 1994).

1. **Context** creates the diversity leader's frame of reference, separating what can be known from what cannot. As Stanley Davis (1982, 66) explains, "Context creates a reality, and the reality it creates is the content." The diversity leader's context is that " 'we' is everyone," and everyone is not the same. Within such a conceptual framework, the diversity leader brings out the flavor of the vegetable stew: the carrot remains a carrot, and the potato a potato, united by a flavorful broth made rich and whole by the contribution of its different parts.

2. **Perspective** is the vantage point from which the diversity leader views the health care organization. The diversity leader's forté is flexibility—the ability to reconsider situations from different vantage points and to appreciate different perspectives. Perspective creates fresh insight and helps to resolve seemingly unsolvable diversity dilemmas. Because the diversity leader can see the performance review from the perspective of the minority employee who wants feedback *and* the majority supervisor who is reluctant to give it, the dilemma is seen as a pathway to understanding, rather than as a battle line.

3. **Continuity** is "the unbroken chain of processes that constitute the exchange between order and chaos" (Dreachslin, Kobrinski, and Passen 1994, 19). While others may feel that the lawsuit filed by a Filipino nurse forbidden to speak Tagalog at work, the premature departure of the first African American vice president amid accusations of racism, or the disparaging

comments about the health care organization made by gay and lesbian spokespeople on the local news came "out of nowhere," the diversity leader sees the continuity of events and the inevitability of such incidents. While the health care organization's diversity climate may have seemed calm and uneventful, the diversity leader sees the pattern of behaviors, beliefs, and values that led to such critical incidents.

ORGANIZATIONAL TRANSFORMATION AND THE DIVERSITY LEADER

The diversity leader is faced with the challenging task of recreating the context for transformation in each department, each employee, and each constituent of the health care organization. Movement from "not knowing that you don't know" to "knowing that you don't know" occurs in "a flash of insight" (Davis 1982, 77). The diversity leader cannot know what might trigger the "flash" for someone else that creates the context for reframing diversity to occur. Diversity leadership, therefore, involves creating multiple opportunities and contexts for discovery—formal training, informational articles on other cultures, brown bag lunches to explore dimensions of diversity, lecture series, and other avenues for self-exploration and communication about differences.

When will the diversity leader and the health care organization know that transformation has occurred? Here is Davis' (1982) answer.

The occurrence of transformation is not dependent upon the relative mix of old and new behavior (content). For the first ones to apprehend this transformed context, there may be only a scintilla of evidence of the new culture; for the last ones to come to it, it may be as aftermath. Somewhere between is probably an irrelevant and unidentifiable moment when the body corporate will have been transformed. Working on a new plan, both as formulation (strategy) and as implementation (structure, people, systems, and culture—that is, organization), I have often been asked and have often asked myself, "How do you know when you're there?" The answer, it appears, is "When you don't have to ask the question any more." When this occurs, people have moved from confusion (knowing that they don't know) to composure (knowing) (p. 77).

During the often chaotic process of transformation, everything—including the health care organization's sacred cows—is open to question. Conflict and differences of opinion are inevitable consequences of growth and exploration, and "being comfortable with contradictory formulations (thesis and antithesis) is the only path to resolution in a larger synthesis" (Davis 1982, 74).

The diversity leader is the pioneer of a new way of seeing the health care organization's diversity potential—potential unseen by others. The diversity leader's belief in this discovery must remain steadfast, despite evidence (content) to the contrary; this is the key difference between discovery and invention.

> Competitors can imitate inventions; they cannot imitate discoveries. Each competing institution will have to make the same discovery for it to have the same power. In the beginning, most people will ignore the discovery when it is made known to them. Again, they will not know that they don't know. The first-in will have to keep communicating the discovery until more and more members discover the new context. And one institution, as leader, will have to keep communicating the discovery until more and more institutions discover the new context (Davis 1982, 79).

The diversity leader will find organizational allies who have made the shift from "knowing that they don't know" to "knowing," and these **change agents**, the harbingers of the health care organization's new identity, are key to successful diversity leadership.

CHANGE AGENTS

Change agents often present themselves, and they are diversity leadership's "paradigm pioneers" (Barker 1989). Health care organizations that value diversity will see them, support them, and learn from their insight and initiative. Alva Wheatley, vice president and manager of Kaiser Permanente's Cultural Diversity Project tells how Kaiser's extensive diversity initiatives began seven or eight years ago with the work of Jerry Lew, a trainer in Kaiser Permanente's northern California region. Lew began diversity awareness training for employees because "no one ever told him he couldn't." His pioneering efforts began the process of organizational transformation that continues to result in fundamental changes in policies, practices, and behaviors in Kaiser Permanente's 12 regions nationwide. As a result of Lew's pioneering work, Kaiser Permanente's corporate commitment to diversity is now embodied in a strategic plan because diversity is seen as a business imperative.

A similar situation occurred at United Hospital in St. Paul, where the director of education services, Jeanne Bailey, was the change agent. She engaged both employees and administration to assist in identifying the issues, selecting the consultant, developing a needs assessment, projecting and obtaining budget commitment, and monitoring the ongoing diversity training process.

United Hospital and Children's Health Care–St. Paul discovered an opportunity for transformation when faced with union issues arising from incidents at the hospitals that brought into question their success in managing diversity. A grass-roots response to the incidents by members of Union Local 113 resulted in the formation of a Cultural Diversity Study Team in 1992, which has since evolved into the current Diversity Action Council that is responsible for coordinating a wide array of diversity initiatives at the hospitals.

Mary Ann Newman, operations vice president from United Hospital and a member of the Diversity Action Council, reports that United and Children's–St. Paul, which share a building, have begun a peer trainer program that utilizes self-selected, volunteer change agents who represent a cross-section of the hospitals' workforces. The use of peer trainers was in direct response to employee preferences expressed in a paper and pencil diversity survey conducted by the grass-roots Diversity Study Team.

United Hospital's and Children's–St. Paul's peer trainers have formed dyads composed of two employees based on the hospitals' goal to form balanced teams in terms of job type, race, gender, sexual orientation, and ethnicity. An external consultant, Miriam V. Lee, president of Vaughn-Lee & Associates, led the peer trainers through two days of intensive diversity training, and trainers were given the opportunity to practice their presentation before an audience prior to conducting training sessions for fellow employees. Each diversity training team assumed responsibility for conducting ongoing diversity training sessions throughout the hospitals.

Peer diversity trainers were interviewed prior to selection by members of the Diversity Action Council, and completed an application that included questions such as,

1. Why is diversity important at United and Children's Hospitals?
2. Describe experiences you have had that would prepare you to be a diversity trainer.
3. What are important qualities and strengths a diversity trainer must have?

Then through self-selection of volunteer applicants and a screening process, the Diversity Action Council, with advice from consultant Lee, selected applicants most likely to serve as effective peer trainers.

A caveat if your facility decides to undertake a project of this sort: because diversity initiatives bring up deeply held feelings and call standard practices and behaviors into question and can shake the foundations of the institution and its employees, change agents cannot be put in the position of sinking or swimming on their own. This approach is likely to derail a well-intentioned diversity effort. United and Children's–St. Paul's model combines management facilitation with the efforts of volunteer change agents, guided by an external consultant who was selected for her skill and experience in diversity leadership.

Change agents in health care organizations like United and Children's–St. Paul can come from all levels of the organization, but executive management's commitment and active involvement in modeling the new culture of diversity leadership is key to its success. Grass-roots initiatives don't work without commitment from the top; recall that United Hospital's vice president for operations, Mary Ann Newman, is a member of the Diversity Action Council. In addition, commitment must be evidenced by the allocation of resources, rewards for participation, and active involvement in training and other diversity-related efforts by the entire executive management team. Health care executives who aspire to diversity leadership must "walk their talk."

LIVING WITH PARADOX AND CONTRADICTION

Remnants of the old way are difficult to extinguish. Consequently, the diversity leader in today's health care organization must learn to live with paradox and contradiction. Be aware that diversity initiatives will galvanize opposition as well as support. Anne Arundel Medical Center spokesperson, Joyce Phillip, director of employee relations, describes the employee response to a newly introduced scholarship program earmarked for African Americans: "We received so much backlash about it. We were accused of reverse discrimination." The Medical Center's response was to focus attention on basic interventions to heighten awareness of other cultures.

Another example is presented by Steve Barney, senior vice president for human resources at SSM Health Care System's corporate headquarters in St. Louis, Missouri, who reported mixed reaction to SSM's diversity initiatives. Some white males, he said, see SSM's commitment to change as career limiting for them, but the overall acceptance is excellent.

At IHC's corporate offices in Salt Lake City, Utah, Mary Ann Holladay, assistant vice president of human resources, described the initial reaction to the diversity issue from her white male counterparts as one of "disinterest and denial of the importance of the issue." Women and minorities, in her experience, are more aware of diversity issues and supportive of diversity initiatives than white men, probably because of their personal experiences with being "different" from the norm. Holladay said that white women at Intermountain would talk about diversity with minority men before they would broach the issue with white men.

Now, however, disinterest and denial have been largely replaced by awareness and commitment to diversity leadership, according to Holladay. The team focus of IHC's total quality management (TQM) and continuous quality improvement (CQI) initiatives contributed to the attitudinal and behavioral shifts that Holladay has seen over the past five years.

If diversity is seen as a zero-sum game, producing winners and losers in a battle over limited resources, negative reactions, particularly from constituencies who feel they have something to lose in the change process, are inevitable. Diversity leaders must be careful not to fall into the trap of approaching the change process as a battle of "us versus them." If white men are seen as perpetrators and everyone else as victims, then white men have nothing to gain from participation in diversity initiatives. What must be stressed then is that we are all victims and perpetrators, depending on the diversity issue at hand. Each of us, because of our uniqueness and difference, can therefore thrive in a culture that values diversity.

Direct action or opposition isn't always the most effective way to address institutional relics. Change is a natural, but chaotic, process. Because disorganization and confusion are part and parcel of transformation, enforcing a standard of "politically correct" speech will only move your opposition underground. Diversity leadership's aim is otherwise—to make the invisible visible.

Certain recalcitrant individuals take action beyond speech that is oppositional to behavior that is oppositional. Behaviors that violate Equal Employment Office/Affirmative Action (EEO/AA) guidelines, the Americans With Disabilities Act or other legislation are legally prohibited and must be addressed accordingly. But behaviors that are not illegal, but are contradictory to valuing diversity, must be addressed in a different way. Actually, behavior is easier to change than attitude. The key to extinguishing speech or behavior that is oppositional, but not illegal, is social pressure. For example, in an experiment to determine the effect of exposure to antiracist norms on the expression of racial prejudice, researchers (Blanchard, Lilly, and Vaughn 1991, 103) found that a "favorable normative influence can contribute to the establishment of a social climate that condemns racism." They drew the following conclusion:

> Antiracist sentiment is malleable. Our findings offer promise to an orientation toward eliminating racism that emphasizes relatively more the public behavior of well-intentioned, yet inexperienced whites than the private attitudes of such people. The goal of creating social settings that maximize the public expression of strong, antiracist opinions and minimize the public expression of all forms of discriminatory and insensitive behavior might be advanced by the efforts of a few outspoken persons who vigorously advocate antiracist positions and by the presence of norms consistent with those views (p. 105).

Generalizing these findings regarding racism to other dimensions of diversity, we can conclude that health care organizations that support and encourage key individuals who model strong prodiversity norms and set corporate policy that is consistent with those norms, will see less oppositional behavior. Essential to this strategy is that executive management be among the health care organization's prodiversity models.

DEALING WITH FEELINGS OF LOSS

Futurist Joel Barker (1989) has reminded us that when a paradigm shifts, "everyone goes back to zero." Accordingly, change can bring loss—whether it's positive or negative change. Staff, patients, executives, and the board need to be permitted to voice their feelings of loss and disappointment without fear of reprisal. The trap of "political correctness" must be avoided by the health care organization that values diversity.

To deal with loss, Terrence E. Deal and Allan A. Kennedy (1983, 5) explain that organizations undergoing fundamental cultural change must allow for a transitional mourning period and acknowledge that "with change comes the loss of tangible and intangible attachments—to offices, heroes, work rituals, or symbols." Health care organizations that value diversity must provide forums for representatives of the new and old context to interact. As Deal and Kennedy (1983, 5–6) explain, "the main objective of the transition is to maintain a healthy tension—a continuing dialogue between old and emerging ways."

Valuing diversity is a way of thinking and being: i.e., a context. It is more than a series of behaviors or content. Health care organizations making the transition to valuing diversity will need to support management, staff, board, and patients as they make the transition from "confusion to composure" (Davis 1982, 77).

During the transition, there's confusion in terms what can and cannot be said and done. For example, men newly aware of sexism, who have recently made the transition from "not knowing that they don't know" to "knowing that they don't know," may no longer know how to behave toward their women colleagues. Should I open the door or shouldn't I? Was the remark I just made in the department meeting sexist or not? Similarly, white employees with new insight into racism may become paralyzed with fear and stilted in their interactions with African or Asian Americans. Should I ask what they want to be called or shouldn't I? Could my question about this patient's diet be construed as racist?

The transformation and change process is neither straightforward nor linear, but when enough individuals and departments have discovered how to value diversity, then the health care organization is transformed. Beware that fear of reprisals or misinterpretation as individuals move from "confusion to composure" (Davis 1982, 77) can lead to disengagement and abort the change process. It is for this reason that the diversity leader must provide an environment in which attitudes and behaviors can be voiced and explored without fear. To assist the diversity leader, some suggestions follow from the authors of *Driving Fear out of the Workplace* (Ryan and Oestreich 1991).

1. If you want people to disclose their fears, recognize and be able to talk about some of your own.

2. If you want people to speak up about sensitive issues, demonstrate that you can communicate about such issues. Perhaps more importantly, show that you are willing to listen to the concerns of others—even if what they present is difficult for you to hear.

3. If you want people to stop making negative assumptions, freeze those assumptions in yourself. Notice them as they come to mind and consciously bypass them in favor of a more constructive, accurate view of people and their motives.

4. If you want others to ask questions about fear's presence, be willing to ask those same questions first (p. 129).

BENCHMARKING, DISCOVERY, AND INVENTION

Benchmarking is an increasingly popular strategy to measure performance in key areas of management and clinical practice. Health care organizations select the practice to be benchmarked, compare their performance to best demonstrated practice, and take action based on the results of the comparison. Benchmarking can provide invaluable information in the process of evaluating the effectiveness of your organization's diversity leadership. But, as Stanley Davis (1982) points out, although inventions can be copied, discovery cannot.

As competitors in the computing industry have learned, Hewlett Packard's policies, procedures, products, and other content can be copied, but other organizations cannot imitate the 'Hewlett Packard way', i.e., the context. Each health care organization must discover its own path to diversity leadership. Once your health care organization's unique path has been discovered, you can benefit from benchmarking, i.e., from one another's inventions.

TEAM DEVELOPMENT DURING TRANSFORMATION

Teams are essential to the high-performing health care organization. In today's hospitals, we see transdisciplinary health care teams responsible for the care of patients. We see teams composed of individuals from all levels of the health care organization come together to solve problems using the principles of TQM. We see how patient-centered care models are built on the team concept. We see admissions clerks, parking lot attendents, maintenance staff, nurses, allied health professionals, administrators, and physicians all working together to influence the patient's experience with the health care organization. With teams playing such an integral role in the operation of the health care organization, diversity issues are certain to affect the functioning of teams.

Health care organizations that have recently initiated a program of diversity leadership may find team issues that they had thought to have been resolved surfacing again. Issues of identity, influence, acceptance, suspicion, roles, trust, and interdependence may resurface, with the newly discovered theme of diversity as the key issue in successful resolution. A fundamental shift to diversity leadership will cause the organization to recycle through the stages of group development (Weber 1982) and cannot occur without backlash.

TRANSFORMATION
PRODUCES CHANGES ············

As we have seen, changes will occur in the transformed health care organization, emanating from and affecting all aspects of the organization. Chapters 9 and 10 discuss the types of new business initiatives, policies and procedures, and approaches to clinical practice found in transformed health care organizations.

REFERENCES ············

Barker, J. 1989. *Discovering the Future: The Business of Paradigms*, 2d ed. Videotape. Burnsville, MN: Charthouse Learning Corporation.

Blanchard, F. A., T. Lilly, and L. A. Vaughn. 1991. "Reducing the Expression of Racial Prejudice." *Psychological Science* 2 (2): 101–5.

Bruhn, J. G., H. G. Levine, and P. L. Levine. 1993. *Managing Boundaries in the Health Professions*. Springfield, IL: Charles C. Thomas Publisher.

Davis, S. M. 1982. "Transforming Organizations: The Key to Strategy Is Context." *Organizational Dynamics* 10 (3): 64–80.

Deal, T. E., and A. A. Kennedy. 1983. "Corporate Culture: Carrier or Barrier to Success." *Impact* 1 (2): 2–6.

Dreachslin, J. L., E. J. Kobrinski, and A. J. Passen. 1994. "The Boundary Path of Exchange: A New Metaphor for Leadership." *Journal of Leadership and Organization Development* 15 (6): 16–23.

Ryan, K. D., and D. K. Oestreich. 1991. *Driving Fear Out of the Workplace*. San Francisco: Jossey-Bass.

Thomas, R. R. 1990. "From Affirmative Action to Affirming Diversity." *Harvard Business Review* 68 (2): 107–17.

Weber, R. C. 1982. "The Group: A Cycle from Birth to Death." In *NTL Reading Book for Human Relations Training*, edited by L. Porter and B. Mohr, 68–71. Alexandria, VA: NTL Institute.

CHAPTER 9

Invention of the New Content:
Health Care Delivery

NEW CONTENT—policies, procedures, strategies, and ways of doing things—is an inevitable consequence of transformation and reflects the organization's new vision of diversity leadership. Can change happen without transformation? Undoubtedly, the answer to that question is yes. But change without transformation has a hollow ring to it. Well-intentioned changes conceived and implemented in the context of an affirmative action–based vision will be seen as "window dressing" by employees, customers, and the community. On the other hand health care organizations that truly value diversity have discovered a **new context** and, within their new diversity paradigm, have invented new content that not only *looks*, but also *feels* different to the organization's constituents.

This chapter illustrates the changes that health care organizations have made in their move from an affirmative action paradigm to one of valuing diversity. It focuses on changes in health care delivery and the relationship between the health care organization and its market. Recall Stanley Davis' (1982) model (see pp. 145–146). The changes to be discussed here refer to the movement from "knowing that you don't know" (which includes research, development, exploration, and planning) to "knowing" (which encompasses operations, action, and implementation).

Three specific arenas for change in health care delivery are discussed: niche marketing, community service, and patient care.

NICHE MARKETING

With the advent of DRGs, health care organizations discovered the niche marketing strategy. Women's health centers and heart institutes were the inevitable result of an era of increasing competition for a shrinking pool of hospital inpatient days and Medicare reimbursement dollars, played out in the context of "winner and loser" DRGs. Health care organizations that have discovered the diversity paradigm have transformed their view of the marketplace and have uncovered new applications of the niche marketing strategy.

A case in point is Good Samaritan Hospital and Health Center of Dayton, Ohio. Good Samaritan has tailored a line of services to meet the needs of local Japanese-owned companies and the Japanese nationals, usually senior-level executive managers who are living in the hospital's service area. Key to success has been Good Samaritan's thorough planning and research into marketing and service delivery strategies that are culturally appropriate.

In the late 1980s, Good Samaritan Hospital discovered untapped potential in the growing number of Japanese-owned companies and Japanese nationals in its service area when a serendipitous event triggered the discovery that resulted in substantive change in the way the hospital, which had been established in 1932 by the Sisters of Charity of Cincinnati, Ohio, viewed its marketplace.

Here's the story: Tomiko Cross, an employee at Good Samaritan for more than 20 years, who immigrated to the United States from Japan over 30 years ago, remains fluent in Japanese. She played a central role in Good Samaritan's discovery and change process. One day, as she walked in a Dayton park, she began talking with a young Japanese woman who had recently experienced a miscarriage and was treated at Good Samaritan. The young woman, who spoke little English, told Cross that she wished she had known her while being treated at Good Samaritan because she would have found comfort in talking in Japanese with someone during her stay. The young woman's comment produced a flash of insight for Cross: she could serve as a communications bridge between the hospital and the growing community of Japanese nationals in its service area. Cross shared her insight with the Good Samaritan administrators and was appointed Japanese Relations Coordinator in 1990.

Luckily for Good Samaritan, Cross' insight coincided with opportunity. Approximately 50 Japanese companies are situated in the Dayton-Cincinnati-Columbus triangle, attracted, in part, by the Interstates 70 and 75 corridor. Honda has parts distribution plants and an engine assembly plant about one hour north of Dayton, and Matsushita Electronics, producer of Panasonic brand-name products, built a picture tube assembly plant in the same area. HealthPark, a Good Samaritan Hospital and Health Center's primary care facility, was, coincidentally, strategically located to serve the growing Japanese community.

John Marzano, director of communications and marketing at Good Samaritan Hospital in Dayton, Ohio describes their foray into the realm of diversity leadership like this: "The patient-focused care model helped spur this kind of thinking. This was a niche opportunity and a niche market for us. The wives and children of Japanese executives had particular problems accessing care because they usually didn't have the facility with English that their husbands did. Good Samaritan Hospital and Health Center saw this as an opportunity to bring its mission and values to life, while capitalizing on a favorable business opportunity." Good Samaritan, along with other health care organizations that value diversity, discovered that good business and community service go hand in hand.

Good Samaritan Hospital and Health Center's first public initiative in its Japanese outreach program was a seminar entitled, "How to Access Health Care in the United States." Japanese executives, representing over 30 Japanese-owned companies in the area, were invited to attend. The seminar was held at HealthPark, the hospital's satellite facility in southern Miami County that was to serve as the central access point for the hospital's package of services to the Japanese companies and community.

Good Samaritan had done a considerable amount of behind-the-scenes planning prior to the seminar. Communication issues were central to the planning process. A Japanese consultant was engaged to assist the hospital in creating an appropriate infrastructure for the new service line as well as to help create the official approach to marketing the service line. The consultant familiarized hospital management and staff with Japanese etiquette, including the importance of the business card exchange, and translation of health care materials and correspondence.

Good Samaritan also designed an approach to communicate about this initiative to American-owned companies like General Motors that were sensitive to the Japanese presence in the Dayton area. The hospital was prepared to explain that they were not doing something 'better' for the Japanese, but, rather, they were redesigning standard services to fit another cultural paradigm.

The hospital's Japanese strategy involved two phases. In phase one, the needs of Japanese nationals, both employees and their families, would be addressed. This is a relatively small population because the workforce in the Japanese-owned, Dayton-area companies is predominantly American. In phase two, the hospital would negotiate preferred provider arrangements to supply the health care needs of *all* of the companies' employees.

At this writing, Good Samaritan Hospital and Health Center is well into phase one of its niche marketing strategy. The infrastructure developed to support phase one includes the following:

1. a full-time Japanese Relations Coordinator, fluent in Japanese language and culture, who serves as the key liaison between Japanese patients and the hospital's service providers;

2. a Japanese-American family physician who serves as the primary health care services access point in a growing primary care network called Samaritan Family Care;

3. a wide range of dual-language materials including brochures, medical record forms, and information packets;

4. round-the-clock access to care through the use of a mobile telephone staffed by a hospital representative who is fluent in Japanese; and

5. a training and orientation program for physicians, employees, emergency room staff, and outpatient services staff, each of whom is provided with a telephone card and information on accessing the Japanese interpreter.

The results to date are quite impressive: 25 Japanese-owned firms have contracted with Good Samaritan to provide physicals for their Japanese employees and families, more than 50 families utilize the services of Good Samaritan's interpreter and physician; in excess of $250,000 in incremental hospital revenue has been generated by the program. Start-up costs were low; the Japanese Relations Coordinator position became full-time, after beginning as a 20 percent position. Radiology services, the family birthing center, surgery, cardiac, emergency trauma center, and outpatient services are among those used by participants in the program; a communication link has been established between the hospital and Ohio's Office of Economic Development in Tokyo; and the hospital has entered into an agreement with Tokio Marine Insurance Company to accept its traveler's health insurance for Japanese visitors to the Dayton area.

The hospital has taken preliminary steps to set in motion the phase two plan to sell preferred provider contracts to the Japanese-owned companies that participated in phase one. The establishment of direct contract relationships with those Japanese-owned companies that are self-insured is a central aim. Market pressures for managed care and preferred provider arrangements have just begun to affect the Dayton health care marketplace, and as those pressures increase, Good Samaritan Hospital and Health Center expects that its already successful niche marketing strategy will continue to bear fruit. Marzano explains:

> Since the Japanese are long-range decision makers, the hospital designed our marketing strategy for the long run. The Japanese pride themselves on a preventive approach to health care. This approach coincides with the current trend toward managed care, health care networks, and preferred provider arrangements. We have found that the Japanese patients and companies are very loyal and that word of mouth is a powerful marketing tool in the Japanese community. If you provide a worthwhile service, the response will be continued support for your efforts.

Good Samaritan Hospital has put into practice in a health care setting the same advice that Catherine A. Novak, a senior editor of *Best's Review*, offers to the insurance industry. In summarizing the benefits of niche marketing efforts instituted by various insurance companies, Novak (1992, 18) says, "Profiting from demographic trends takes marketing savvy and an appreciation of the need to tailor sales approaches to various market segments, including women and diverse ethnic groups."

COMMUNITY SERVICE

As health care organizations realign to form health care networks and capitation becomes an increasingly common reimbursement mechanism, health care providers have focused on prevention and early detection as preferred strategies to improve the health status of their patients, while containing costs by reducing their reliance on expensive hospital inpatient care. Diversity leaders see culturally appropriate community outreach as an essential component of this new service delivery model.

Paradise Valley Hospital, like Good Samaritan, discovered the convergence of mission and market in its model for community and patient service. A 228-bed community hospital, Paradise Valley is one of the most ethnically and culturally diverse hospitals in San Diego County. Founded in 1904, it is a religious-based Adventist facility that has always focused on wellness and community outreach. Kathy Wilson, executive director of outpatient services, explains that Paradise Valley recently revised its mission and vision statements to "reflect collaboration with the community we serve. We feel very strongly that we are a part of the community and that, without a community partnership, health care is not effective."

Paradise Valley is an inner-city hospital located ten miles from the Mexican border in National City, with a population that is 51 percent Latino. The hospital's service area is 12 percent Asian, 13 percent African American, 35 percent Latino, and 40 percent Caucasian. The hospital's patients are even more diverse— 34 percent Asian, 26 percent African American, 19 percent Latino, and 21 percent Caucasian.

In 1992, Paradise Valley Hospital formed a cultural diversity task force because one of the hospital's key goals is "to meet customers' needs by providing services that are culturally and lingually appropriate." The task force, composed of employees who represent the diversity of the hospital's service area, provides guidance in the implementation of actions designed to further this and other diversity goals. Some of the changes implemented under the task force's direction are:

1. **Cultural diversity and customer service training,** a one-day course all hospital employees attend, designed to improve service to patients from diverse cultural groups. The course familiarizes staff with culturally based beliefs, values, and behaviors that can affect patients' treatment preferences and their relationships with health care providers. Participants are provided with strategies to use this new knowledge to improve their ability to deliver excellence in customer service to a culturally diverse patient mix.

2. **Center for Health Promotion Outreach,** which was established in southeast San Diego to meet the disease prevention and wellness needs of member of the African American and Latino communities. The staff is bilingual, reflecting the racial and ethnic composition of the service area. A women's health services program, including mobile mammography, was implemented in 1992. The center uses communication networks that are trusted and established in the neighborhood as a key component of their marketing strategy. The center has begun working through the African American churches and sororities, for instance, to increase the utilization of center services by African American women.

3. **A senior membership program called Premier 65,** which offers lectures and billing assistance in English and Spanish. The office staff is bilingual, and volunteers who speak Tagalog are available to help Filipino members.

4. **Partners for Prevention,** which is a coalition of representatives from business, government, social service agencies, health care, educational institutions, and churches spearheaded by Paradise Valley Hospital. Partners for Prevention held four community

forums in 1993, all in both English and Spanish. The purpose of the forums was to identify the most significant health problem affecting the community. Paradise Valley used the information gleaned from the forums to improve its strategy for meeting the health care needs of the community. In the future, the needs assessment will include asset mapping to show resources available within the community.

5. **Healthy Beginnings,** which is a program to help expectant and parenting mothers become drug and alcohol free. It uses culturally sensitive approaches and a culturally diverse staff to improve patient participation and success in treatment.

Paradise Valley Hospital's efforts have not gone unnoticed by the community. Tony Inocentes, author of a popular column in the San Diego *Star-News* entitled "The Latino Perspective," is among those who have publicly recognized the hospital's distinction as a diversity leader. In one column titled "Hospital Organizations Need Reinvestment Mandate," he offered the following:

> After examining the three South Bay hospitals, it becomes clear that Paradise Valley Hospital's devotion to the community as a whole remains genuine. I believe this is primarily due to the hospital's president, Fred Harder, and its governing board's ability to maintain its overwhelmingly local membership, thus giving it the ability to be sensitive to diversity issues, changing demographics, and its community's economic needs (Inocentes 1994).

Community service initiatives, like those in place at Paradise Valley Hospital, are best designed with community input. Yale–New Haven Hospital recognized this and began its efforts to improve customer service by holding focus groups in the spring of 1994. Focus group participants reflected the diversity of the community—49 percent white, 35 percent African American, 13 percent Latino, and 2.3 percent Asian/Pacific Islander.

A transdisciplinary team has used the focus group data to reengineer ambulatory care delivery and improve the health status of the community. New Haven is the third largest city in Connecticut and, although it is the seventh poorest city in the country, it is located in the wealthiest state. The high school dropout rate in New Haven is over 40 percent.

Yale–New Haven Hospital is building important linkages between itself, a traditional academic medical center, and the people of New Haven's inner city. These linkages are increasingly important to today's health care organization. Suzanne Boyle, clinical director for ambulatory services at Yale–New Haven Hospital, said,

"Valuing diversity in patient care calls for a cultural shift. If we have a city with many health needs, we'll be unable to meet the demands and health goals of a managed care environment."

Because of its diverse patient mix, Yale–New Haven Hospital is working with an external consultant to develop culturally sensitive patient care literature. For Example, brochures describing the hospital's Women's and Primary Care Centers are available in Spanish as well as English. The hospital has also canvassed patient care literature nationwide and is developing a prenatal teaching guide geared to the needs of the local community.

In addition, Yale–New Haven has redesigned its ambulatory clinics, creating spacious waiting rooms and offering day care for children in a space contiguous to the women's center in an attempt to address a major barrier to mothers seeking health care. The hospital is also currently retooling its approach to patient service in order to address concerns expressed by focus group members about waiting time, lack of cultural sensitivity on the part of caregivers, miscommunication about billing, and other customer service issues.

Changes in a health care organization's approach to community relations are highly visible reflections of the value placed on diverse groups within the health care organization's service area. Visual images in advertising and health education materials, for example, reflect the health care organization's view of its marketplace. Potential customers can be lost if print and other media don't include images that reflect them, their community, and their experience. Truman Medical Center in Kansas City, Missouri, follows this advice. "We will not allow photographs or other advertisements to be published unless they represent the diversity of our service area," according to Sherell Tyree, corporate director of personnel.

Involvement of hospital representatives in community service is another highly visible reflection of a health care organization's position vis-à-vis diversity leadership. Truman Medical Center, which comprises two facilities with very different service area demographics, has an active program of community service. Truman Medical Center works with a health care magnet school in its service area in order to encourage African American and Mexican American young people to consider careers in the health care industry. Truman also offers seventh and eighth grade students from a local middle school an intensive two-week summer program designed to familiarize them and their public school teachers with the inner workings of the hospital.

The medical center also has a scholarship program for physical therapists, and efforts are underway to form a partnership with Langston University, an historically black university, to encourage local African American students to enter the field of physical therapy and work at the hospital. Involvement with the public schools in health career awareness can address the diversity imperative and reflects the health care organization's commitment to community involvement and diversity leadership. Similar programs are in place at Yale–New Haven Hospital.

Special events sponsored by health care organizations can be marketed in ways to attract and welcome attendance from diverse community members. Expectant single mothers or lesbian couples, for example, may not avail themselves of prenatal education programs if all of the hospital's informational material on the program depicts heterosexual couples. Similarly, a health fair for seniors isn't likely to attract working class Latino or African American participants if the planned activities, menu, and services are designed to meet the preferences of white middle-class participants. Community service involves outreach that uses the medium and delivers the message appropriate to the audience. The African American church, for example, can be an effective medium for health education and participation in screening and wellness programs.

Effective diversity leaders will be familiar with service area demographics and, through the use of culturally appropriate messages and media, will expand the health care organization's ability to meet the community's health care needs. As David Jones, president of United Hospital in St. Paul, Minnesota explains,

> Community roots are essential to our success. We're looking broadly at health status for our community. It's part of our mission. Some services will make money, while others will not. There are constant threats to the tax exempt status of hospitals across the nation. Hospitals lost sight of our mission in the 1980s in response to the pressure of DRGs and the changing nature of the health care delivery system. It's time to recognize again that the hospital is more than just a money making institution.

PATIENT CARE ···········

As President Jones points out, some diversity efforts won't make money but need to be done because not-for-profit health care providers are mission and community service–driven. As United and Children's Health Care–St. Paul learned, mission and community service–driven health care can save the institution money and prevent any bad press. Prior to the redesigned care model for the Hmong community, briefly discussed in Chapter 4, court orders to force Hmong parents to submit their children to the hospital's treatment plan were occurring far too often.

With the redesigned care model, Jane Persoon, nurse manager of Children's–St. Paul's neonatal ICU says, "I can't remember the last time we had to get a court order to treat a Hmong patient. It is easier to work with, rather than against, the Hmong and their culture." It's easier and less expensive. The new culturally sensitive approach to patient care allows Children's to avoid the costly and time-consuming process of litigation. Administrative and clinical staff, as well as physicians, now reflect a new awareness and respect for Hmong culture in all aspects of patient care.

Signs above the beds of tiny Hmong patients in the neonatal ICU now read, "Please respect my Southeast Asian heritage and put IVs in my hands and feet only." At an earlier stage in the learning curve, however, caregivers stood by in dismay while Hmong parents vociferously objected to IVs in their children's head, a common practice with pediatric inpatients whose tiny veins are more accessible in the head. That common practice doesn't present a problem for most of Children's–St. Paul's patients. Hmong families, on the other hand, commonly share a cultural belief that leads to concern that needles in the head will injure the brain. Children's–St. Paul has now altered its standard operating procedure to respond to this deeply held cultural belief. In so doing, a barrier to family cooperation with children's medical care has been removed. As Deb Ciriacy, a nurse in the hospital's neonatal ICU explains, such beliefs are "different, not wrong."

Previously, Hmong patients were asked to check their cultural beliefs at the door. Now the the goal at Children's–St. Paul's is to balance the beliefs and practices of Western medicine with the health and spiritual beliefs of the Hmong. Staff still take the hand and footprints of Hmong babies who die in the hospital, but the traditional lock of hair is not routinely taken. Many Hmong believe, Deb Ciriacy explains, that the hair of the deceased should not be cut because a person needs to be intact when he or she moves on to the next world.

A number of policies and procedures and culturally based assumptions needed to be questioned in order to deliver culturally sensitive and appropriate medical care to Hmong patients. While in the traditional European American nuclear family, the parents make medical care decisions for their children, in the traditional

Hmong family, explains Dr. Drew Ozolins, pediatric ICU medical director at Children's–St. Paul, the extended family more often is involved in decision making, especially when surgery is the recommended treatment path. "The vast majority of the time," Dr. Ozolins reports, "the Hmong family agrees with medical judgment. They just use a wider process to make the decision. In most cases, treatment is not urgent and it is possible to let Hmong families make decisions as dictated by their culture. A ten-minute decision for another family may take hours or days for a Hmong family. The path to a decision is different, but if the goal of a healthy child is achieved, we have all succeeded."

Ozolins feels that "in a broad sense, each cooperatively made decision builds a bridge to future relationships with the Hmong community." He and the hospital staff accommodate the use of alternative medicine insofar as it is medically possible without putting the patient at risk. Hmong families often want their children to wear special bracelets or anklets when they go to surgery, so Children's–St. Paul makes an extra effort to permit this. Some patients' families also request that specially prepared teas are given by mouth or through the nasal gastric feeding tube. Whenever possible, hospital staff cooperate.

According to Ozolins, who completed his residency in a San Diego hospital that served a large Latino, especially Mexican, population, "In that setting, I also needed to adjust my thinking to cultural differences. The Hmong, like all of us, find illness stressful. Their need for support is on a par with any family's needs. The great differences in medical tradition create the need for an enormous leap in understanding. We're trying to meet the Hmong halfway."

Jane Persoon, nurse manager in the neonatal ICU, has taken advantage of the opportunities that the hospital provides to learn more about the Hmong language and culture. Hmong patients would shake their heads affirmatively and say yes to the doctor, and then vociferously refuse the very treatment to which they had apparently agreed. Beda Lewis, director of quality management at Children's–St. Paul, explains that there isn't a word for "no" in the Hmong language because to say "no" is considered very disrespectful. As a result, traditional Hmong family members may give you the answer you want to hear because they do not want to show disrespect. Caregivers have had to become more aware of Hmong cultural norms in order to know when yes means no.

Lewis credits Children's–St. Paul's two Hmong interpreters, Cher Vang and Ai Vang, for serving as a bridge of understanding between the Hmong community and the hospital. Ai Vang, for example, was called to the emergency room at United Hospital, the adult acute care facility that shares a building with Children's–St. Paul when a doctor, who was decidedly frustrated, was trying to get an adult woman Hmong patient to consent to surgery. All the distraught Hmong woman could see was the doctor's anger. Ai Vang asked the doctor to step out into the hallway with her and told the doctor that the patient would not follow his advice unless he was supportive and kind. The doctor changed his approach, and the patient consented to surgery and recovered.

The Birth Center, a shared service of United and Children's–St. Paul, has also made changes in labor and delivery to accommodate Hmong culture and medical tradition: Hmong women traditionally give birth in a squatting position. Hmong family members may bring chicken and rice for the new mother, which the patient will eat instead of the standard hospital fare. The hospitals now accept and value these differences in the Birth Center.

Lewis illustrated the importance of moving beyond judgment and ethnocentrism in the delivery of care when the caregiver and the patient have different cultural backgrounds. Men are traditionally the key decision makers in Hmong culture, Lewis explains. Hmong women traditionally had no say in birth control. Some nurses felt it was their duty to "liberate" the Hmong women. A more effective approach, says Lewis, is to work with, rather than against, the patient's culture. Rigid thinking on the part of caregivers, Lewis says, can only produce problems.

Teaching sheets used in patient education and parent guides are available in the Hmong language. Signs in the elevators at Children's–St. Paul are in Hmong, English, and Spanish. The hospitals have moved from inflexible to flexible in their rules about the number of visitors a patient may have in order to better serve large Hmong families.

The expertise of Children's–St. Paul's Hmong interpreters is essential to the hospital's continuing success in delivering patient-focused, culturally appropriate care. Cher Vang, the hospital's first Hmong interpreter, explains that the nuances of Hmong culture can sometimes produce misunderstandings between the patient's family and the caregivers. Cher Vang sees his role as developing trust with both patient and physician. Families will sometimes ask him to vouch for the doctor. The doctors and nurses rely upon him and the hospital's other Hmong interpreter, Ai Vang, to explain Hmong culture and guide them through the communication process. Serving as an interpreter between two very different cultures can be challenging. There's no word for ventilator or other common medical terminology in the Hmong language. Cher Vang and Ai Vang must, nevertheless, be able to explain medical treatment so that Hmong patients and their families can give informed consent. Doctors must develop trust in their ability to do so.

Cher Vang and Ai Vang conduct in-services for residents and nurses to familiarize them with Hmong culture and tradition as it relates to medical care. As a result of their work, the interpreters have developed a network of former patients in the Hmong community who have undergone successful treatment at United and Children's–St. Paul. Current patients and their families are put in touch with former patients and their families to discuss recommended medical procedures. Trust, explains Cher Vang, is very important in Hmong culture. Without trust, relationship is impossible. The key to success, explains Cher Vang, is to understand and accept Hmong culture, to be flexible, and to give patients and their families time to think and adjust.

Cher Vang's advice is pertinent to health care providers that strive to deliver culturally appropriate patient care across a broad range of differences. United and Children's–St. Paul are transferring knowledge gleaned from their Hmong initiatives to improve patient care delivery to other diverse communities within their service areas. The principles of understanding, respect, and inclusion that are reflected in United and Children's–St. Paul's Hmong initiatives can be applied to other constituencies as well.

REFERENCES

Inocentes, T. 1994. "Hospital Organizations Need Reinvestment Mandate." *The Star News*, May 21–22.

Novak, C. A. 1992. "Profiting from Diversity." *Best's Review* 92 (11): 18–22, 99–100.

CHAPTER 10

Invention of the New Content: Human Resource Management

PERSONNEL POLICIES, benefits packages, and job and organization design are aspects of human resource management in which changes will occur in health care organizations that discover the diversity leadership paradigm. These changes will have a measurable impact on recruitment and retention of a diverse workforce. This chapter discusses the central issues of recruitment and retention and describes practices observers are likely to see in health care organizations that accept and work within the diversity leadership paradigm.

RECRUITMENT

Recruitment of a workforce that reflects the health care organization's customer base is both part of and a prerequisite for diversity leadership. To have effective diversity leadership requires diverse leaders; change doesn't occur without change agents. Niche marketing strategies like those implemented by Good Samaritan Hospital, changes in customer and community service like those used by Paradise Valley Hospital, and the approaches to culturally sensitive patient care in place at Children's Health Care–St. Paul all occurred because change agents who represent the community are employed by the health care organization. Building a culturally sensitive cadre of caregivers and administrators who are predominantly white isn't sufficient when your customer base is 30 percent Asian or 25 percent Latino.

The oft-used maxim, "What you believe, you can achieve" is relevant here. To understand how relevant, consider the converse,

"What you don't believe, you can't achieve." Many health care organizations have stopped diversity-focused recruitment efforts before they started because of beliefs such as the following: We can't hire an Asian administrator; there just aren't any available; or African American nurses are too difficult to find, and the competition is too stiff; or A female building engineer? We will never find one. Health care organizations are cautioned not to let beliefs such as these become self-fulfilling prophecies. In order to recruit a diverse workforce, an organization must believe it can recruit one.

Some strategies for recruiting for diversity are:

1. **Diversify advertising efforts.** How and where you advertise has an important effect on who is recruited to fill a position. Recruiting for diversity requires that health care organizations expand their horizons by advertising through nontraditional sources. Newspapers, journals, and professional newsletters that target a minority audience are all potential outlets for announcements of available positions. Airing radio spots on stations that attract a minority audience, posting position descriptions in languages other than English, and advertising in gay and lesbian publications are among the alternative advertising approaches used by health care organizations that value diversity.

2. **Develop relationships with organizations that represent minority professionals.** Being African American isn't a requirement to join the National Association of Health Services Executives (NASHE). Sending white as well as racial and ethnic minority representatives to minority organizations' professional conferences or heterosexuals to gay and lesbian events will not only help your organization build the networks needed to recruit a diverse workforce, but it will also provide multicultural experiences that will benefit majority group members in your current workforce.

3. **Pressure executive search firms to present a more diverse mix of candidates.** A January 26, 1993, *Wall Street Journal* article quotes Richard Clarke Associates, a New York–based firm that specializes in searches for minority managers, as saying that the firm's search assignments increased by 50 percent from September 1992–September 1993 because companies have realized that they must diversify their top ranks to be competitive

in recruiting at lower levels. Many established search firms, the article reports, have set up separate arms for minority recruitment.

4. **Heed the advice in Chapter 4 about interviewing high-context communicators.** Health care organizations must implement interviewing strategies and applicant screening processes that overcome style differences and focus on the skills needed to get the job done.

RETENTION

Diversity leaders have been encouraged to quantify the value of effective retention strategies by Lewis Griggs, president and CEO of Griggs Productions, producers and distributors of the highly acclaimed "Valuing Diversity" videotapes. To see the value of managing diversity, says Griggs, measure what is spent on entry-level training, recruiting, and defending EEO lawsuits (Geber 1990). Some ways to determine how turnover affects your organization are discussed.

Analyzing turnover ratios by dimensions of diversity

The reduction of turnover costs is a clear benefit of effective retention strategies and the valuing diversity paradigm. Turnover costs have three components—those of separation, replacement, and training.

In his book, *Cultural Diversity in Organizations: Theory, Research, and Practice*, Dr. Taylor Cox summarizes turnover ratio analysis results that are relevant to diversity leaders in health care organizations. For instance, Cox (1993) explains that Corning Glass reported a turnover rate for women in professional positions that was two times that of men during the period 1980–1987, and during that same period at Corning, turnover for blacks was two and one half times that of whites. Cox's (1993) conservative figure for replacement costs would be $15,000 per loss. This is the type of data that led to Corning's focus on diversity leadership. What are the costs to your organization of differential turnover by race, gender, ethnicity, age, or other dimensions of diversity?

A Bureau of National Affairs survey of 303 companies found an average annualized turnover rate of 12 percent (Mercer 1988). According to Mercer (1988, 37–38), "Managers should realize that this money is subtracted directly from company profits. A company whose turnover rate increases automatically slashes its profits; on the other hand, an organization that lowers its turnover enhances its bottom line." Therefore, effective diversity leadership requires that health care organizations analyze and address differential turnover rates as a diversity imperative.

Uncovering the Causes of Differential Turnover Ratios

In order to address differential turnover ratios, the causes of turnover must be uncovered. For instance, the results of one survey studying the incidence of verbal abuse in nursing practice in West Texas and its implications for turnover support the conclusion that at least 18 percent of turnover among nursing directors and staff nurses is related to verbal abuse; 82 percent of staff nurses and 77 percent of nursing directors reported experience with verbal abuse (Cox 1987). Droste (1987) estimates the cost of nursing recruitment at approximately $20,000, making the implications for the diversity leader clear.

ADDRESSING DIFFERENTIAL TURNOVER RATIOS

Another study supports the contention that organizational development (OD) intervention can work in a health care setting to achieve the goal of reduced turnover. In this study, the focus of the organization development intervention was nursing services. The study hospital's conservative estimate is that it saved $1.5 million in replacement/turnover costs during the two-year post-organization development intervention period, using an $8,500 per nurse estimate for replacement costs (Boss et al. 1989).

The researchers (Boss et al. 1989) also credit the intervention with stopping a union movement by implementing quality-of-worklife initiatives designed to foster improvement as operationalized by Likert's System 4, a typology that categorizes management into four types—exploitative, coercive authoritarian; benevolent authoritarian; consultative; and participative group-based management. The desired management style in Likert's paradigm is participative group-based management. Pre- and post-OD intervention scores on Likert's Profile of Organizational and Performance Characteristics showed statistically significant improvement for the study hospital along the six dimensions assessed by the instrument—leadership, motivation, communication, decision making, goal setting, and control processes. A matched comparison hospital showed no change.

Turnover ratios also improved for the study hospital and worsened for the comparison or control hospital. One year before the intervention, the study hospital's turnover rate was 31.3

percent. One year after the intervention, the rate dropped to 17.8 percent and then rose to 20.6 percent two years after the intervention. Comparable figures for the control hospital were 22.6 percent, 26.3 percent, and 25.6 percent, respectively.

Although the study hospital's OD intervention was not diversity-related, the techniques used can be adapted to focus on diversity leadership. The hospital held confrontation and team-building meetings in which issues of power, staffing, flex-time, budgeting, and working effectively were explored. Structural interventions resulted in the reengineering of nursing units and the redesign of jobs. Role negotiations meetings were held between the director of nursing and each unit coordinator to clarify roles and expectations, and 75 specific action items resulted. All unit co-ordinators held similar meetings with their respective head nurses.

Management training covered a myriad of topics, including time management, organizational change, communication, conflict management, process analysis, and meeting management. Members of administration were trained as change agents, developing new behavioral norms designed to change the culture. External consultants mediated disputes and taught the nurses process consultation skills. Sociotechnical interventions and changes in budgetary and financial procedures were also introduced. Managers were coached and counseled on issues such as leadership and problem resolution. Administrative update meetings were regularly held by the hospital's CEO.

Clearly, some turnover is not only unavoidable, but desirable. But when turnover ratios are different across dimensions of diversity, health care organizations must respond with appropriate analysis and action. Suggested actions are described in subsequent sections of this chapter.

Absenteeism: A Hidden Cost of Failed Diversity Leadership

The U.S. Department of Labor's Current Population Survey (CPS) data on absenteeism produced findings with implications for diversity leadership. CPS sample data showed a national average absentee rate of 5.1 percent, but when data were analyzed by gender, distinct differences in absentee rates between men and women were uncovered (Meisenheimer 1990). Age and family status, other important dimensions of diversity, were also associated with different absenteeism rates (Meisenheimer 1990).

Only absences for full-time workers are analyzed in the CPS; Meisenheimer (1990) reports two measures of absenteeism— absence rate and lost worktime rate. **Absence rate** is the proportion of workers who have an absence in a given week, regardless of the length of that absence. **Lost worktime rate** is hours absent from work given as a percentage of total work hours.

The absence rate for women was, on the average, 65 percent higher than that of men workers, and women had higher absence rates than men regardless of the age group analyzed. Except for the 55 and older age group, women's lost worktime rate was also higher than that of men. The highest absence rates were found among mothers of children under six years of age; the lowest, among fathers of preschool children. Lost worktime rates followed a similar pattern (Meisenheimer 1990).

The changing demographics of America's workforce make analysis and management of different rates of absenteeism a critical diversity imperative. Human resource departments in health care organizations that value diversity analyze absenteeism by key dimensions of diversity and calculate the costs of differential rates of absenteeism.

As Meisenheimer (1990) points out, the costs of absenteeism include expenses for replacement workers; sick, vacation, and personal leave pay; and lost productivity and reduced output capacity. These incremental costs result in decreased efficiency and ultimately in increased costs of health care delivery.

Only through quantitative analysis can the success of changes in personnel practices that are implemented to address absenteeism be evaluated. Because the health care industry's workforce is composed of a relatively large proportion of women, analyzing and addressing employee absence data like those reported by Meisenheimer (1990) is especially critical for health care organizations in the current era of reengineering and cost containment.

LESSONS FROM CORPORATE AMERICA

Corporate pioneers such as Digital Equipment Corporation, Hewlett-Packard, McDonald's, Proctor and Gamble, Avon, and Xerox responded to the diversity imperative much sooner than did health care organizations. Consequently, organizations such as these have progressed much further in exploring and implementing changes that reflect a strong commitment to diversity leadership. Health care organizations can benefit from studying the diversity initiatives of these corporate pioneers.

Digital Equipment Corporation

Digital Equipment Corporation, based in Massachusetts, was among the first organizations to explore movement from an affirmative action to a valuing diversity paradigm. The evolution of Digital's approach to diversity leadership began in 1979, with a strong white male backlash against the EEO and high tensions (Piturro and Mahoney 1991). Digital hired Barbara Walker, a diversity consultant and attorney, whose mandate was to help the manufacturing division deal with the "black/white thing." Her approach was to set up a small discussion group of seven senior managers that frankly and openly discussed racial and cultural stereotypes, eventually moving beyond the issue to explore multiple dimensions of diversity. As word of the discussion group spread throughout the manufacturing division, managers who were not included in the first group lobbied with Walker to involve them, leading her to develop additional groups. The early informal groups have been replaced by a formal program of core groups led by trained in-house facilitators. Participation, although encouraged, is voluntary (Piturro and Mahoney 1991).

As a result of this action, productivity has increased in the manufacturing division, the number of women in management has increased 20-fold in the past ten years, diversity in the workforce has resulted in a more diverse customer base, and sexual orientation is among the dimensions of diversity that are now included in its Valuing Diversity Program.

The district managers Walker originally worked with at Digital are now vice presidents and senior managers (Solomon 1989). These leaders, all well schooled in diversity, now occupy key decision-making roles in a corporation that, due to its foresight, is well positioned to address the diversity imperative.

Other corporate diversity programs that were firmly established in the late 1980s and their benefits were highlighted in Solomon's (1989) article and offer important information for health care executives.

Hewlett-Packard

Hewlett-Packard developed a flexible approach to diversity training, key to which is a computerized course intended for use by first-line and new managers. A condensed version is used to train senior management. About 200 trainers are qualified to teach the course, which consists of modules on disk that can be modified to include local demographic data and other statistics. Each module is organized around a different theme and is designed to teach the corporate diversity philosophy as well as strategies for managing a diverse workforce. A rich array of diversity issues are covered including gender, race, disability, and age. In addition to the computer modules, a workshop varying from one to three days in length is offered to help managers see how their management style and expectations of staff are influenced by their own culturally based assumptions, beliefs, and values (Solomon 1989).

Honeywell

By the end of 1988, about 90 percent of Honeywell's employees had undergone workforce diversity awareness training, which for management included an experiential learning exercise in which Honeywell's predominantly white men managers worked for two days with the predominantly African American management teams at Johnson Publishing Company. Honeywell managers who participated in this experience reported an enhanced understanding of the difficulties women and minorities experience in networking to establish the relationships necessary to move ahead at Honeywell (Solomon 1989). Health care organizations might consider establishing similar programs.

McDonald's

McDonald's executive leadership began attending diversity training programs in the late 1970s. Its early focus on executive-level commitment to the development of skills in managing diversity is reflected in its programs for recruiting and retaining a diverse workforce (Solomon 1989).

Procter and Gamble

Procter and Gamble began exploring the complex issues involved in managing a multicultural workforce in the early 1970s when the company opened a division in Albany, Georgia, with the promise that its workforce would reflect the local community, which was about 40 percent minority–based. Diversity initiatives included leadership training, employee development, support for women and minorities, and a commitment to measuring and continually improving diversity leadership (Solomon 1989).

Avon

Executive leadership played a key role in initiating the diversity program at Avon Products. By the mid-1980s, Avon's Minorities and Women's Participation Council included the CEO and division presidents. Seventy-three percent of Avon's managers are women (Solomon 1989).

Xerox

Xerox has successfully recruited a very diverse workforce and is now working on breaking the glass ceiling, according to its corporate affirmative action/equal opportunity officer (Geber 1990). The company has identified "pivotal jobs" that would appear on the resume of any successful top manager at Xerox and then ensures that minorities and women are considered for these positions (Geber 1990).

Solomon (1989) describes Xerox's success in recruiting and retaining an increasingly diverse employee base despite a decrease in the size of its workforce. In the ten years after its managing diversity efforts began in 1978, the percentage of women in Xerox's workforce increased from 29 percent to 32 percent, while the percentage of management positions held by women increased from 10 percent to 20 percent. Minority representation in Xerox's workforce increased from 18 percent to 24 percent, with the percentage of management positions filled by minorities increasing from 11 percent to 19 percent (Solomon 1989).

U S West

U S West (Caudron 1992) developed a Pluralism Performance Menu to appraise the company's top 125 corporate officers based on how well they meet pluralism-related criteria. Corporate officers have to demonstrate what they have done to support pluralism at U S West. Diversity initiatives at U S West have their roots in sexism and racism workshops developed in the mid-1970s at Northwestern Bell under the direction of President Jack MacAllister, who brought his commitment to diversity leadership to his new position as CEO of U S West.

If managers at U S West continue to hire and promote only white men from a diverse labor pool or otherwise not support the company's diversity efforts, they may lose their annual bonus or experience a salary reduction. Search firms employed by U S West must provide a diverse mix of candidates, and colleges from which U S West recruits employees are reviewed to ensure that these graduates represent a good ethnic mix.

In addition to linking financial rewards with diversity leadership through the Pluralism Performance Menu, U S West (Caudron 1992) supports eight employee resource groups (ERGs) that were organized by employees with shared interests and concerns. Among the ERGs are groups for veterans, disabled workers, and Native Americans, as well as gays and lesbians. These groups not only provide support to their members but also help the Denver-based communications company relate to an increasingly diverse marketplace.

Juanita Cox-Burton (1988) describes U S West's Accelerated Development Program as being designed to identify women of color with leadership potential and provide them with special training in management skills, career planning assistance, challenging job assignments after completion, and a mentor from within the organization. She says, "We felt that a program of this type is long overdue. There has always been an accelerated development program for white males; the only difference is that it hasn't been called the 'White Male Program'. It does have a name, however, the 'old-boy network' that informal network of cooperative relationships, that works silently but diligently. Friendships, help from colleagues, customers, superiors, and developmental assignments—these are the keys to success" (Cox-Burton, 1988, 41).

Northern States Power Company

Northern States Power Company (NSP) serves 1.7 million gas and electric customers in parts of Minnesota, Wisconsin, North and South Dakota, and Michigan's Upper Peninsula. Its diversity initiatives, as described by Nancy Weidenfeller (1992), director of workforce services, can serve as a benchmark for health care organizations as they implement changes that reflect the valuing diversity paradigm:

1. Commitment to diversity begins at the top with chairperson and CEO James J. Howard. CEO Howard personally took the lead in communicating diversity as a company priority. Diversity must be addressed as an essential component of every business plan at the company.

2. NSP's precept is that its 7,100 employees should mirror the population in its service areas.

3. Diversity is a major focus of NSP's strategic plan.

4. Rewards and advancement at NSP depend, in part, on an employee's contribution to the achievement of NSP's diversity goals. Annual employee performance reviews include an assessment of how well the employee creates an environment that cultivates workforce diversity and measures each person's active participation in meeting departmental goals.

5. Contribution to diversity initiatives is factored into the selection of candidates for promotion into management and to identify those managers who will become the future officers and executives of the company. Diversity is a "genuine bottom-line issue" for employees.

6. In 1990, NSP established a companywide diversity council whose 15 volunteer members work with more than 36

diversity coordinators in all operating units to identify potential barriers to the effective performance of a diverse workforce. CEO Howard participates actively in the council.

7. NSP has increased its contracting with women and minority business. The 1991 level of such contracting was four times the level in 1988.

8. Programs such as maternity and paternity leave, child and elder care referral programs, flexible hours and job sharing, sick child care, and adoption assistance were instituted.

9. NSP and several other large Minneapolis-area employers entered into a cooperative agreement with the school system to plan and fund a "downtown open school" near its headquarters for children in kindergarten through the second grade. NSP employees whose children attend say that the school has been a major factor in enabling them to continue their employment.

NSP's efforts have resulted in an increasingly diverse workforce: 7 percent of NSP's employees are racial minorities, compared to 5.4 percent in the Minneapolis–St. Paul service area; 23 percent of NSP's employees are women, with an increasing percentage of women holding nontraditional jobs; nearly one in every four meter-readers is a woman; more than 15 percent of bargaining unit labor positions such as coal and ash handlers and warehouse workers are filled by women. Weidenfeller (1992, 22) concludes that, "Ultimately, diversity—with all its many positive implications—simply makes good business sense."

Security Pacific Bancorporation Northwest

In a *Healthcare Forum Journal* article, Shea and Okada (1992) suggest that the award-winning diversity leadership program at Security Pacific Bancorporation Northwest, a Seattle-based multibank holding company and an affiliate of Security Pacific Corporation, the nation's fifth largest banking company, is a model for health care organizations. This program began in 1988 with a 19-member multilevel task force appointed by the chair to explore issues surrounding diversity and make recommendations for action. The task force recommended five goals, and then Security Pacific hired a diversity manager to develop and implement an action plan to achieve the goals. The goals, as outlined by Shea and Okada (1992), were:

1. Develop a program to communicate the diversity mission throughout the organization.

2. Create an organization-wide system of career development and training to ensure employee development (especially of minorities and women).

3. Identify high-potential individuals, including ethnic minorities and women, and develop a program to mentor them into senior positions.

4. Create a diversification plan for all business units. The plan identifies each unit's diversity profile (its employee base, the needs of the publics it serves) and outlines expectations for progress toward improving competitiveness through diversity.

5. Develop a credible evaluation process for a manager's diversity performance and ensure that unit managers are rewarded for superior results. Each manager sets annual diversity goals and is measured against these goals throughout the year (pp. 25–26).

Shea, a consultant with the Hay Group, and Okada, vice president and diversity manager of Security Pacific Bancorporation (1992), advise health care organizations to tailor a diversity program to their organization and to have business reasons for diversity leadership. Health care organizations, explain Shea and Okada (1992), must make a long-term commitment, tie rewards to performance, and make line management—not human resources—responsible for the program.

MORE CHANGES IN HUMAN RESOURCES MANAGEMENT

Changes in human resource management, as evidenced by the experience of the companies whose initiatives were previously described, must be fundamental and far-reaching if organizational transformation is to occur. This section provides some additional suggestions for change in health care organizations that wish to reflect the valuing diversity paradigm.

Results of a recent survey demonstrate the increasingly widespread commitment of a broad spectrum of organizations to change in human resource management. Over 400 Society for Human Resource Management members were surveyed, and representatives of health care organizations were included in the sample. The survey found that in nearly one of every three of the respondents' companies, managers were held accountable for increasing diversity in the managerial ranks, and an additional 65.5 percent said they needed such an accountability for performance policy; 58 percent of the organizations surveyed had minority internships, and nearly 42 percent encouraged networking among minority groups (Rosen and Lovelace 1991).

Health care organizations can assess their diversity leadership performance against results of surveys like this. Additional avenues to pursue for health care organizations that are moving from an affirmative action to a valuing diversity paradigm follow:

Establish Support Groups

One successful retention strategy is to form support groups for minority workers (Schwartz and Sullivan 1993); these are particularly effective within health care organizations that are just beginning to recruit for diversity.

Dr. Schmieding (1991) describes how the formation of a minority nurse group aided in recruitment, retention, and advancement of minority nurses in a midwestern health care organization. Minority nurses constituted 7 percent of the 1,500 nurses in the health care organization, 3 percent of the head nurses were minority group members; and there were no minority clinical nurse specialists and few minorities in administration; and minorities made up about 47 percent of all patients (Schmieding 1991). Clearly, the workforce and the customer base demographics were distinctly different.

The majority of the support group members in this particular hospital were black, but there were also Asian, Latino, and white members. The group reviewed representation of minorities in the health care organization's publications and found that minorities constituted only 12 percent of the people portrayed in the photographs and were seen in a dominant position about 7 percent of the time in two-person photos. With hospital funding, the group sent a representative to the National Black Nurses Association's national convention, and two minority clinical nurse specialists and a minority staff development instructor were hired as a result of the group's efforts (Schmieding 1991).

Support groups such as this one not only provide needed camaraderie for employees who share a particular dimension of diversity, but also benefit the health care organization as a valuable resource for ideas as well as assistance with implementation of diversity-friendly changes in human resource management, customer relations, and patient care.

Customize Diversity Initiatives

One size doesn't fit all when it comes to implementing human resource management practices that adjust to a diverse workforce. Each dimension of diversity produces a different set of needs and preferences with respect to management practices, benefits packages, and job design. Tailor your programs to the unique needs of your workforce.

In some health care organizations, for example, sexual orientation is a dimension of diversity that requires focused attention and change in practices of the health care organization. Several hospitals have extended benefits to the domestic partners of their gay and lesbian employees. David Jones, president of United Hospital in St. Paul, feels that such changes are an inevitable consequence of diversity leadership.

Gays and lesbians, older workers, single parents, Latinos, African Americans, and the disabled are among the diverse groups your health care organization may need to specifically consider as you explore alternative practices in human resource management. As health care organizations deal with today's workforce diversity, keep one eye on the future and be prepared to change focus as the diversity of the organization's employee base continually changes.

Consider Job Redesign

Health care facilities tend to be hierarchical in organization design and relatively inflexible in job design. Tradition and historical precedence as well as licensure requirements that restrict particular tasks to certain classes of caregivers have served to limit flexibility. Even in the context of these constraints, alternatives are available to health care organizations that wish to redesign jobs. Age, physical ability, and communication style are among the factors that may call for job redesign, which is also an essential component of the current movement to patient-focused care.

Health care organizations such as Yale–New Haven Hospital are emphasizing the connection between diversity leadership and job redesign as they explore and implement patient-focused care. Purposeful overlap is designed into the jobs of patient care team members. Interdependence is encouraged, and meeting the needs of the patients becomes the primary concern, with status, roles, and job descriptions becoming secondary in importance.

Yale–New Haven Hospital's patient-focused operational redesign (PFOR) goes hand in hand with diversity leadership, according to Pat Burke and Pat Worthy. Ms. Burke and Mrs. Worthy are staff support to the hospital's redesign effort. Pat Worthy is a black registered nurse, and Pat Burke is a white human resources professional. Both are also graduates of the intensive consulting pairs diversity training program in place at Yale–New Haven Hospital.

Yale–New Haven Hospital's PFOR approach teams registered nurses with patient care, environmental, and business associates. Environmental associates are primarily responsible for functions such as transportation, supplies, equipment, and housekeeping, while patient care associates handle certain nonlicensed patient care functions, as well as phlebotomy and EKG; the role of a business associate is primarily clerical, encompassing the former unit secretary function.

As in the majority of our nation's urban health care organizations, Yale–New Haven's service workers—patient care and environmental and business associates—are disproportionately black and Latino and live in the local community, while the registered nurses are predominantly white women who live in white neighborhoods. Environmental associates are predominantly men.

Pat Worthy and Pat Burke are enthusiastic when they describe the growing cross-cultural awareness that is evidenced by PFOR team members. Yale's PFOR design focuses on team rather than individual performance, is patient- rather than caregiver-centered, and includes a purposeful overlap in the duties and functions of PFOR team members. Communication among nurses, patient care associates, and employees in other new roles on the PFOR units has improved. Pat Worthy describes one incident where a young white female nurse, realizing that the male Latino environmental associate on her team was busy, transported a patient herself.

Assumptions about commitment to the job, previously held but not spoken, are now being openly discussed and resolved. Prior to PFOR, explains Worthy, a white nurse saw a black unit housekeeper staring out the window seemingly doing nothing and pointed this out to Worthy. The nurse assumed that the unit housekeeper was trying to get out of work, but when Worthy asked the housekeeper what she was doing, she learned that the housekeeper's supervisor scheduled breaks to be taken at a particular time or not at all, which explained the housekeeper's apparent inactivity. There were many such preconceived assumptions operating prior to PFOR, but since PFOR, team building and the consulting pairs diversity training program are helping to address issues that might interfere with patient care and PFOR teamwork or reinforce racist stereotypes.

Rethink Compensation and Job Redesign

Changes in compensation, when combined with increased flexibility in job design, can help organizations develop the skills and adaptability of their current workforce:

> A potential shortage of workers requires employers to build a versatile, flexible labor force through cross-training and compensation systems that encourage employees to develop skills beyond those required for their own jobs. One technique to achieve this goal is a "pay for skill" compensation system. The employee's compensation is increased when he or she demonstrates proficiency at each progressive skill level, allowing employees to be rewarded for what they know and what they can do, as well as giving them incentive to grow (Wozniak 1991, 22).

In health care organizations, new approaches to organization and job design, such as those motivated by movement to a patient-centered care approach, afford valuable opportunities for health care executives to make changes that are diversity-friendly and provide a career ladder for the organization's service workers.

Like other businesses, health care organizations are becoming flatter, and opportunities for advancement will increasingly involve lateral movement rather than promotion to the next rung of a hierarchical organizational ladder. In the flatter and leaner organizations of the future, diversity leaders will face new challenges (Kanin-Lovers 1990):

- Determining and managing salaries will be increasingly challenging in reengineered organizations.

- Appropriate compensation can be difficult to determine for employees 'promoted' laterally due to increased technical expertise.

- Job rotation, wherein workers perform a number of different jobs, creates staffing flexibility for the manager and the worker but presents a challenge for the human resource manager who needs to set compensation based on internal and external equity.

- Classification of people who participate in job rotation is based on the depth and breadth of their skill and knowledge base, not their job classification, making it increasingly difficult to conduct valid market-based studies of equity.

- Increasingly, employees of health care organizations and others will work outside of the office, or will share jobs or work flexible schedules. Under such circumstances should the organization pay by project completed or by type of work done? (Kanin-Lovers 1990) Should at-home workers be paid the same as office workers? (Kanin-Lovers 1990) These and other vexing questions will confront the diversity leader in the health care organization of the future.

Salary surveys to assess external equity must be broadened to allow for more flexible job boundaries (Kanin-Lovers 1990). Encouraging employees to develop their skills will be essential. One technique, **vertical skill development,** requires that the organization establish a technical career ladder. Employees move up the ladder as they develop new skills, and compensation increases with each rung of the ladder. Another technique is **horizontal skill development,** which allows for advancement and increased compensation as the breadth of the employee's expertise in one area increases. Some organizations, explains Kanin-Lovers (1990) reward skill development with bonuses instead of increases to base pay, thereby avoiding the long-term effect that increases in base salary have on the organization's operating expenses.

Retool the Organizational Reward System

The more diverse the workers, the more they are motivated by different incentives or rewards. Health care organizations that value diversity tailor rewards to the worker's preferences. As Vroom's (1964) well-known expectancy theory of motivation explains, different outcomes or rewards are associated with different **valences** for workers. Workers must, according to Vroom's model, believe that their efforts will result in high performance *and* believe that high performance will lead to a reward that they value in order to motivate behavior.

Human resource management practices in health care organizations that value diversity require clear performance standards and a visible link between valued rewards and desired performance. Many well-meaning diversity efforts have been derailed by organizations' failure to link rewards to desired behavior. Patient-focused care, for example, requires teamwork as a desired behavior. Rewards, therefore, must reinforce teamwork, not just individual accomplishment.

Health care organizations that practice diversity leadership are evaluating their current reward systems and are instituting policies that reinforce diversity leadership and recognize that diverse workers value different rewards.

Institute Mentoring Programs

Health care organizations that value diversity institute formal mentoring programs. At the same time, health care executives who value diversity understand that formal mentoring programs cannot "fix" the inability or unwillingness of managers to truly mentor anyone who is not like them.

Formal mentoring programs are just one piece of the diversity leadership puzzle. Mentoring programs go hand in hand with succession planning and emphasize the importance of creating and maintaining a career ladder. Health care organizations can model their programs on those of the corporate diversity pioneers previously described.

Promotion from within can be an especially effective strategy for the diversity leader. When combined with tuition reimbursement and mentoring programs, such a policy can be an effective approach to increasing the diversity of the organization's professional and technical workforce while filling positions in allied health professions where national shortages exist. For example, although occupational therapists are predominantly white, occupational therapy assistants are generally more racially and ethnically diverse.

Too often mentoring and career development are thought to be only for younger workers. As Anthony Buonocore (1992b, 55) explains, "The word 'young' with respect to individuals, connotes chronological age. By definition, the older employee is certainly not young. However, young also may be defined as 'being in the early or undeveloped period of growth,' and that definition can be just as appropriate for an older employee."

Buonocore (1992b) compares the mentoring needs of the older worker to the mentoring needs implicit in MIT professor Edgar Schein's definition of early career development as the process of finding a "career anchor." Buonocore (1992b, 55) explains that "the person who undergoes a period of mid-life reflection often develops new motives, needs and values. And yet it is the rare organization that embarks on a new program of mutual discovery to determine what might be the best path for that employee to follow to establish a new anchor." Career development, Buonocore (1992b) says, should be thought of as a lifelong process.

Health care organizations that value diversity do not restrict mentoring to just younger employees, and they acknowledge that workers who wish to move laterally rather than vertically can also benefit from mentoring programs. Job rotation or exchange programs are human resource strategies that can encourage career development and help older or underrepresented workers expand their horizons.

A U.S. Department of Labor study of the glass ceiling phenomenon in corporate America found that the ceiling was lower than previously thought, and that minorities plateaued at lower levels than women (Zachiariasiewicz 1993). The glass ceiling can feel like a cement wall to people of color or like a mountain to disabled people. Formal mentoring programs are among the strategies that can held eradicate institutional barriers to the optimal achievement of a diverse workforce.

Expand the Flexibility of Benefits

As family structure changes and the workforce becomes more diverse, flexible benefits become increasingly important. Demographic trends such as the following are reported in *Employee Benefit Plan Review* (1989) and continue today: the median age of mothers giving birth for the first time is increasing. By 1987, 56 percent of women with preschool children were in the workforce, and 73 percent of married women with school-age children held jobs outside the home. Between 1985–2000, the over-age-85 population is expected to grow from 2.8 million to almost 5 million, putting increasing demands on middle-age working women who also act as the primary caregivers for their aging parents.

Health care organizations, with a predominantly female workforce, must be especially responsive to the needs of working women. Expanding the flexibility of benefits is among the strategies being implemented by health care organizations that value diversity.

Ensure a Climate That Values Diversity

Although organizational climate was discussed extensively in Part 2, its fundamental importance justifies mentioning it again here. A study of homophobia among physicians and nurses in a large urban teaching hospital reemphasizes the importance of organizational climate to diversity leadership.

Douglas, Kalman, and Kalman (1985) studied 91 interns and residents and 261 registered nurses in a large urban teaching hospital. Respondents completed an Index of Homophobia scale (IHP), a 21-item self-administered, Likert-type instrument. Homophobia, in terms of the scale, is defined as "the constellation of affective responses, including fear, disgust, anger, discomfort, and aversion, that individuals may experience in contacts with homosexuals" (Douglas, Kalman, and Kalman 1985).

The study showed that mean scores for both doctors and nurses fell in the low-grade homophobic range with no significant differences between nurses and doctors. Approximately 31 percent of the respondents said they felt more negatively about homosexuality since the emergence of AIDS and almost one in ten agreed with the statement that homosexuals who get AIDS are "getting what they deserve" (Douglas, Kalman, and Kalman 1985). Results of studies like these highlight the challenges faced by health care executives who are charged with developing an institutional climate that values diversity. And those organizations that value diversity make a commitment to periodic assessment of their diversity climate, using the tools and techniques described in Part 2.

Recall the Chapter 8 discussion of how behavior is much more amenable to change than are beliefs or feelings. In response to its diversity climate assessment, United Hospital and Children's Health Care–St. Paul adopted a general harassment policy that prohibits hostile, abusive, or disrespectful behavior in the workplace, thereby targeting behavior, not beliefs or feelings. A formal harassment policy is one approach to creating an institutional climate that is comfortable for diverse workers.

Conflicts between nurses and physicians are often complicated by accusations of sexism and well-documented gender differences in communication style and intent (Tannen 1990), especially since the vast majority of practicing nurses are women and practicing physicians are men. Katzman and Roberts (1988) present results of a study of physician-nurse conflict conducted in a 350-bed, nonprofit, nonsectarian hospital in the northeastern United States. The researchers observed 14 women nurses in traditional nursing roles and 11 women nurse practitioners. Subjects ranged in age from 22 to 60. Their qualitative analysis of data collected through observational and interview techniques reveal that

> Contrary to the hopes and the predictions of nursing leaders, the innovative functions of nurses in expanded roles have not prevented the common problems of discrimination they share with nurses in traditional roles. For example, the nurse practitioners in this study had exhibited traditional behaviors, such as deference to males and passivity, and they expressed feelings of inferiority to physicians. On an overt level, the nurse practitioners were

largely unaware of these behaviors, so counterproductive to their professional goals. And so, two groups of health professionals—male physicians and female nurses—come together daily for the common purpose of patient care. . . . They are dependent on one another; yet they often fail to communicate directly. When direct communication does occur, the male physician dominates the subservient, female nurse. In general, physicians are bosses; nurses take orders . . . if stereotypical sex or gender role relationships are unrecognized and unresolved, conflict and controversy will continue (Katzman and Roberts 1988, 588–589).

Nurse-physician relationships are just one of the many challenges facing the diversity leader. Involving physicians in the process of diversity assessment, training, and change is a key factor in creating and maintaining a positive diversity climate.

Understand Interpersonal Communication Style and Diversity Climate

Diverse workers bring with them differences in communication style. These differences can and do influence employees' comfort with and perception of the quality of the climate in health care organizations. In addition, employees' success in progressing vertically or laterally in the organization is also affected by these differences.

Edward T. Hall's (Hall and Hall 1990) framework for describing certain key differences in communication style was presented and related to the health care industry in Chapter 4. Ethnographic researchers have documented communication differences between racial, ethnic, or gender groups that can produce conflict in the context of cross-cultural communication. Cross-cultural communication is increasingly common in today's health care organizations.

Dr. Thomas Kochman, sociologist and president of Kochman Communication Consultants, Ltd., is author of the book, *Black and White Styles in Conflict* (1981), which presents key dimensions of communication along which black and white communicators differ and describes the potential for conflict around communication intent that such differences present. Kochman and his colleagues have since expanded his ethnographic study of black and white communication style differences to include Latino and Asian styles.

Health care executives who value diversity will familiarize themselves and their staff with such differences in communication style, sometimes referred to as **ethnic markers**. It is important to remember, however, that there is a wider range of differences within than between groups in communication style. Health care executives who value diversity are careful not to use new information about ethnic markers and communication style to stereotype individuals based on their group memberships.

Like research and development groups, transdisciplinary health care teams are composed of professionals who are well versed in their fields and must cooperate to accomplish a goal. One study of diversity management in research and development groups is especially relevant to diversity leaders in health care organizations who are exploring the linkages between communication style and organizational climate. The study was conducted in 1989 in five major research laboratories in four states, three of which were in the Northeast, representing the communications, petroleum, laser technology, and electronics industries, among others (Gordon, DiTomaso, and Farris 1991). In each company, two focus groups— one homogeneous with respect to race, ethnicity, gender, and national origin, and one heterogeneous on the same dimensions, were formed. Each group consisted of six to eight members of the technical staff. The focus groups discussed these areas: the expectations of managers, one's peers and subordinates, communication, conflict and cooperation, career plans and paths, coordination of work and family life, cultural and subcultural styles of interaction, as well as norms and values. Between five and six managers were also interviewed at each company.

The study revealed that nonwhite men complained that a particular style was being "looked for" and that "if you didn't exhibit it, you weren't given the good assignments." Women and minorities both reported making comments in meetings and work groups that were ignored until repeated by a white man (Gordon, DiTomaso, and Farris 1991).

The communication style that was rewarded, according to focus group participants and managers who were interviewed, consisted of behaviors such as: taking the initiative to seek help, defending ideas to peers and management, writing up and publicizing one's own work, and aggressively pursuing the type of experiences that might help them develop as professionals. Focus group participants agreed that women, racial and ethnic minorities born in the United States, and immigrants were less likely than native-born white men to exhibit the rewarded style. The researchers attributed this to cultural differences in preferred communication style (Gordon, DiTomaso, and Farris 1991).

Managers in health care organizations that value diversity must adopt performance evaluation methods and offer opportunities for growth to employees on the basis of substance and accomplishment, rather than style. Some suggestions for action that are designed to invite and accept communication from diverse workers in a variety of styles (Johnson 1992) are presented, having been gleaned from discussions with Lewis Griggs, producer of the seven-part "Valuing Diversity" videotape series (one of which, "Communicating Across Cultures," presents a series of vignettes that deal specifically with cross-cultural communication). Suggestions for action include the following:

1. Change communication rules to accommodate diverse styles and inform workers of the organization's preferred communication style.

2. Rethink the definition of a meeting. For example, are certain types of people being excluded from important but informal opportunities to communicate in the hallway or during lunch?

3. Review the time and setting for meetings. Do meetings inadvertently exclude certain people? For example, are meetings held in bars, or do they conflict with religious holidays?

4. Review aspects of meetings such as seating arrangements, refreshments, the procedure by which a leader or facilitator is chosen, and the relative importance of punctuality. Consider the effect of these factors on diverse employees. How is setting used to communicate relative status?

5. Reconsider procedures and decision rules commonly used in meetings. For example, who initiates conversation, who asks questions, how are interruptions handled, and what are the rules for brainstorming?

6. Test communication assumptions and rules. For example, how are speakers of English-as-a-second-language perceived, what nonverbal messages are being conveyed through gestures or body language, and when is it acceptable to use a language other than English in the workplace?

Health care executives must be cognizant of these differences as well and communicate with workers in styles and through media that will most effectively carry the message. Preferred communication style differs not only by gender, race, and ethnicity, but by other dimensions of diversity, such as employee age. In fact, Towers Perrin's Workforce 2000 research uncovered important differences in communication preferences by age group. Age groups studied were as follows: radio babies, with birthdates between 1924 and 1942; TV babies, with birthdates between 1942 and 1960; and computer babies, born between 1961 and 1979 (Nies 1991). Radio babies and computer babies each represent 25 percent of the workforce, while TV babies comprise the remaining 50 percent (Nies 1991).

The communication media preferences uncovered by the Nies (1991) study were: radio babies prefer print media, while TV babies prefer video, and computer babies interactive media: computer babies prefer one-on-one meetings, while TV babies prefer small group meetings, and radio babies are most comfortable with mass meetings; radio babies prefer question and answer sessions, TV babies listening, and computer babies involvement.

As a result of these findings, Nies (1991, 29) says of the task of the diversity leader: "The challenge you have is to reach all employees with effective media and methods to help them achieve the organization's goals, as well as their own individual goals. To do this, you'll need to understand each group's orientation." Health care executives who value diversity are learning about all types of differences and similarities in communication style and are using their knowledge to alter standard operating procedures in order to communicate more effectively.

REENGINEERING: THE IMPACT OF VALUING DIVERSITY

Health care providers are increasingly engaged in reengineering—moving from a task to a process focus, from a provider to a patient focus. **Reengineering,** as described by the approach's originator, Dr. Michael Hammer and his colleague, James Champy (1993), involves transformation of organizations that were designed in accordance with Adam Smith's fundamental principle of greater productivity and efficiency through the division of labor. Mass production, in health care as well as other industries, is giving way to individualized customer service. Departmental structures are giving way to organizational designs that are structured around processes such as patient-focused care.

Reengineering has involved fundamental restructuring and, in the short run, has necessitated downsizing or rightsizing, particularly on the inpatient side of health care delivery, which represents a declining proportion of the business of health care providers. Many organizations, in health care as well as other industries, have rightsized largely through early retirement and other approaches aimed at the long-term, older employee—that is, Nies' (1991) radio babies.

Eliminating older workers may produce a short-term gain at the expense of long-term problems. As labor shortages increase, traditional new entrants to the labor force decline in numbers, and the skills gap increases, short-term gains may appear decidedly short-sighted. In an article entitled, "Older and Wiser: Senior Employees Offer Untapped Capabilities," Anthony J. Buonocore (1992a) offers some alternative approaches to managing older workers in this era of downsized, reengineered organizations. Among the strategies he recommends are retirement rehearsal where employees, with the right to return, can try out retirement to see if they like it, elimination of mandatory retirement age, and the adoption of programs to employ retirees part-time during peak periods (Buonocore 1992a).

Health care organizations that value diversity must also ensure that downsizing and reengineering do not disproportionately disadvantage particular groups. For example, Alvin R. Johnson, vice president of employee relations at Yale–New Haven Hospital, explains that the hospital's initial design for patient-focused care involved changing a number of service worker roles from full- to part-time. The hospital retooled the design so that the costs of reengineering would not be disproportionately felt by lower-income minority workers from the hospital's local community.

Reengineering and, in the short run, downsizing, are necessary responses to a changing health care marketplace. Health care executives who value diversity will consider the impact of reengineering and downsizing on diverse groups of workers and on the organization's long-term needs.

THE CHANGING ROLE OF HUMAN RESOURCE MANAGEMENT

The human resource function plays a central role in diversity leadership, as it did in the earlier era of EEO/AA. One key indication of the success of diversity leadership is when operations, not human resources, takes ownership of the issue. Human resource's task is to facilitate this transition.

Effective diversity leadership requires a transformation such as this: a vision of change in the human resource function from "a personnel management system focused on paper to a human resource management system focused on people. Facilitating the continued growth and development of individual workers will be a major objective. In this scenario, personnelists will become full human resource partners with line managers, especially with regard to organizational strategic planning" (Teasley and Williams 1991, 137).

DIVERSITY LEADERSHIP AND TQM/CQI

Diversity leadership is essential to effective implementation of TQM/CQI, management approaches that are the cornerstone of the Joint Commission on Accreditation of Healthcare Organizations (JCAHO) Agenda for Change. As discussed in Chapter 4, the teamwork involved in worker empowerment and implementation of TQM will cause diversity issues to surface, and these must be addressed if TQM/CQI are to be effectively used as management strategies.

Determining the reasons for special cause variation cannot occur in an atmosphere of mistrust. Successful implementation of TQM/CQI requires a focus on improving processes rather than blaming departments or individuals. Service workers, nurses, physicians, and administrators must work as a team to uncover and address problems that affect the quality of care and other aspects of service delivery in health care organizations. Health care organizations, which tend to be segregated by discipline along significant and sensitive dimensions of diversity such as race, ethnicity, gender, and social class, must recognize that diversity leadership and TQM/CQI are complementary processes.

ROLE OF THE CEO IN THE CHANGE PROCESS

David M. Jones, president of United Hospital in St. Paul, Minnesota, sees his role as a model and facilitator, not an enforcer, of diversity leadership: "If you have a process that is driven from the top as a directive, if you order employees to value diversity, you will be ineffective," explains Jones. "Our process is employee-driven, and the focus is on involvement. Administration provides support and shares leadership with our employees. The diversity agenda at United Hospital was set by the employees themselves."

Brock Nelson, CEO of Children's Health Care, whose St. Paul campus shares a building with United Hospital, concurs: "The fuel that drives our diversity initiative has been the employees." It is important that employees see the CEO model behavior that is consistent with the message being stated. The CEO cannot be perceived as giving double messages about the value of diversity. One of the ways in which Nelson "walks his talk" is through attending and actively participating in diversity awareness training. The CEO, Nelson emphasizes, must be a truth-teller; this involves having a personal understanding of diversity and the process of cross-cultural communication and change.

Visible personal support and involvement in diversity leadership by the CEO, coupled with employee-driven diversity agendas, are key to the change process.

BACK TO THE BEGINNING

Changes in human resource management like those discussed in this chapter are means not ends. The desired end is the highest possible quality of care delivered to the patient. Improved health status in the community, patient loyalty, and patient satisfaction are among the key measures of a health care organization's success.

Even the most committed change agent or health care organization can become "battle weary." Diversity leadership is a process that is never finished, presenting the challenge of entropy to diversity's strongest advocates. Diversity leadership can be likened to peeling an onion: every time you think you're finished, there is another layer of issues, and more tears to be shed.

How do diversity leaders keep themselves and the health care organizations they serve energized for the long haul? The final section of this book, Part 5: Revitalization, addresses this question by discussing the challenge of entropy and the process of continual renewal.

REFERENCES

Boss, R. W., L. S. Boss, M. W. Dundon, and A. E. Johnson 1989. "A Crisis in Nursing: The Impact of OD as a Remedy." *Public Administration Quarterly* 13 (1): 140–55.

Buonocore, A. J. 1992a. "Older and Wiser: Senior Employees Offer Untapped Capabilities." *Management Review* 81 (7): 49–52.

———. 1992b. "Older and Wiser: Mature Employees and Career Guidance." *Management Review* 81 (9): 54–57.

Caudron, S. 1992. "U S West Finds Strength in Diversity." *Personnel Journal* 71 (3): 40–43.

Cox, H. C. 1987. "Verbal Abuse in Nursing: Report of a Study." *Nursing Management* 18 (11): 47–50

Cox, T. 1993. *Cultural Diversity in Organizations: Theory, Research, and Practice.* San Francisco: Berrett-Koehler.

Cox-Burton, J. 1988. "Leadership in the Future—A Quality Issue." *Advanced Management Journal* 53 (4): 39–43.

Douglas, C. J., C. M. Kalman, and T. P. Kalman. 1985. "Homophobia among Physicians and Nurses: An Empirical Study." *Hospital and Community Psychiatry* 36 (12): 1309–11.

Droste, T. 1987. "High Price Tag on Nursing Recruitment." *Hospitals* 61 (19): 150.

Employee Benefit Plan Review. 1989. "Demographics: Driving Force behind Flexible Plans." *Employee Benefit Plan Review* 43 (10): 14–16.

Geber, B. 1990. "Managing Diversity." *Training* 27 (7): 23–30.

Gordon, G. G., N. DiTomaso, and G. F. Farris. 1991. "Managing Diversity in R&D Groups." *Research Technology Management* 34 (1): 18–23.

Hall, E. T., and M. R. Hall. 1990. *Understanding Cultural Differences.* Yarmouth, ME: Intercultural Press.

Hammer, M., and J. Champy. 1993. *Reengineering the Corporation: A Manifesto for Business Revolution.* New York: Harper-Collins.

Johnson, V. 1992. "Workforce Diversity: Creating a Meeting Environment Where Everyone Can Be Productive." *Successful Meetings* 41 (5): 122–26.

Kanin-Lovers, J. 1990. "Meeting the Challenge of Workforce 2000." *Journal of Compensation and Benefits* 5 (4): 233–36.

Katzman, E. M., and J. I. Roberts. 1988. "Nurse-Physician Conflicts as Barriers to the Enactment of Nursing Roles." *Western Journal of Nursing Research* 10 (5): 576–90.

Kochman, T. 1981. *Black and White Styles in Conflict.* Chicago: University of Chicago Press.

Meisenheimer, J. R. 1990. "Employee Absences in 1989: A New Look at Data from the CPS." *Monthly Labor Review* 113 (8): 28–33.

Mercer, M. W. 1988. "Turnover: Reducing the Costs." *Personnel* 65 (12): 36–42.

Nies, M. C. 1991. "Baby Talk Helps Bridge Generation Gaps." *Communication World* 8 (12): 27–29.

Piturro, M., and S. S. Mahoney 1991. "Managing Diversity." *Executive Female* 14 (3): 45–48.

Rosen, B., and K. Lovelace 1991. "Piecing Together the Diversity Puzzle." *HRMagazine* 36 (6): 78–84.

Schmieding, N. J. 1991. "A Novel Approach to Recruitment, Retention, and Advancement of Minority Nurses in a Health Care Organization." *Nursing Administration Quarterly* 15 (4): 69–76.

Schwartz, R. I., and D. B. Sullivan. 1993. "Managing Diversity in Hospitals." *Health Care Management Review* 18 (2): 51–56.

Shea, S., and R. K. Okada. 1992. "Benefiting from Workforce Diversity." *Healthcare Forum Journal* 35 (1): 23–26.

Solomon, C. M. 1989. "The Corporate Response to Work Force Diversity." *Personnel Journal* 68 (8): 43–53.

Tannen, D. 1990. *You Just Don't Understand: Women and Men in Conversation.* New York: Ballantine Books.

Teasley, C. E., and L. Williams 1991. "The Future Is Nearly Now: Managing Personnel in the Twenty-First Century." *Review of Public Personnel Administration* 11 (1–2): 131–38.

Vroom, V. H. 1964. *Work and Motivation.* New York: John Wiley & Sons.

Wall Street Journal. 1993. "Seeking Minority Talent for Higher Levels." 26 January.

Weidenfeller, N. 1992. "Celebrating Diversity." *Public Utilities Fortnightly* 129 (12): 20–22.

Wozniak, T. 1991. "Attracting and Retaining the 'Baby Bust' Generation." *Journal of Compensation and Benefits* 6 (5): 20–24.

Zachariasiewicz, R. 1993. "Breaking the Glass Ceiling: A Review of U. S. Department of Labor Efforts." *Credit World* 81 (5): 21–23.

PART V

Revitalization

I t is well after dark, and CEO Bryant is sitting alone in his office, holding his head in his hands, feeling tired and dejected. He's been feeling like this a lot lately, and he knows that he isn't alone. His vice president of human resources and several of the long-term members of the center's diversity action team also seem to have lost their enthusiasm. Even his recent vacation didn't produce the renewed sense of energy he so desperately needs.

Bryant has seen this happen before with other change initiatives. People, and ultimately the organization itself, seem to reach a point where the energy and the will to move forward dissipate. Bryant turns off the light and slowly heads out the door, shaking his head and mumbling, "Something has to be done. We need a burst of energy from somewhere."

CHAPTER 11

The Challenge of Overcoming Entropy and Revitalizing

DIVERSITY LEADERSHIP is a continual process of transformation and change. Realization follows realization, and each new insight produces more changes in the values, beliefs, and behaviors of individuals and organizations. The process of organizational or personal transformation and change "combines false starts with striking success and order with confusion. The change process can be replete with lapses and relapses, often defying a rational model which would have the change-maker stepping easily from goal clarity into action" (Gross 1994, 89).

The process, while exciting and enlightening, is also difficult and can result in organizational or personal entropy. When entropy is followed by revitalization, the change process moves participants to new levels of understanding and expression. However, if the health care organization or its change agents remain in entropy too long, the commitment to diversity leadership can wither on the vine and relapse is likely to occur.

What is entropy, and why does it occur? How can diversity leaders recognize entropy in themselves, others, and the health care organization? Are there strategies to lessen the depth and duration of entropy—to revitalize change agents and the organization? This chapter addresses these questions.

ENTROPY

Transformation, change, and the establishment of a new order precede entropy in the change process. Transformation, discussed in Chapter 8, moves organizations and individuals from "not knowing that they don't know" to "knowing that they don't know" (Davis 1982). Transformed organizations and individuals then cross the boundary path (Dreachslin, Kobrinski, and Passen 1994) between the known and the unknown, the familiar and the unfamiliar. When the boundary path is crossed, the traveler has moved from order to chaos, and it is from the chaos that a new order will emerge. Chaos is described as:

> A state of flux—the eruption of the tension to both resist and move toward change, which upsets the status quo. A sudden disarrangement of what was previously known occurs, along with the disappearance of the prior predictability—the familiar has become strange. In chaos we may experience heightened fear about the loss of security, or anger over the change imposed, or sadness over the loss of an imagined future (Gross 1994, 101).

The changes that follow transformation and chaos result in the establishment of a new order, which in turn must yield to future cycles of transformation, chaos, and change. **Entropy** is the phase in the change process that follows periods of fundamental cultural transformation. Entropy provides a much-needed hiatus, slowing the process of continuing transformation, change, and individual as well as organizational adaptation. Entropy manifests itself as a period of stagnation, disinterest, and active questioning.

Webster's Unabridged Dictionary defines entropy as "a thermodynamic measure of the amount of energy unavailable for useful work in a system undergoing change" and further states that "entropy always increases as the available energy diminishes in a closed system, as the universe." Entropy is to be expected in organizations, groups, and individuals who have expended significant levels of energy and resources into redesigning practices, procedures, and policies.

ENTROPY IN CHANGE AGENTS

Paradoxically, the individuals or groups who were the forerunners of transformation and change, the champions of diversity, are most vulnerable to entropy. Change agents' energy tends to diminish after the organization appears to have gotten the message and is well into the process of implementing a diversity strategy. Entropy is often experienced as burnout by organizational change agents.

Change agents have expended tremendous energy in keeping the organization focused on the need for transformation and change. They have engaged in many struggles, led the organization through the turmoil and confusion of chaos, kept management committed to diversity leadership, and ensured that representatives of both the emerging and the established cultures remained motivated and engaged. It is no wonder that change agents are generally the first to experience entropy.

Champions who invest early on in the process may suddenly find themselves vulnerable to entropy in the form of depression, loss of energy, and disillusionment. The task of guiding the organization through the process of evaluating and altering the ways it deals internally with its human resources and externally with its customer base begins to feel overwhelming and unachievable. Change agents begin to question their commitment to the process of diversity leadership itself and may experience a longing to return to the era that preceded diversity leadership. Champions of diversity may begin asking themselves questions like the following: Why did we do this in the first place? Weren't things easier to manage before we opened up diversity issues? Withdrawal from active involvement in diversity leadership or from the health care organization itself is often the response that change agents make to entropy.

ORGANIZATION-WIDE ENTROPY

Organizations are open, not closed, systems. Consequently, the influx of new energy and the emergence of new champions of diversity is always possible. But, if current diversity leaders are not revitalized and new change agents do not emerge to replace those experiencing entropy, organization-wide entropy can result.

Widespread burnout, relapse as evidenced by the resurgence of old attitudes and behaviors, and the overwhelming pressure of continued challenges to the boundaries of diversity leadership can lead to organizational depression. During the entropy stage, the health care organization's energy is drained, resulting in widespread exhaustion and apathy. The organization can experience **compassion fatigue** (Taylor 1991)—the pressure to understand yet another subculture, to welcome yet another dimension of diversity into the fabric of organizational life, can feel overwhelming.

Entropy in organizations parallels individual and group processes in that it generally follows periods of heightened activity. Health care organizations may experience entropy after serious commitment to diversity leadership has been in place for several years. Some manifestations of organizational entropy follow:

- Employees in the organization appear to be in a rut, complaining of exhaustion and burnout.
- Complaints about services are resurfacing, but from new identity groups.

- Employees seem impervious to the concerns of the new and emerging identity groups.
- Employee reactions to proposed diversity initiatives and concerns appear to be canned, with the perception that "We've been there and done that" being voiced with increasing frequency.
- Excitement about moving forward seems to have diminished and employees reminisce about the past.
- Identity groups that actively fought for their own inclusion become uninvolved or resist the inclusion of new and emerging identity groups.
- Employees express a longing to find similarity and familiarity in a sea of differences.

Visible changes are dramatic; the organization has made great strides in changing the climate and culture, but the energy to maintain a steady course of action has diminished and the employees and the organization have seemingly lost their passion for diversity leadership. Leadership may begin to question the wisdom of its investment of human and financial resources in diversity training and other initiatives. Entropy sometimes manifests as relapse, leading individuals and organizations to question whether change occurred anywhere except in their imaginations. But change *did* occur. Organizations are dynamic systems, and periods in which accomplishment appears to vanish always accompany fundamental shifts in awareness and behavior. The energy to maintain deep structural change is difficult for both individuals and organizations to sustain. Recidivism, or attempts to return to the way things were, can occur when old, familiar ways compete with the desire to sustain new behaviors.

How can momentum be maintained in a context of diminished energy? The seeds of renewal and revitalization are in the morass of organizational depression, making revitalization diversity leadership's new challenge.

REVITALIZATION

Revitalization literally gives new life, vitality, and vigor to diversity leadership. The energy drain experienced during entropy is replaced by a period of reawakening; the energy stores of change agents and the health care organization are replenished and the process of diversity leadership is renewed. Through their actions, leaders can increase the depth and the duration of entropy or speed the transition to revitalization and renewal. Some strategies, culled from the experience of successful change agents and transformed organizations, are presented to help speed the transition from entropy to revitalization.

- **Diversity leaders must accept, and even welcome, entropy as a natural and necessary part of the change process.** Change agents and the health care organization itself must be permitted to experience the diminished energy and enthusiasm as well as the concomitant reduction in diversity-related actions that accompany entropy. The movement to revitalization will not occur in response to guilt, shame, or denial of entropy. Diversity leaders must allow change agents and the health care organization some time away from the process of continual organization and personal change and adaptation. If diversity initiatives temporarily lose their champion, leaders must let the initiatives wither until new champions emerge or new initiatives replace the old. Acceptance of entropy is different from complacency— while accepting entropy as natural and understandable in themselves and others, diversity leaders must provide opportunities for renewal and revitalization. A short-term hiatus could otherwise become permanent, signaling an end to the continual process of diversity leadership.

- **Movement from entropy to revitalization requires an influx of new energy and enthusiasm in individuals and the organization.** While the trigger for renewal is different for each change agent and each health care organization, frequently used strategies include introducing a new and dynamic lecture series, sending change agents to conferences or training seminars where exposure to new ideas can occur, and organizing site visits to other health care organizations that are active in diversity leadership.

- **Change agents or organizations in entropy may rediscover their own lost enthusiasm when offered the opportunity to mentor others who are beginning the process of diversity leadership.** The enthusiasm expressed by beginners is often contagious.

- **The introduction of a new or challenging project has also sparked renewal in change agents and health care organizations.** The new status quo (Gross 1994) can lull individuals and organizations into a complacency that is as ineffective as that which existed before diversity leadership was first introduced. Through the introduction of another initiative, properly timed and resourced, change agents and organizations can be catapulted from entropy to renewal and revitalization.

- **Uncovering the next wave of diversity leaders is key to success.** It's essential that leaders encourage increasing levels of involvement on the part of emerging change agents and highlight and support the new diversity initiatives of individuals and departments that may have stood on the sidelines or have had only peripheral involvement in earlier diversity initiatives.

- **Sometimes it's necessary to recruit change agents from outside the organization.** New hires can provide a fresh perspective on old dilemmas and move the organization from inaction to action, from disillusionment to renewed enthusiasm.

- **Allowing revitalized change agents to re-assume central roles in the process is wise in the long run.** If entropy is viewed as a necessary and natural part of the change process, then those experiencing it are not punished as a consequence.

- **Because people and organizations simultaneously resist and welcome change, it's necessary to provide opportunities for change agents who are experiencing entropy to assume new roles.** A change agent whose work was performed behind the scenes might be offered an opportunity to move to center stage, or vice versa. Role changes can often rekindle enthusiasm and catapult individuals and organizations from entropy to revitalization.

- **Rewarding those who step up to lead the diversity initiatives is key.** Entropy can be reinforced and prolonged by health care organizations that fail to properly recognize and reward change agents. Invite change agents to share your organization's successes and challenges with others. Initiatives that may no longer seem impressive to an internal audience may be recognized as innovative and exciting by outsiders. Enthusiasm, like disillusionment, is contagious.

Strategies such as these allow the natural process of entropy to unfold, but encourage individuals and organizations to move on to renewal and revitalization. Renewal and revitalization are key to effective diversity leadership, which, by nature, is a process rather than an outcome.

Throughout the diversity leadership process, from discovery to revitalization, the role of the CEO is critical. In the next and final chapter, five CEOs share their perspectives on diversity leadership.

REFERENCES ············

Davis, S. M. 1982. "Transforming Organizations: The Key to Strategy Is Context." *Organizational Dynamics* 10 (3): 64–80.

Dreachslin, J. L., E. J. Kobrinski, and A. J. Passen. 1994. "The Boundary Path of Exchange: A New Metaphor for Leadership." *Journal of Leadership and Organization Development* 15 (6): 16–23.

Gross, S. J. 1994. "The Process of Change: Variations on a Theme by Virginia Satir." *Journal of Humanistic Psychology* 34 (3): 87–110.

Taylor, J. 1991. "Don't Blame Me! The New Culture of Victimization." *New York* 24 (22): 26–34.

CHAPTER 12

CEOs' Perspectives on Diversity Leadership

I N T H I S chapter, the following five nationally prominent CEOs share their perspectives on diversity leadership: Thomas Chapman of the George Washington University Hospital in Washington, DC; Pamela Meyer Davis of Edward Hospital in Naperville, Illinois; Consuelo (Connie) Diaz of Rancho Los Amigos Medical Center in Downey, California; Michael Jhin of St. Luke's Episcopal Hospital in Houston, Texas; and David M. Lawrence of the Kaiser Foundation Health Plan, Inc. and Kaiser Foundation Hospitals, headquartered in Oakland, California. These five CEOs, each of whom has over 20 years experience in the health care industry, are themselves a microcosm of America's diversity.

Five open-ended questions were posed to each of the CEOs.

1. Why should the health care executive address diversity?
2. What is the CEO's role in diversity leadership?
3. How and why did you become involved in diversity leadership?
4. Which aspects of diversity are of particular concern in your health care organization and its community?
5. How can executives encourage organization-wide commitment to diversity leadership?

Their answers to these questions provide important personal insights into diversity leadership and follow their brief biographical sketches.

MEET THE CEOS

Thomas Chapman, CEO of the George Washington University Hospital in Washington, DC, has been actively involved in developing and shaping the careers of hundreds of racially and ethnically diverse men and women health care administrators. Chapman, a founder of the Group Health Association of America's managed care fellowship program for minority administrators, is actively involved in working with universities, hospitals, and industry to identify and employ minority talent. Chapman, an African American man, is a Fellow of the American College of Healthcare Executives who earned his M.P.H. from the Yale University School of Public Health.

Pamela Meyer Davis, president and CEO of Edward Hospital in Naperville, Illinois, attributes her interest and involvement in diversity leadership to the personal challenges she faced as an aspiring woman health care administrator. A Fellow of the American College of Healthcare Executives, she has mentored health care administrators from diverse backgrounds as well as designed and implemented innovative approaches to job and organization design that facilitated the advancement of women and men by providing the flexibility to combine active parenthood with career growth. Meyer Davis, a white woman, earned her M.H.A. from the University of Iowa.

Consuelo (Connie) Diaz is CEO of Rancho Los Amigos Medical Center in Downey, California. Diaz's conviction that providers and administrators should mirror the consumer profile has led her to participate in the development, chartering, and growth of programs and organizations that share that objective. She is president of the Association of Hispanic Healthcare Executives. Diaz, an Hispanic woman, earned an M.P.A. in health services administration from the University of Southern California.

Michael Jhin is president and CEO of St. Luke's Episcopal Hospital in Houston, Texas. His personal commitment to diversity leadership is reflected in his role as a mentor to aspiring health care administrators and in his own management style. Jhin is an advocate of "ultimate diversity leadership" through recognizing and rewarding each individual's uniqueness. Jhin, an Asian American man, is a Fellow of the American College of Healthcare Executives and earned his M.B.A. from Boston University.

David M. Lawrence, M.D., is chairman of the board and CEO of Kaiser Foundation Health Plan, Inc. and Kaiser Foundation Hospitals. Lawrence has devoted his career to bringing high-quality and compassionate medical care to a diverse patient mix. He credits his stint in the Peace Corps with piquing his interest in diversity leadership. A white man, Lawrence is a graduate of the University of Kentucky's College of Medicine in Lexington, specializing in internal medicine and pediatrics; he earned his M.P.H. from the University of Washington.

THE CEOS' PERSPECTIVES ON DIVERSITY

Why Should Health Care Executives Address Diversity?

Chapman: It's good for business. The nation's population is becoming more diverse, and there are tremendous talents that can contribute to improved performance of most organizations. It's also the right approach to building a healthy organization.

Meyer Davis: Hospital employees reflect today's workforce by representing various ages, sexes, work values, religions, and cultural backgrounds. By the year 2000, according to the Bureau of Labor Statistics, women will make up 47 percent of workers, and minorities will hold 26 percent of all jobs, up from 22 percent in 1990.

For that reason, it is the responsibility of hospital administration and its management team to create an organizational culture that encourages this diverse group of individuals to work cooperatively toward a common goal of providing high-quality health care at the most cost-effective price.

For hospitals to remain competitive and preserve their viability in the marketplace, they must discover ways to adapt their organizational culture to the emerging demographic realities. People will use hospitals that are responsive to their needs and with which they feel most comfortable. As a result, admissions, patient satisfaction, and financial success will be tied more closely to health care environments that reflect diversity.

Diaz: The pat answer would be "because it is right and just." However, that and 75 cents might get me a good cup of coffee. The only answer that works is that it makes good business sense. For any business to be successful, its sales force must know its market, must understand its market, and must be able to communicate effectively with its market. To believe that health care is any different is to court disaster. Collectively, the health care industry interacts millions of times daily with our market—our patients.

On far too many occasions, we don't know who they really are, don't understand their concerns from their perspective, and cannot communicate with them in a language or in a context that means something to them.

Jhin: A health care organization is an enterprise of people taking care of people. As health care executives, we are stewards of the health of our community. We have an obligation to the community we serve to enhance their health status via superior value in high-quality, cost-effective health services. Service is best when the staff delivering the care have a true understanding of the patient receiving the care.

To foster sincere understanding requires that we address the diversity of our workforce, as well as our patient population. To be truly effective, we must go beyond diversity leadership as it is commonly perceived, to *ultimate diversity leadership*, treating each individual as a subculture of one.

The traditional metaphor of the "melting pot" often used to describe our American way of life is no longer where we want to be. We do not want to melt away our differences; we want, instead, to weave a "tapestry," where the rich, complex uniqueness of each social group and individual is woven into the fabric of the commonality to create a beautiful mosaic.

Lawrence: At the moment there is quite a bit of discussion in every industry about diversity as a business imperative, but the real issues extend well beyond that. We must recognize that we are increasingly part of a "global village." Addressing diversity simply is part of being a good global citizen, regardless of the business you happen to be in.

That being said, I think we do have to call attention to the fact that in health care there is a special impetus for diversity awareness. Health care is a highly personal issue, and so preferences, perceptions, needs, and norms are even more influenced by culture and background than in most other services or industries. Cultural activities, customs, preferences, and so forth can have an impact on an individual's health in general, on the health problems they face, on the health care choices that they make, and on the way they want their health problems addressed. The population is diverse and will be more so in the future. The only way to provide meaningful, effective health care services is through understanding the differing needs of our customers individually and as members of different "groups"—whether ethnic, racial, religious, gender, age-related, what have you. The best way to build that understanding is to have a workforce—both at the executive level and in direct patient care—that mirrors the diversity of the people you serve.

What Is the CEO's Role in Diversity Leadership?

Chapman: The CEO's role is to establish the moral tone and business objectives as well as set the pace and energy required to implement the action plan. CEOs must make the organization believe they are serious.

Meyer Davis: The CEO, the management team, and medical staff must work together to develop a vision for managing diversity that involves strategically planning how the organizational culture should be modified to support the diverse workforce.

Managing a diverse workforce is demanding and will require a strong leadership commitment. One way to ensure success is to conduct a diversity assessment among organization members, which includes an in-depth look at policies, procedures, and internal systems that have been in place for many years. This could be accomplished through interviews, focus groups, and questionnaires. This assessment is crucial before a change in internal systems takes place.

The CEO should appoint a cultural diversity task force to evaluate the assessment and to make recommendations for future directions the organization should take.

Diaz: The CEO has to lead by example. Rhetoric about affirmative action goals and objectives—no matter how vehement—means nothing if the CEO's key staff reflects something different. Hiring minorities and women as custodians, attendants, and clerks is laudable, but it is not enough. It is the CEO's responsibility to ensure diversity at all levels in the organization—from front-line staff, to back office support, to the management ranks. It is the CEO's responsibility to develop a diverse cadre of supervisory, management, administrative, and executive talent, either through outside recruitment or by creating an environment for growth within the organization. It is the CEO's responsibility to influence institutions that prepare the workforce to recognize the diversity in the consumer pool that workforce will serve and to turn out a workforce that represents it. Appointing authorities below the CEO have to know that their commitment to diversity in their workforce will be a factor in assessment of their performance.

Jhin: The CEO's role is critical in building a top-performing organization with a synergistic workforce. The CEO is both the role model and the change agent in leading the organization to synergy.

First, let me say that it is not necessary for a champion of diversity to be a minority. But it is necessary to be a "culturally competent" individual, an excellent listener, and a strong relationship-builder, able to transcend barriers to find the common elements that bind all people together.

The CEO is the *champion of diversity*, celebrating the differences that make our employees and customers unique. The effective CEO weaves diversity principles into all of the hospital's systems. At St. Luke's Episcopal Hospital, for example, we do not have a specific Diversity Program. Rather, our daily activities reflect our commitment to treat each member of our St. Luke's family, customer or employee, as someone unique, worthy of dignity and respect. We celebrate our uniqueness through various activities such as International Nurse's Day and our lecture series on aging.

The CEO must be sure that we treat everyone equivalently or fairly, but not the same. There must be a delicate balance of consistency and flexibility. Each person's needs are different. When we fail to recognize our differences and attempt to treat everyone the same, we fail to maximize our full potential.

While leading the organization as a champion of diversity, the CEO must also be a *champion of commonality*. Our essential sameness as human beings is the glue that binds us as a community. We are all part of a vast and beautiful tapestry, held together by the common thread of humanity. It is this thread that forms the basis for understanding, becoming more binding as we build to higher levels of trust.

By integrating the advocacy of diversity and commonality, one may then become a *champion of meritocracy*. Members of our organization are judged by what they contribute that adds value to the hospital's mission.

Lawrence: The CEO has the opportunity to underscore the need for diversity awareness and to model the seriousness with which the issues need to be addressed. CEOs are well positioned to be champions for diversity, by making it a priority and a key strategic piece of the vision of their organizations.

How and Why Did You Become Involved in Diversity Leadership?

Chapman: It's obvious how badly the field needs this and how poorly it was pursued. Historically, the existing composition of health care leadership drove me to this challenge. It was very clear from the beginning that there were opportunities to improve diversity in health care leadership—consistent with the evolving demographic trends of the nation.

Meyer Davis: Managing diversity will be critical to all employers in the future, especially in health care environments. A review of U.S. Labor Department statistics confirms this. Between 1989 and 2000, 42.8 million people will enter the U.S. workforce, but only 32 percent of those will be white males, while the other 68 percent will include women, blacks, Hispanics, Asians, Native Americans, and others. The health care industry reflects these changing demographics with foreign-born and foreign-educated physicians representing some 20 percent of all licensed physicians in the United States. In addition, clinical professionals trained in their home countries currently occupy a significant share of technical and laboratory positions throughout the United States.

A visible administrative commitment is critical to managing diversity. Working together to develop an environment that works for all of our employees, physicians, and patients is crucial to positioning the hospital for the future.

As patients will use hospitals that are responsive to their needs and with which they feel most comfortable, cooperation among our key players (i.e., management team, medical staff, and employees) is essential to offer our consumers the highest-quality health care at the most cost-effective price.

Diaz: The timing of my entry into health care management coincided with the dawning of the political correctness of affirmative action. There were probably two sentinel events that pushed me into this arena.

First, as entry-level as my position was at the time, I was among the very few Hispanic women in the management workforce of the Los Angeles County Department of Health Services. This guaranteed me a seat on just about every focus group, task force, and committee looking at improving the affirmative action performance of the department. It was an enlightening period in my life. It shook my consciousness into the realization that my road in this new field I'd chosen was to be a very bumpy one.

Second, soon after my appointment, a colleague who was a man approached me to ask if it didn't bother me that the only reason I had that job was that I was a woman and a Hispanic. The implication was obvious. It became for me a matter of honor to educate like minds to the fact that women and minorities could think and govern and lead on a level with white men. It became a matter of expediency to identify, recruit, and/or develop women and minorities who could think and govern and lead on a level with white men.

Jhin: When an organization such as St. Luke's exists in a diverse community such as Houston, Texas, a mixing of cultures naturally occurs both inside and outside the organization. Since health care executives are the stewards of the health of our communities, we must employ our critical assets, particularly human resources, to the greatest strategic and community advantages. Becoming involved in diversity leadership is simply a natural adjunct to St. Luke's core value of "valuing people," which allows us to use the creativity and diverse thinking processes of our people to become the most effective organization possible in serving our diverse community.

Because *ultimate diversity leadership* requires an investment of the hospital's resources, we must look at the benefits derived from this investment to justify our commitment to this path. *Ultimate diversity leadership* leads us to respect the "minority of one," to truly value the subculture that exists within each individual. *Ultimate diversity* has as its credo the acceptance of each person's genuine self.

I believe that many of the current diversity programs fall short of the kind of *ultimate diversity* I have described above. Using myself as an example, a typical diversity program would recognize me as Asian and ask that people come to know me as a person of Asian cultural heritage. While it is true that my Asian heritage is an integral part of who I am, it is also true that throughout my life I have sought out exposure to other cultures and groups throughout the United States and Europe. I have consciously made efforts to incorporate aspects of all of these cultures and groups into my own individuality, thus making me a sort of "tapestry within the organization's tapestry." One cannot begin to know me by simply knowing I am Asian. The same fact is true for each member of our hospital family.

I can say that becoming part of this wonderful tapestry is a conscious decision, not an accident. It requires a willingness to open oneself to all of the people who make up our community, and subsequently, to meet the challenges that will inevitably arise.

Being a welcomed member of a truly diverse hospital family unleashes performance energy. Diverse organizations are fluid and more able to respond quickly to the changing needs of the community. *Ultimate diversity* is the key to our strategic "thrival."

Lawrence: My time with the Peace Corps gave me a deep appreciation of how much we can all learn from one another.

My work with Kaiser Permanente has given me an understanding of both the business imperative and the service imperative of diversity.

Which Aspects of Diversity Are of Particular Concern in Your Health Care Organization and Its Community?

Chapman: Race and gender are the two most important issues for me to work with because of the related community pressures and service dynamics to achieving good health status. The issues of sociocultural and socioeconomic barriers as major obstacles for many people of color should be critical for all health institutions and communities.

Meyer Davis: At Edward Hospital, our employees are our greatest resource. We strive to create an environment in which all employees feel empowered and realize their individual potential. On a monthly basis, I meet with various employee groups to discuss future plans for the hospital as well as to answer questions and listen to their needs or concerns.

Edward Hospital is in the process of developing various educational programs that are tailored to the learning styles and customs of its employees, while also working diligently to prepare internal communications materials that are meaningful to all employees.

Diaz: In my particular experience, race and gender have been the most troubling hurdles. I'll address gender first because I have seen the most progress on that level.

Being a woman of color generally complicated my advancement through the management ranks. Interestingly enough, the strongest encouragement, my most stalwart support, the most consistent opening of doors came from white mentors who were men. With the exception of my current position, every promotion was effected by a white man. Of interest—and concern—is that, with the exception of my current chain of command (Hispanic man, African American man), the most consistent challenges to my advancement were at the hands of men of color, particularly Hispanics. I could expound endlessly on my perception of the reasons for this, but I won't. Suffice to say that they are all gone, and I am not.

The issue of race or ethnicity is more difficult. Particularly in the government sector, with an increasingly shrinking pie, the scramble for the bigger slice has served to pit minority against minority, diverting our energies from the real task at hand—increasing (1) opportunities for the advancement of minorities in leadership roles and (2) awareness of the contributions minorities are making. The current effort to dismantle affirmative action programs is witness to the consequences of turning our energies against each other instead of remaining vigilant to circumstances that threaten achievement of our mutual goals.

Jhin: The hospital community is a microcosm of our larger community. Each individual brings to us a subculture of one. Within that subculture of one, we may find a combination of several or even all of the aspects of diversity—race, gender, age, disability, etc. It would be far too simplistic to say that any one of these aspects is of particular concern, because to do so fails to recognize the complexity and uniqueness of each member of our hospital family.

The challenge, therefore, becomes to define diversity beyond race, gender, or age so that it becomes inclusive of all people. Accomplishing this removes the barriers to understanding, and the concept of diversity becomes less of a threat. We live in a world of limited resources, where to "give" to one often produces fear that something is being "taken" from another. *Ultimate diversity* challenges us to develop balance in order to optimize the benefits to the groups as a whole.

Lawrence: Essentially, every aspect of diversity—whether it's gender or disability, race or sexual orientation, age or culture—has a direct impact on health issues and health care needs. This, and the fact that our "community" spans 16 states and covers 6.6 million members, means that all aspects of diversity are of concern to us.

We have substantial diversity among our membership, and providing excellent service and health care that matters to all of our members demands not just a theoretical "awareness" of diversity or an acceptance of it, but concrete steps such as health education materials in a variety of languages, the use of translators, and an understanding of cultural values that influence perceptions of health and treatment. The issues that can arise are exceedingly delicate—what does a physician with Western training and a Western medical mindset do when his or her clinical opinion runs against the cultural values, norms, or preferences of a patient, for example? The proper resolution of such situations can't be "taught" by any kind of generic diversity training. You must have a provider and staff population that mirrors the population you are trying to serve.

How Can Executives Encourage Organization-wide Commitment to Diversity Leadership?

Chapman: It starts with a commitment by the governing board. Led by the CEO, the medical staff must be encouraged through leadership also. As long as health care is capitalistic, an economic rationale must be developed to support this philosophy; otherwise, it could fail in a competitive society.

Please remember diversity is not about numbers or affirmative action quotas. It is about putting talent in the right places to change "the culture of the status quo" and help an organization evoke and adapt to a changing world. It's to provide positive images that give the next generation of graduate students a chance to see the world with different inspiration and possibilities. Finally, it's about changing the philosophy, policy, and behavior of institutions by giving them multiple perspectives from different races, cultures, classes, and genders.

Meyer Davis: Encouraging workplace diversity involves building an organizational culture that fosters personal differences and heterogeneous groups of people working together toward a common end.

To achieve the shared goal, hospital executives should involve the management team, all employees, and the medical staff to contribute to the organization's overall direction and vision. In order for this to be effective, the direction must be understood, accepted, and set in motion by the entire organization.

At first, employees may resist a change in the status quo or feel threatened because they may not understand the changes being made, but managing diversity is a long-term process that includes awareness-building coupled with comprehensive education and training programs for all employees.

The strategic planning process at Edward Hospital stems from basic communication principles. First, we solicit input regarding the direction of the hospital from all groups, including the medical staff, management team, and employees. After the input is received and the planning process has begun, administrative staff hold strategic vision sessions to discuss potential initiatives for the next few years, as well as to solicit feedback.

Effective communication of the hospital's strategic initiatives is essential as it helps everyone understand, accept, and help to implement necessary changes to continue our mission of providing high-quality health care at the most cost-effective price.

Diaz: The answer to the question is, again, "by example." The rank and file listen to what their leaders say, then observe what they do. They will emulate deeds, not words.

With regard to the medical staff as the primary providers, diversity in the physician ranks that mirrors the community served is a critical objective. Given the statistics on medical school admissions, however, we should not expect that to occur any time soon. Absent ability to recruit a medical leadership comprised of diverse ethnicity and gender, the effort should focus on educating leadership—and the medical staff rank and file—to the issues and concerns of the community they serve.

Jhin: Our approach to diversity at St. Luke's is to value people as individuals. Along with integrity, excellence, and goal orientation, valuing people is one of the core values of our organization. When we talk about valuing people we are referring to the patients—our reason for being—and to our employees—our most valuable asset.

It is commonly believed that building a diverse workforce that mirrors the community fulfills an organization's commitment to diversity. Unfortunately, it is not that easy. Each employee of St. Luke's regardless of age, race, or gender will interact with patients and coworkers of all other ages, races, or genders. It would be impractical on an ongoing basis to generate the perfect match of employee to either patient or coworker. To be effective, employees must reach beyond understanding diversity, as commonly perceived, because its broad-brush approach fails to adequately address the individuality of each person we serve. Employees must embrace and understand all forms of diversity, delving into the unique subculture of one. This is a goal that requires a commitment well beyond today's traditional diversity programs.

To encourage organizational commitment to diversity efforts requires that *ultimate diversity leadership* becomes a strong thread in the fabric of organization, interwoven throughout its mission, values, and human resource systems: organizational planning and design, selection, performance management, compensation/benefits, employee communications, and employee education. Through this type of integrated approach, organizations can better formulate an approach to diversity based on individual relationships. This avoids pitting minority groups against one another, which can occur in traditional diversity programs utilizing race or gender as a criteria for participation.

To be a truly effective provider of health care services requires not only a diverse workforce in terms of cultural characteristics, but one that is diverse in terms of skills, education, and specialization. While championing each employee's uniqueness as an individual, we also need to champion his or her unique contributions to the health care team in roles as the staff physician, nurse, physical therapist, admitting clerk, or diet service aide, etc. The basis for teamwork is trust, the basis for trust is understanding, and the basis for understanding is language. We must, therefore, remove the language barriers, in terms of spoken, body, cultural, and technical languages. Methods such as picture card, interpretive phone services, multilingual written communication pieces, and multilingual staff and volunteers have been effective at St. Luke's.

As health care executives, as health care workers, and as members of the world community, we must all come to an understanding that being a member of the human race is fundamental to membership in any sub-race or sub-group. I'm not saying that differences don't count. Although my hands are similar, my left hand is different in important ways from my right hand, but they meet each other nicely palm to palm, and together, accomplish a good many tasks. However, if I had two left hands or two right hands, I would lose the functionality that is created through the differences. To have *ultimate diversity*, each of us should use the differences in our own hands to join with the differences in another's hands. By valuing the unique difference in each hand, whether it be male, female, black, white, red, yellow, or brown, we can weave strong threads that truly create a vast tapestry of humanity—each strand recognized for its individual beauty while the overall design is appreciated for its synergistic strength and grace.

Lawrence: Executives can encourage organization-wide commitment to diversity leadership by consistently and openly supporting it; by identifying, recognizing, and rewarding excellence in diversity leadership in their organizations; and by modeling the commitment to diversity. Medical staff must be involved; in fact, they should be at the forefront, as many of the challenges and the rewards of diversity affect them directly or indirectly through the impact on their patients.

Epilogue

DIVERSITY LEADERSHIP, like change itself, is complex and multifaceted. Success can be difficult to measure or, sometimes, even recognize. The excitement of discovery and exploration results in the insights produced by transformation. The initial enthusiasm generated by visible changes in organizational and personal values, beliefs, and behaviors gives way to entropy and yields to complacency. Entropy, in turn, sets the stage for renewal and revitalization, producing ever more fundamental change. Every time we think that we have arrived at the pinnacle, another challenge arises to move us beyond. Diversity leadership is more a path than a destination.

Diversity leadership's fundamental challenge is to simultaneously acknowledge and value differences and similarities. Individual uniqueness and human commonality must both be celebrated. Our differences provide a rich and varied base of needs and resources, while our similarities provide the sense of community that is essential to individual and collective cooperation and accomplishment. As CEO Michael Jhin explained, diversity leaders must be champions of commonality as well as of diversity.

The path of diversity leadership is traversed most successfully together. Only through relationships with one another can we uncover the richness of our diversity and the comfort of our similarity. Success begins with the first step.

Index

About the Author

Dr. Janice L. Dreachslin is Associate Professor of Health Policy and Administration in the Management Program at the Penn State University Graduate Center in Malvern, Pennsylvania. Her Ph.D. was awarded in 1979 by Wayne State University in Detroit, Michigan. She also holds a B.A. in Sociology from Wayne State University and was made a member of Phi Beta Kappa in 1970. Dr. Dreachslin teaches U.S. and international health policy courses as well as organization behavior, and is the recipient of the 1994 Penn State Great Valley Award for Teaching Excellence.

Dr. Dreachslin has been active in the fields of health and human service administration and diversity for over twenty years. She has consulted in the United States, Canada, and Great Britain and is the author of numerous publications and presentations on health care administration and general management. She has published articles in *Health Policy, Medical Care, The International Journal of Health Services,* and *Quality Assurance in Health Care,* among others. She serves on the editorial boards of *Journal of Management in Medicine, Issues and Inquiry in College Teaching and Learning,* and *Journal of Clinical Outcomes Management.* Dr. Dreachslin is a member of the Academy of Management, the Association of University Programs in Health Administration, the American Public Health Association, and the International Society for Health Care Quality Assurance.

Dr. Dreachslin has extensive practitioner as well as academic teaching and research experience, having served as Director of Consulting Services at the private, not-for-profit Commission on Professional and Hospital Activities (CPHA) and as Associate Director of a federally funded training institute for desegregated education at Wayne State University. She is currently an active organization development consultant specializing in the process of diversity leadership.

Contributing author, **Dr. Portia L. Hunt,** Professor of Counseling Psychology at Temple University, received her Ph.D. from Indiana State University in Terre Haute. Dr. Hunt is founder and president of the Eclipse Consultant Group.

237